WHITE WATER!

WHITE WATER!

THE THRILL AND SKILL
OF RUNNING THE WORLD'S GREAT RIVERS

MARK BLAINE

BLACK DOG
& LEVENTHAL
PUBLISHERS
NEW YORK

Copyright © 2001 Black Dog & Leventhal Publishers, Inc.

All rights reserved. No part of this book may be
reproduced in any form or by any electronic or
mechanical means including information storage and
retrieval systems without the written permission of the
copyright holder.

Published by
Black Dog & Leventhal Publishers, Inc.
151 W 19th Street
New York, NY 10011

Distributed by
Workman Publishing Company
708 Broadway
New York, NY 10003

Designed by Dutton & Sherman
Photo Research by Kimberley Mangun

Book Manufactured in China

ISBN: 1-57912-211-6
h g f e d c b a

Library of Congress CIP data is on file at the offices of
Black Dog & Leventhal.

This book is intended to be a resource for river
runners—it should in no way serve as a substitute for
experience and instruction. Whitewater paddling is an
inherently dangerous activity. If you choose to get on
the water, you assume the risks.

Contents

Acknowledgments

Thanks to Jennifer Savage for copyediting the manuscript and her critical analysis of paddlespeak, Jenny Wierschem for her sharp eye, Kim Mangun for her thorough photo research, Lee Peterson for his photographic skill and general support, Oregon River Sports for their gear and good humor, and Dutton & Sherman for such a clear, engaging layout of the book. Thanks also to Laura Ross and especially J.P. Leventhal, who saw opportunity in a book about whitewater. I also must thank Lauren Kessler, who taught me that real writers really write.

Finally, Jessica MacMurray's support, energy and focus made *Whitewater!* a reality. My life in recent years has been filled with a lot of writing and a lot of paddling, but the two didn't really mix. Jessica saw that I could combine them, and that we could have fun putting together a book. From late-night photo editing at the kitchen table to roll sessions on the Willamette River, we did.

To Dad, who taught me to point my feet downstream when I swim in the river.

To Mom, who should read no further in this book, lest she get too clear a picture of what I do in my spare time. Take it instead as confirmation that I took Dad's advice.

Introduction

I can still remember the first time my father pushed me off the beach and I took my first few awkward strokes across the waters of Washington's Puget Sound. I didn't know, at the time, that those halting strokes would lead to a lifetime on the water. I remember—and am reminded from time to time by the gleam in the eyes of paddlers I meet around the world—the challenge of trying to surf my first wave. I remember the thrill of finally sitting on that wave, feeling the water coursing around me. I have a lifetime filled with incredible memories from spectacular rivers around the world. Whether it's a crowded competition, fans on the banks and friends and competitors in the water or just a quiet paddle on a warm summer afternoon, there is so much to be enjoyed, celebrated and learned on the river.

Whitewater offers so much and has been discovered by so few—but, as a sport, is enjoying new-found popularity. Paddling, whether in a raft, kayak or canoe, can be a family sport, an extreme sport, a personal challenge and so much more. If you're looking for fun in the water, you'll find it on the river—or if you're looking for challenge and adrenaline, you can find that, too. For the uninitiated, whitewater can be exciting at any level—but also intimidating and dangerous. *Whitewater! The Thrill and Skill of Running the World's Great Rivers*, is a fantastic introduction to whitewater and an essential guide for paddlers of all abilities. Mark Blaine has filled this book with useful information, concise instruction and enticing profiles of whitewater rivers from just about everywhere. Enjoy the lessons found on these pages. I'll see you on the river.

Scott Shipley
Atlanta, Georgia 2001

Preface

The edge of the world is off U.S. 441 in north Georgia. There, at Oceana Falls on the Tallulah River, a glossy pool tumbles over the horizon. One April Saturday a few years ago, I stood in ankle-deep water on the edge of that flat-earth pool, looking for a line, or more precisely, looking for a treetop down the gorge to line up on before I pointed the nose of my boat over the edge.

I could spit, and that was good. Dry mouth is a sign of terminal anxiety, a good objective test of your state of mind. About three-fourths of the way down the 56-foot slide, a large flat rock called the Thing stuck up in the path of the current, obstructing most of the river-left edge and shooting a vertical column of water a dozen or more feet into the air. The line I needed to take was left of the Thing, a 10-foot slot I would have to hit after my toboggan ride over a few inches of water and smooth granite. I would be going 35 miles per hour when I hit the pool at the bottom, but I didn't calculate that then. Instead, I watched a canoeist flip near the top and sickeningly scrape on his side all the way down. His helmet and paddle on the rock sounded like the muffler dragging from the underbelly of an old Buick. He hit the hole at the bottom, flushed through and rolled sluggishly up. People cheered. I just stood in the ankle deep water, antsy, thinking that this was the biggest thing I'd ever run, looking back up the gorge to where I'd put in only a few minutes ago, taking small comfort in my ability to spit.

Where I started would be critical. Falling over was not an option. From the pool I would line up on that seam in the water that led to the peak of a little curling wave a few feet over the edge. I would hold this line all the way down, and try to keep a little bit of left angle so that I could deflect off the pressure wave of water spraying off the Thing. I decided to forget about the trees in the distance: the clean line on Oceana started at the lip when you caught the exact flow that would carry you past, not into, the Thing. So my decision about where to drop off the edge would be based on the nuances of the ripples just a few feet from where I stood. Besides, the treetops gave me vertigo.

Boats were stacked like firewood on the little beach at the top of the falls. About a dozen other paddlers were stopped here as well. Georgia Power had agreed to recreational releases from the dam upstream of the Tallulah Gorge and it was one of the first weekends that the river had run in 80 years. The run was by permit only and a few hundred lucky boaters would get the chance to paddle it. For most, it was an exploratory run with a few hundred other adrenaline-soaked Tallulah newbies. Nearly everybody had a camera, and a few people were shooting video. Since nobody really knew the lines, there was a lot of carnage.

"Go on, let it slurp you back in," Hank, a kayaking emergency room doctor, hollered in east Tennessee twang as he videotaped a paddler who failed to clear the hole at the bottom of Oceana. The hole tumbled the boater, dunking him, churning him like a washing machine. "Surf that bastard," Hank yelled. "Surf it." Oceana finally let go and everybody cheered.

I pulled my kayak out of the pile, put the nose into the water and wiggled in. I paddled out into the pool and did a few twists to loosen up. Two other paddlers sat in the placid water with me. "After you?" one joked to his buddy. "No, after you," the other retorted and peeled his kayak into flow that would take him over the edge.

He disappeared. There was a pause, then, later than I expected, cheers. He was through. His buddy went immediately after. Fewer cheers, but apparently a clean run. One of my friends nodded that the run was clear.

I spotted the seam and eased into the surprisingly gentle current. Angle set, my boap tilted over the edge and I accelerated. I hit the curling wave and was blinded by a spray of water. Skipping across the rock face, I held my line, sat up straight and in two beats of my heart hit the water spraying off the Thing. I felt myself deflect off the foaming pile on the rock and, half a beat later, I hit the hole. Water surged up my nose and around my eyeballs on impact and I surfaced beyond the hole, bow pointing skyward. Cheers.

The intent of this book is to be a resource for people interested in whitewater paddling, describing what paddlers need to head to the river and giving them a sense of what to expect when they get there. *Whitewater!* covers this information broadly, and I have described the equipment and techniques for rafting, canoeing and kayaking—the three most common ways of getting down whitewater rivers. It's neither a rafting book, a kayaking book nor a canoeing book. People come to the sport in different ways, and while the techniques and equipment may vary between each boat type, it's limiting to think only in terms of one way of doing it being better than another. It's fun to be part of a team running rapids in a raft; it's also fun to depend on yourself in a solo boat. Kayaks offer a thrilling ride on a surfing wave; rafts easily carry the gear you need for a two-week expedition to remote canyons of the world. Paddling isn't all like that run on the Tallulah Gorge, and it doesn't have to be scary or big to be fun. The most important thing to learn about paddling is to learn to assess where you are as a paddler, to understand your limits and paddle safely. I hope this book will be a good resource for you, but it's no substitute for quality instruction and experience. Seek both, and your days on the river will be exciting and fulfilling.

Mark Blaine
Eugene, Oregon 2001

EQUIPMENT

Boats

RAFTS

Early whitewater rafts were World War II surplus inflatables that made their way to rivers. From these early boats, basic paddle and oar-rig rafts have evolved for different rivers and different styles of paddling and rowing. Lacking the traditional forms of canoes and kayaks, rafters have been open to some elegant, and some funky, designs over the years. These refinements have made modern inflatables safe, durable and a lot of fun.

A basic whitewater raft consists of tubes, a floor and thwarts (tubes that attach inside the boat for stability). Most river rafts are between 10 and 18 feet long and made of strong fabric coated with various plastics and rubber:

Catarafts are maneuverable inflatable boats that are particularly suited for running difficult water. They are usually configured for rowing and can carry much gear, though space for passengers is limited.

There's nothing...absolutely nothing...half so much worth doing as simply messing around in boats.
—Kenneth Grahame,
The Wind in the Willows

hypalon, urethane, PVC and neoprene. Raft size is generally determined by application: small rafts are more common on small rivers and creeks while large rafts, sometimes several of the biggest models lashed together, are standard on the biggest rivers. Small rafts are more maneuverable and responsive, but hold fewer people, less gear and are less stable. Big rafts are stable and hold vast quantities of food and gear, but take longer to move and maneuver

Rafts rigged with rowing frames can haul a lot of gear for multiday river trips. Rowing a gear boat requires a river runner with skill and experience to negotiate rapids with the extra weight.

Grand Canyon of the Colorado River, Arizona

HEADWATERS: *Rocky Mountains of Colorado*

LENGTH: *280 miles from Lees Ferry to Pierce Ferry*

DIFFICULTY: *Class 4+*

CHARACTER: *It's the Grand Canyon, looking up. Rapids are big and the river can change flow quickly. The water is cold, even on 100-degree summer days, as the flow is drawn from the bottom of Glen Canyon Dam. Access is limited to about 20,000 boaters a year, and the river is remote, to say the least. Trips run for multiple weeks with few options for resupply or take-out.*

The Grand Canyon of the Colorado River is the trip of a lifetime. First run by John Wesley Powell in 1869, it has become a classic of whitewater paddling. Private boaters can wait a decade or more for their name to be assigned a put-in time in the prime months, though it's possible to get on more expeditiously in winter. Either way, the trip is one of the most spectacular adventures to be found in the U.S. Crystal-clear desert air, stacked mesas of multi-colored rock and the enormity of the Grand Canyon will blow your mind at every turn—and it's a much quieter way to see the Canyon than in the RV park on the South Rim.

Most who run the Grand Canyon choose to do so with an outfitter, as few have the trip management skills and equipment in their garage to plan such an undertaking. An outfitter deals with the logistics of the run, from shuttle to food, giving paddlers a chance to enjoy the canyon undistracted (except for the numerous big rapids). Expect to pay a lot for this piece of mind. Trips range upward from $1,000 for a bare-bones excursion. Paddlers also may find a spot on a private group going down the canyon that has a seat to fill. Look around and plan months or even years in advance. The trip is a major undertaking if you go—you'll have to check out of civilization for three weeks or so (you lucky dog)—but there aren't many better ways to spend time and money.

The rapids are big and pushy. Granite and Crystal are better known among the big-water Class 4 rapids. Lava Falls is Class 5. The Grand Canyon has its own rating scale (which goes up to 10) so you might need to translate between the standard system used on every other river and the numbers assigned to the canyon's many rapids. Any ratings you see in this book are based on the

Lava Falls is the biggest of the big rapids in the Grand Canyon.

standard system. Rapids, however, aren't the only thing the Grand Canyon has going for it. Day after day, rafters can goggle at the incredible scenery or take off on one of numerous side hikes. There are also long flat stretches and upcanyon winds that make progress slow and arduous at times.

Verdon River, France

HEADWATERS: *French Alps*

LENGTH: *20 miles*

DIFFICULTY: *Class 5*

CHARACTER: *The Grand Canyon of the Verdon is a dam-fed but largely inaccessible river canyon that is one of Europe's classic whitewater runs. Passages are tight and flows are low, usually just a few hundred cfs. The river at times runs underground and there are several mandatory portages.*

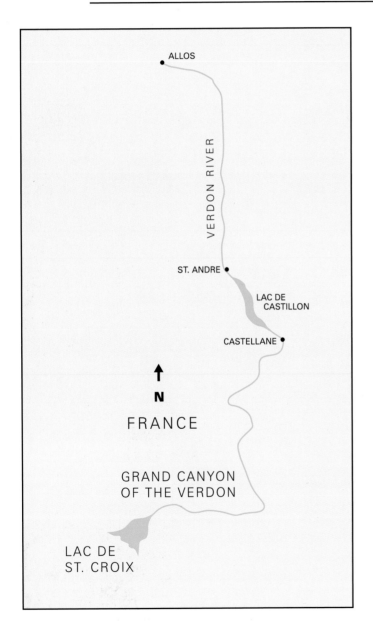

The Verdon is a European classic. Called the Grand Canyon of the Verdon, the river follows a spectacular course between vertical canyon walls, through and under limestone. At one point paddlers will follow the river course underground, paddling the river's green waters through an eerily lit cave.

Flows are low, with optimal water levels under 900 cfs. The wild canyon flows between two reservoirs: its flow is determined by releases from Castillon Reservoir and it flows into St. Croix Reservoir. What runs between is unforgettable. There are numerous tight passages, requiring river runners to duck, squeeze and shimmy through. With 1,000-foot cliff walls looming above, this is no place for the claustrophobic, or the unprepared. The Verdon is Class 5 with few places for a paddler to abandon his trip, and your skills should be up to what the river demands: blind drops, tricky rapids, difficult rescue. Scouting opportunities and portage trails are generally labeled on the river with signs. There is an access point about midway through the run that paddlers often use to break the trip into two days, leaving boats and paddling gear down in the gorge and hiking to the rim to camp. The run is 20 miles long and can be paddled in a day, but the experience isn't recommended: the run is just too amazing to bomb through. Plan to slow down and enjoy it. The Verdon is one of few European rivers that doesn't have a road or town or other sights of civilization edging up to its banks.

The Verdon River runs greenish blue out of the French Alps. Several runs are possible on the river, but the most famous is the Grand Canyon of the Verdon.

through rapids. On some smaller rivers, big rafts won't even fit through the narrow passages of some of the rapids. When picking the size of a raft, consider how many people and how much gear you'll be carrying, whether you'll use the raft on big water or technical creeks and whether you'll row or paddle.

Big or small, traditional rafts incorporate several other design innovations that whitewater paddlers should be aware of when running them downriver. The upswept ends of a raft, the rise or kick that's similar to rocker on a canoe or kayak, shortens the effective length of the boat, making some moves easier and allowing it to ride over waves and holes. Too much kick and a boat will tend to bend like a taco going through the rapid—too little and it will dive at the bottom of steep drops and cut into waves. Floors are also a key consideration. Self-bailing floors are a recent innovation that allow water to drain out of the bottom rather than accumulate like older-style standard-floor rafts. Self-bailers are expensive, however, and may not be necessary depending on the rivers you plan to run.

Beyond traditional rafts, a number of other inflatables are effective river runners. Foremost among them are catarafts—the whitewater equivalent of the ocean-going catamaran. A cataraft typically consists of two tubes supported by a rowing frame with commonly 12-, 14- or 16-foot lengths, though very small two person catarafts joined by inflatable thwarts are popular on some rivers. Catarafts are very maneuverable and fast. They can be quite playful, but the downside is there's little room for passengers.

Whether you're using a cataraft or a traditional raft, you may need a rowing frame, depending on what you plan to do with the boat. Rowing frames allow one person to control the boat, and to carry gear instead of passengers. Frames are mounted either in the center of the boat or at its stern and provide extra rigidity to the boat that paddle rigs do not. Oar-rig rafts may not be as convenient on tighter rivers because they require the oars to be shipped into the boat in narrow passages.

> *Bow:* **The part of the boat in front of you. Most of the time you want it pointed downstream.**

> *Kayaks come in a variety of shapes and sizes, especially because designs have been steadily getting smaller and more responsive in the last decade.*

KAYAKS

Modern kayaks are derived from the boats used for thousands of years by native peoples living in the far north of the Northern Hemisphere. The traditional boats were made of skin stretched over a frame of wood or bone and were designed to move fast over long distances but handle rough ocean waters and the rigors of hunting whales. The kayak was adapted for river use in the middle of the 20th century and quickly evolved from canvas or other material stretched over a frame to molded fiberglass. Plastics were incorporated into commercial designs in the 1970s.

C-1: **A decked canoe. The C-1 paddler, a canoeist (never canoer), kneels in his or her boat and uses a one-bladed paddle. The boat looks like a kayak and often is a kayak with the seat removed and a foam pedestal glued in its place.**

Whitewater kayaks have changed vastly in the past decade. Generally the trend has been toward shorter, flat-bottomed, lower volume boats and away from older designs based on longer whitewater slalom kayaks. Kayaks have also become more specialized as designers have refined the abilities of boats to surf and play or maneuver tight creeks and resurface quickly after running waterfalls. Whitewater kayaks are made almost exclusively of plastic, with each manufacturer touting the performance of its special compound. A few boats (usually squirt boats and slalom racing boats) are still made from fiberglass or Kevlar, but these kinds of boats require more care than plastic boats.

Whitewater kayaks today range from just under 7 feet long to 9 feet long. The smallest among new whitewater kayaks is about half the length of the

Whitewater rodeo and surf competitions offer paddlers a chance to test their moves among the best. Here Brian Edmonds sends his bow skyward at the Nugget Rodeo on the Rogue River in Oregon.

Paddlers sometimes have to get creative when they haul their boats to the river and shuttle vehicles between the put-in and take-out. Here bicyclists have been hired to shuttle high-volume creek boats for a river run in Nepal.

classic slalom design. Today, kayaks are generally shaped for playing—surfing and acrobatic paddling—or for the adrenaline spiked vertical drops of creeking. Most manufacturers also make an all-around or river-running design that's a blend of the qualities of slalom and play boats.

Playboats tend to be the shortest of kayak designs with thin ends intended to slice into the water and make vertical moves. They have flat bottoms intended to help them "release," or skip and spin atop the fast moving current on the face of the wave. These boats also have the least volume of standard commercial designs and paddlers can expect them to be a tight (and sometimes painful) fit. More and more of these boats are made for destination paddling—paddlers know a specific spot on a river and drive directly to it to perfect certain moves. These boats can be a lot of fun for running playful rivers, but the tight fit may require a few stops to get out and shake blood back into the feet.

Creek boats are made for the rough-and-tumble demands of paddling on tight tricky waterways with lots of vertical drop. They are the playboats' chunky cousins with blunt, radically upswept bows and sterns (curvature of the hull called rocker) that allow creek boats to spin quickly, snap into eddies and resurface fast after vertical drops. They tend not to be as short as the most radical playboat designs and are usually made with heavier plastic to withstand years of skipping and bouncing off rocks. For beginners, creek boats can be forgiving designs that are easy to roll, however new boaters may find them hard to paddle in a straight line.

Chine: On a kayak or canoe, the chine is the transition between the side of the boat and its bottom. Hard chined boats have sharp corners or edges that define this transition and are made to carve in the water. They are also more edgy and feel more likely to "catch" in a hole and flip the paddler. Soft chines are more subtle and rounded and allow more margin for error but may sacrifice some performance.

River-running boats blend comfort with playful features that make them enjoyable for all-day trips and forgiving for beginners and more experienced paddlers alike. River runners tend to be a bit faster and able to move in a straight line, or track, better than more radical designs, making long ferries and big water moves easier. These boats do everything with a few compromises and there's room to carry lunch.

Several more specialized designs may turn up on your river trip. Squirt boats are ultra-low-volume kayaks that look much like surfboards with a bulge in the middle to fit you inside. They're made to explore the river's currents on eddy lines and disappear completely in subsurface tricks called "mystery moves." These boats are only for advanced paddlers who've mastered other designs and feel at home among the river's most squirrely nooks.

Slalom kayaks are also common on some rivers that serve as training sites for racers. They're designed to move quickly down river while negotiating through suspended gates positioned strategically among the holes, waves and rocks of rapids. Whitewater slalom racing is an Olympic event and because of its fast pace and natural drama, has been popular among world television audiences.

Downriver race boats are a strange-looking design intended to move as fast as possible down tricky rapids. These boats are long and thin, except for a wide bulge behind the cockpit. Unlike their Olympic slalom cousins, downriver race boats don't have to move through gates and, thus, are not easy to turn.

Kayak fit is a balance of comfort and the desire for performance. Some smaller modern boats are more comfortable than their larger predecessors because manufacturers are taking body positioning in the boat into account and forming it to those shapes. Recent innovations include wider boat hulls, footbumps for extra room around the toes, more ergonomically designed thigh braces and comfort-

Whitewater slalom requires the ultimate in control and a fast quick-turning boat. Paddlers must negotiate rapids and weave through gates suspended over the river. Slalom has been among the most widely watched televised events in recent Olympic Games.

able, adjustable back bands. Needless to say, the first time you slip into a kayak it will likely feel tight and contort your legs into what seem to be unnatural positions. You may find pressure points that grow more agonizing the longer you stay in the boat or that the boat feels confining. Relax and try to wiggle around a bit. Let your body settle into the boat. If you can get wet before you try on the boat, do it. It will help you slide in and will tend to loosen everything up.

Remember, too, that the clothing you wear in the boat can have a lot to do with your comfort. Nylon river shorts can catch and bind and booties can add volume to your feet that you didn't account for when you adjusted the foot braces or bulkhead.

The boat fit should be snug but not painfully tight. Your knees should be up under the thigh braces and your feet should be firmly, but not tightly,

Inflatable kayaks offer a versatile, accessible option for river runners. They can be great boats to learn the basic moves, but they will also grow with a paddler. Some IK paddlers have run Class 5 with them.

braced against the foot pegs or bulkhead. If there's a back band in the boat, make sure you're not sitting on it, and position it so it will stay firmly in the small of your back.

Finally, feel how loose your hips are in the boat. The most critical thing with fitting the hips isn't necessarily the tightness of the outfitting but the shape of the hip pads. This is a common place to develop painful pressure points. The hip pads should hook over the tops of the thighs. This will give a much more snug feeling while allowing you to loosen up a bit on the squeeze of the hip pads. It will also keep you from falling out of the boat when you flip over. Several manufacturers sell precut foam blocks for hip pads and you should consider them for outfitting your boat. They make a big difference.

Dry Box: **A box that is used to keep gear, food and clothes dry on the river. As it's usually more durable, dry boxes are often used for more valuable items or gear that might punch a hole in a dry bag.**

Proper boat fit takes a good boat choice and time. As you paddle more you will become more flexible and the yogic contortions that you once needed to make to get in the boat will ease. You'll also get better at boat fitting and learn some tricks—a little duct tape here, some contact cement there—to getting a solid, but not painfully tight, fit. For most paddlers, this is the kind of fit they should seek. If your boat seems unusually tight, you may find that if you get in and warm up in the eddy and then get out of your boat, stretch and get back in, the boat will fit

Whitewater canoes turn easily and are designed to ride over waves and holes. Float bags in the bow and stern displace water and help to keep the canoe riding high in the roughest circumstances.

much more comfortably. If you want to really ramp up the performance of your boat, however, you'll have to make the fit even closer and accept a little discomfort as your body adjusts to its new roto-molded plastic pants.

INFLATABLE KAYAKS

Inflatable kayaks offer a good solution for paddlers looking for versatility and a fairly easy learning curve. Combining the maneuverability and water contact of a kayak with the stability and simplicity of a raft, inflatable kayaks—called IK's or duckies in some parts of the country—are a great way to get a first taste of whitewater. Beyond that, they will grow with you as you become a more experienced paddler. They can run nearly anything. Some paddlers even swear by inflatable kayaks for Class 5 steep creek-ing, touting the benefits of a soft landing and the lower risk of entrapments. Whatever your case, inflatable kayaks offer a number of benefits and design features.

Inflatable kayaks range from wide, stable boats with large tubes to high performance boats with thigh straps that surf and roll. There are tradeoffs with each. Bigger, more stable boats are great for starting out and running rivers that aren't particularly technical. They are slow and don't surf as well as smaller boats but are excellent for a fun float down the river. As the side tubes get smaller on IK's, the performance improves and the boats incorporate features such as foam floors for stiffness and more refined rocker for maneuverability. Thigh straps can be a great addition to the boat as your skill level increases with the difficulty of the river. They help maneuverability and bracing and will let you roll some of the most high-performance designs.

Inflatable kayaks are also handy for travel, espe-cially the ones with inflatable floors, because they roll up into a small package that's easy to check on an airplane or fit into the trunk of a car. (Try doing *that* with a hard-shell kayak or canoe.)

There are a few drawbacks, however. Since you sit on top of the IK, you are exposed to both air and water and will get wet. For summertime trips on warm water this is a welcome relief, but in other sea-sons, on colder rivers, you'll want to bundle up. If you plan on running anything harder than Class 3, you'll definitely want a wetsuit and you might even consid-er a drysuit. The likelihood of a swim from an IK is pretty high and that combined with the all-day splash factor of the boat can get you dangerously cold on all but the warmest rivers in the warmest months.

CANOES

Not just any canoe will do. Canoes come in a wide variety of shapes and sizes, and whitewater canoes have specific characteristics for running rapids that make them more maneuverable and safe than canoes designed for flat water. Whitewater demands quick response and turning, the ability to slip sideways in the water and the ability to ride over waves and holes without taking on too much water. Open canoes and C-1s, decked canoes that share many design characteristics with kayaks are on the extreme end of these demands and are built specifically for surfing holes and waves and running big drops. In fact, C-1s often are just converted kayaks and the discussion of kayak features in this section may be helpful if this is your interest. Whatever the intent or marketing of the boat, canoe designs boil down to several basics that will help you pick what will work for the type of paddling you want to do.

From day trips on demanding water to floats on mellow whitewater to multiday whitewater expedi-tions, you will need to find a length of boat that will carry you, your gear and perhaps another paddler. This boat should also fit the type of water you're headed for. Like other whitewater boat designs, whitewater canoes have been getting shorter in past years.

Long canoes (traditional designs, like lake canoes) track, or hold a straight line, well and can carry a lot of gear for multiday trips into the back-country. However, these long canoes can be a night-mare in whitewater where boats must move into and out of small eddies and be able to turn quickly in difficult water.

Tandem canoeing requires excellent teamwork to coordinate moves in the chaotic whitewater environment.

Shortness helps a boat turn and be maneuverable and is a significant advantage in tougher whitewater. There is a tradeoff: short boats don't track well and can be maddening to manage on long flatwater sections.

On the far end of the boat-length continuum are open canoes, some shorter than 9 feet, designed specifically for surfing and playing. C-1s fall into this category as well, and some kayaks shorter than 7 feet have been converted to C-1 for the thrill of spinning and cartwheeling in a hole or on a wave. These boats aren't designed to carry much gear and their extreme

Dry Bag: A bag usually made of coated nylon with a roll top used to store gear, food and clothes that must remain dry on the river. A must for long day and multi-day trips.

shortness may hinder them on multi-day whitewater trips.

Like boat length, the upswept bow-to-stern curvature of the hull, or rocker, helps a boat turn quickly and spin. When you push down on an end of a heavily rockered boat it will rock along its length. Rocker changes the effective length of the boat, and boats with a lot of rocker will feel shorter.

Traditional long lake canoes have very little rocker, a design feature that keeps more of the hull of the boat in the water and makes them easier to paddle straight and in a strong wind. Going straight over long distances and fighting the wind are only marginally useful traits in a rapid, however, and most whitewater canoes are heavily rockered.

Rocker gives two big advantages to whitewater boats. First it lets them turn quickly because there is little drag from the water on the ends of the boat. This quality also makes them harder to paddle in a

The canoeist kneels in the boat and sits on a foam or plastic pedestal. His legs are held in, and in the hands of a skilled paddler, the canoe can be rolled.

Ducky: An inflatable kayak. See IK.

straight line for any distance. Rocker also serves to help the boat ride over waves and holes rather than cut into them and ship on water over the gunnels, or rail around the top of the canoe. Rocker makes for a drier ride through the rapids—an especially useful feature when the trickiest moves may come at the end of a long stretch of heavy water and you don't want a lot of water making the boat sluggish.

Length and rocker are the main considerations for the design of the boat along its length, but canoes also have different hull shapes that affect their performance from side to side. Whitewater canoes don't have keels, the strips that run the length of the bottom of the boat and help the boat go in a straight line and keep it from being pushed around by the wind.

Instead, they have smooth bottoms that may be rounded or more squared with edges or chines. Chines are the squared edges that separate the side

of the hull from the bottom. Hard chines are more square and abrupt, soft chines are more rounded and gradual. The smooth bottom helps the boat to turn and slip sideways in the water in ferries. It also slides over obstacles better and makes floating sideways in shallow water less of a crapshoot.

Rounded-bottom boats will feel especially tippy, a sensation that hides a more subtle stability. These boats have little primary stability, or the feeling that you won't tip over when you step into them or are just sitting in the water. They often have excellent and consistent secondary stability, however. Secondary stability offers the ability to lean a boat on edge and hold it there or recover from near flips with a brace. These boats may also be a bit easier to roll. Boats with good primary stability often have a point-of-no-return spot beyond which they'll flip when they're put on a radical edge.

Some boats have more squared off bottoms, or harder chines, that offer a little more primary stability and an edge that's useful for carving on waves and snapping into eddies. Harder chines do have a drawback, though, in that they make the boat feel more edgy and may cause a few unwanted flips as you learn to get used to them. Taking the hard chines concept one further, many new tiny open canoes have been designed with flat bottoms and sharp chines. In the hands of a talented paddler, these boats cartwheel easily in holes and spin and carve elegantly on green waves. Finally, most whitewater canoes maintain the rounded-hull shape up to the ends of the boat, making them blunt and less likely to slice into waves and holes and better able to ride over them. Blunt- or shovel-ended canoes, as opposed to narrow-ended ones that you see in lakes and backyards, can provide a pretty dry ride in challenging whitewater.

Nuances of boat shape are held and translated to the water through the material that the canoe is made of. Most whitewater canoes on the river these days are made of some form of plastic. Ultra-tough compared to their forebears, these boats slide off rocks easily, retain their shape over years of hard use and can even be unwrapped from rocks and popped out, ready for another chance at the river. Some materials are more flexible than others and don't form hard edges as well. So, the smallest canoes, the tiny playboats, are made from plastic similar to that used for kayaks.

No matter what plastic a boat is made of, if it's from a major manufacturer it will likely be good stuff that's made for years of service. Fiberglass and Kevlar canoes also make appearances on whitewater rivers from time to time, though these materials won't stand the abuse that plastic will. Kevlar is light for its strength and good for racing designs, but it won't take the rock bashings that a plastic boat will. Kevlar takes a skilled paddler to make its performance benefits shine above its durability issues.

Finally, there's the venerable aluminum canoe. Extremely durable and cheap, aluminum canoes were the boats of choice among river runners a generation ago, but they have limitations that plastic has eclipsed. Aluminum is durable, but when it fails—most commonly when wrapped around a rock—it is difficult to fix and may require welding to return to a shape that looks like a canoe. It will likely never perform the way it did before once its crumpled wound is beaten out. Aluminum sticks to rocks, a troublesome attribute on difficult, shallow rivers. Finally, aluminum canoes tend to be built in more traditional shapes, with shallow rocker and narrow ends that slice into rather than ride over whitewater. Most of these boats are best left to mellow float streams and flat water.

Kayaks have recently undergone a design revolution with flat bottoms that allow boats to spin on waves and chines, or edges, that let a paddler carve with precision.

Chattooga River, Georgia/South Carolina

HEADWATERS: *Flows out of the Blue Ridge Mountains of western North Carolina to form the border between Georgia and South Carolina*

LENGTH: *50 miles*

DROP: *50 ft/mi*

DIFFICULTY: *Class 2, 3, 4, 5*

CHARACTER: *Starts as a steep mountain creek that runs intermittently and then widens as its gradi-ent eases for about 20 miles. In the last 20 miles of the run, the river gets progressively steeper, tighter and more pushy, culminating in the Five Falls of Section IV, a collection of Class 4 and 5 rapids separated only by short pools. Within another mile, the river empties into Tugaloo Lake. The Chattooga River runs all year through some of the most undeveloped land in the southeastern U.S. It's protected under the Wild and Scenic River Act.*

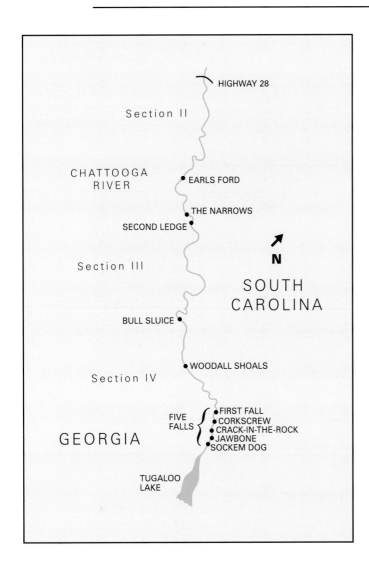

Paddlers find solitude on the Chattooga River like no other river on the East Coast of the U.S. Wild and remote, flowing year-round, the Chattooga demands peak skills from its paddlers and the ability to deal with the unexpected. Roads meet the river in only a few places—so the only escape route for paddlers that have floated beyond the put-in is rough trail over steep ridges.

The Chattooga's hardest rapids are Class 5: steep, tricky drops through and around ominous holes bounded by ghastly undercut rocks. The river offers easier fare in its middle sections where beginning and intermediate paddlers work up to the skills required to paddle the river's more infamous rapids. Paddlers on the Chattooga usually have the river to themselves. It was among the first rivers included in the federal Wild and Scenic River system and, as a result, has been protected from development and damming since 1974. As neighboring towns and nearby cities grew up, the Chattooga remained remote, its wild character undiminished.

As if its rapids aren't enough to send a shiver through most paddlers, the river was also the backdrop for many of the chilling scenes in "Deliverance," the classic 1972 movie starring Burt Reynolds based on the book by South Carolina's James Dickey. The movie brought a surge of tourism to the area in the 1970s and remains a river classic. More than a few paddlers have hummed the opening to "Dueling Banjos" as they've floated around the first bend of the river and out of sight of cars, roads and civilization. Despite the movie depiction, the locals are friendly, and many people gather at access points on the river, particularly

Class 4 Bull Sluice rapid, on hot days to swim and watch occasional river carnage.

Paddling options on the Chattooga are varied. The river is referred to by sections, each about a day-long float. Steep sections 0 and I are restricted by the Forest Service and are illegal to float. Section II is mostly Class 2 water with one Class 3 rapid and is good for beginners and intermediate kayakers and canoeists learning the moves. Section III at low-to-medium river levels is a great run for intermediates kayakers, canoeists and rafters looking for a challenge on rapids such as Second Ledge (a six-foot vertical drop), the Narrows and finishing with Bull Sluice, a swift two-tiered falls. Section III is a popular commercial run and a great way to get acquainted with the challenging whitewater the river offers. Section IV follows and demands solid paddling and rescue skills: this section of river is no place to swim. Most of the rocks are undercut, the rapids are steep and the water is powerful. The first two thirds of the run are a warm-up on diffi-

cult and dangerous rapids like Woodall Shoals and Seven-Foot Falls. It's good to be loose because what follows in the Five Falls is some of the trickiest water commonly paddled in the Southeast. First Falls ends in a pool above Corkscrew, which ends in a moving pool above Crack-in-the-Rock. Crack is followed by a rock garden pool above Jawbone, which flows directly into the nastiest rapid of the five—Sock'em Dog. Commercial trips on Section IV start early and are all-day affairs. Rafts move one at a time through the Five Falls with extra guides and safety boaters below each rapid ready to throw ropes and tow customers (and sometimes guides) to shore. Private boaters should scout thoroughly and find someone who knows the run intimately to follow through the Five Falls. The run is challenging and great fun for the well prepared and experienced, but the Chattooga demands respect. Here, the list of whitewater injuries and fatalities here grows yearly.

River Tryweryn, Wales

HEADWATERS: *Cambria Mountains in northern Wales.*

LENGTH: *1.5 miles is the most common run, but other sections can extend the length of the trip.*

DIFFICULTY: *Class 3+*

CHARACTER: *The dam-controlled River Tryweryn has one of the most consistent flows in the United Kingdom, offering good paddling flows on more than 200 days each year. The river is full of good play spots and a few dicey holes that can recirculate the unfortunate. Commercial raft trips are available.*

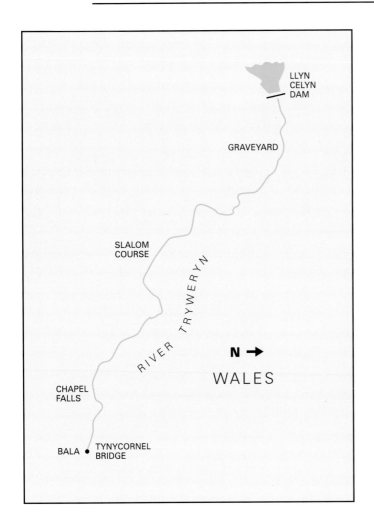

The River Tryweryn flows from Llyn Celyn Dam near Bala and makes a thrilling trip for intermediate and more advanced paddlers. Numerous stoppers, or holes, pepper the rapids of this run and may require scouting, or "inspection" if you want to sound like a local. The steep Graveyard section is memorable among the rapids, a long boulder garden. Fedw'r Gog Falls is another notable rapid that comes after several play spots. Another, perhaps the most popular, play spot follows where kayakers line up to show off their stuff. Chapel Falls ends the run with a potentially nasty hole for the unwary or daredevil playboater. All of it is Class 3, but fast with a few opportunities for carnage. The river is managed for flood control, so flows are consistent despite recent rain or dry weather. Longer runs can be made down to Bala in the winter and a few drops may make the trip worthwhile, though the focus of the whitewater action is on the upper section.

The commonly paddled section of the river is managed for whitewater paddling by a private river club and there's a charge to run the river. The Tryweryn is also a training site for Britain's national team slalom paddlers and the revenue from the fees goes toward keeping the slalom course and river facilities world-class. Because of this, access is good and there's a shower and café.

The waters of the River Tryweryn offer some of Wales's best paddling. Several sticky holes and technical sections challenge paddlers from across Great Britain.

Paddles and Oars

Paddles and oars are simple, yet crucial, pieces of gear. Except for a few fringe kayakers, the river runner caught without a paddle or oars is without means of propulsion, so care should be taken to select serviceable, high quality paddles and oars. River runners need to consider the types of water they'll be running and find the right balance of durability and features that fit, and they should always consider carrying a spare.

First, a simple distinction. Paddles are used to propel kayaks, canoes and rafts, are held with both hands and are used one blade at a time. Oars are used on rafts and drift boats, require fulcrum-like devices called oar locks and are held one in each hand. Paddles are lighter and shorter than oars and usually have broader blades. Paddles may have one or two blades, depending on the application. Oars are much heavier and longer with narrow hand grips at their ends and usually long narrow blades. Both paddles and oars may be made of a combination of wood, plastic, aluminum, fiberglass, carbon and Kevlar fibers and even more exotic materials.

Paddles and oars are available in a wide price range, usually depending on the materials used and the design. They have no moving parts and structural damage is usually obvious, so inspect paddles and

This paddle raft crew takes a break between whitewater action. Everyone on the crew must follow the direction of the raft captain, who sits in the stern.

oars regularly for damage and replace or repair suspect paddles and oars before they break on the river. As always, inspect used equipment carefully before buying and ask what kind of water the paddle or oars were used on. A used "creek paddle," what kayakers and canoeists call the rock-bashing, log-stabbing instruments they use to negotiate steep and rocky creeks, may not have the structural integrity of a used one that's seen only Class 2 water.

Thin bladed paddles often wear down around the edges and within a year of steady use may have noticeably smaller surface area, wear that is not covered under warranty. Wooden paddles and oars, without a durable finish or that are subjected to rough treatment, may crack after water seeps into the wood grain. Local shops and especially local boaters can be invaluable for paddle and oar advice. Ask about a paddle or oar's durability before you buy. Have many been returned to the shop? What's the company's repair and warranty policy? Try several different models, blade shapes and lengths and see what you like.

CANOE AND KAYAK PADDLES

Among whitewater paddles there's a basic distinction. Whitewater canoeists kneel and use one-bladed paddles—descendants of what native people around the world use to propel log, bark and skin canoes and other craft. Whitewater kayakers sit in their boats and use two bladed paddles much like those used by native people of the Arctic who historically used skin-covered kayaks to fish and hunt.

Whitewater canoe paddles are distinguished from other types of canoe paddles by a few telling features. The paddle's grip is the most important feature. Whitewater canoe paddles use some form of the t-grip at the end of the shaft. This grip offers more positive control for the paddler and a good handle to hang onto when things get rough.

Durability is also important for whitewater canoe paddles. Many wood and some fiberglass and graphite composite paddles have edges of a more durable material to keep them from splitting, cracking and delaminating.

The shafts of these paddles are usually stiffer than cheaper aluminum and plastic recreational pad-

Paddles come in different shapes, sizes and materials. Wood is a classic choice while plastic is most economical. More exotic fibers offer paddlers a variety of different characteristics from light weight to flexibility.

dles intended for lakes and slow moving rivers. The shafts of whitewater canoe paddles may also be "indexed," or molded into an oval shape at the hold points. Indexing lets the paddler know the blade is oriented correctly to her grip, a helpful feature in a chaotic environment.

Whitewater canoe paddle sizing is a matter of preference, but a loose standard is to choose a paddle that reaches to the paddler's clavicle when the blade

Float bags: **Inflated bags in kayaks and canoes intended to displace water in the event the boat fills with water, usually after a flip or swim. Float bags make recovering boats much simpler.**

Grab Loop: **The loop of nylon webbing or rope at the bow and stern of kayaks and whitewater canoes.**

Kayak paddles are made with a variety of different blade shapes for different effects in the water. Asymmetrical blades have become popular in recent years.

is on the floor. This standard may vary by several inches and depend on the type of boat—high volume open canoes usually require longer paddles, while lower volume C-1s are paddled better with shorter models.

Whitewater kayak paddles incorporate many of the same features that canoe paddles use—edging, stiff materials and indexing.

The selection of a kayak paddle may be a little more complex than that of a whitewater canoe paddle, however, because the nature of the kayak paddle itself in that two blades offer more opportunity for innovation.

In recent years paddle manufacturers have experimented with blade shapes and different "feathers," or how the blades are oriented to each other. For many paddlers, older style, straight-shaft kayak paddles feathered 80 or 90 degrees (blade faces perpendicular or nearly perpendicular to each other) work fine. Many of the changes, though, are in response to complaints of carpal tunnel syndrome and other signs of stress on paddlers' wrists, elbows

and shoulders from paddles that must be twisted radically with each stroke.

Now, most whitewater kayak paddles come with a 45-degree (or less) feather that requires a paddler only to subtly twist the paddle shaft with each stroke.

Paddles, like boats, are getting shorter as well. Most whitewater kayak paddles range in length from about 194 centimeters to about 204 centimeters, but paddlers are favoring shorter lengths for more maneuverability. Longer paddles may provide more leverage and reach, and long paddles are better for reaching out and over the wide tubes of inflatable kayaks (where lengths offered often go up to about 210 centimeters).

Some manufacturers are even experimenting with bent-shaft designs that put the paddler's wrists

Gunnel: **The rail that goes along the top edge of a canoe's hull. Usually gunnels are made of wood or plastic.**

High side: Rafters move to the high side of the boat when it gets up against a rock or in a hole. Highsiding keeps the downstream current from catching a tube and flipping the raft.

in a more ergonomic position. New blade shapes are designed to minimize flutter in the water, speed up strokes and give better leverage for the cartwheeling rodeo kayaker. The choices can be dizzying. Try several different paddle designs to see what works best for you. What feels comfortable to roll and brace?

How does the paddle perform while surfing a hole? Will it be comfortable to stroke downriver all day? Will it stand up to the rocks and other hard knocks that your local river dishes out?

Both canoe and kayak paddles are made from a variety of materials, and preference and price will dictate what the paddler will choose. Wood has long been a standard, but in recent years ash and hickory have given way to carbon fiber and Kevlar. Wood remains an excellent paddle material, however. It's flexible, easy on the joints and makes an aesthetically beautiful paddle. Wood has a feel that other pad-

Oars are made of similar materials as paddles, with wood, carbon fiber and plastic among popular varieties.

Carbon fiber and Kevlar paddles are fiberglass's more expensive cousins. Lighter than fiberglass and more durable, carbon fiber and Kevlar are common materials in bent-shaft kayak paddle designs and also serve to reinforce some wood paddles.

Aluminum and even titanium show up in a few paddle designs, as well. Metals are durable and lightweight, and aluminum-shaft paddles tend to be less expensive than those made with other materials. Be careful of metal edging on paddle blades because it can tear and leave sharp burrs that can turn your paddle into an eddy-clearing weapon.

Some manufacturers mix plastic blades with other shaft materials. While plastic is usually heavier than fiberglass, carbon or Kevlar, it is durable and economical and is a good choice for the cost conscious entry-level boater.

RAFTING PADDLES AND OARS

Many of the same considerations for canoe and kayak paddles can be applied to paddles and oars used in rafting. Paddles and oars share the same materials with similar questions of cost, durability and comfort.

Rafting paddles tend to be made of more durable, less expensive, aluminum and plastic, partly because paddle rafts often have crews of four to eight people, and for the raft owner or outfitter, tough but inexpensive paddles make economic sense. Raft paddles are commonly 60 inches long, but versions are available between 54 inches and 72 inches. There are exceptions to the one-size-fits-all raft paddle: rafters who want the better performance of stiffer, lighter materials may choose more expensive paddle designs used by whitewater canoeists. The guide, or captain of the raft, may want a longer,

dle materials don't. It's also heavier and may take a bit more care than other materials (or maybe because it looks so good, you'll care about it more).

Fiberglass is probably the most common paddle material. It's lightweight, durable and less expensive than wood and more technologically advanced fibers. Fiberglass feels stiffer than wood but might have more flex than carbon fiber, Kevlar or metal.

Rodeo kayakers have been refining paddle shapes to better fit their quick acrobatic moves. Here kayakers wait for their turn in the play hole.

Steep, rocky creeks and rivers demand durable equipment. Some paddlers use thicker, more durable paddles in such environments because contact with rocks is inevitable.

Indexing: Most whitewater paddles are slightly oval-shaped at the point where the hand grips the shaft. This indexing allows the paddler to feel the orientation of his blades without looking at them.

Oar lock: The attachment point for oars to the rowing frame on a raft.

bigger bladed paddle for powerful rudder strokes and a long reach from the top of the stern tube.

Oars used in whitewater rafting are, like canoe and kayak paddles, the subject of much personal preference and taste. Wood has long been a favorite material of whitewater oars, and its weight is less of an issue than with paddles. Wooden oars have some flex and "feel" to them, but they also must be taken care of. The river environment will make short work of an uncared-for wood oar. Regular inspection and maintenance will help wooden oars have a long life. Combinations of aluminum and plastic are popular because they are durable, less expensive and come in breakdown models that are easier to transport and offer interchangeable blades. Carbon fiber is a tough, lightweight, but expensive material that's also a popular material for oars. Some oars are also counterbalanced with weighted handles to make them feel lighter in the rower's hands.

Oar length should be matched to raft size. A good rule to use is to find an oar that is two-thirds the length of the boat. Thus, a 12-foot raft would require an 8-foot oar, and a 16-foot raft would need an oar between 10 and 12 feet long. Raft width, tube height and frame location will change this equation, and of course, oar length also is a matter of personal preference and whitewater application. Shorter oars may be more maneuverable on tighter, technical rivers but may be harder to drive heavy loads through big water.

Oars require some sort of fulcrum to work. Oar locks and pin-and-clip systems serve this purpose, each offering its own advantage. Oar locks are horse-shoe-shaped pieces of metal with a pin at the bottom that fits into an oarstand fixed to the rowing frame. The oar locks cradle the oar in the horseshoe bend and rotate on the pin. Oar locks offer maneuverability: oars can slide into the boat in tight passages and they can be feathered for more efficient strokes. That maneuverability has a price, however, in a learning curve for the rower trying to orient the oar to the water for a strong stroke in chaotic water. Until the rower gets the feel of using oarlocks, he may find his oar slicing through the water rather than pulling against it when critical strokes are needed. With pins and clips the oar is always in the correct position for stroking, but it can't be feathered for smoother stroking into the wind and the oars can't be pulled into the boat when squeezing through a tight slot.

Deschutes River, Oregon

HEADWATERS: *East slope of the Cascade Mountains in Oregon*

LENGTH: *98 miles on the lower section, multiple shorter sections closer to Bend.*

DROP: *Nearly flat to 200 feet per mile, depending on the section.*

DIFFICULTY: *Class 1, 2, 3, 4, 5, 6*

CHARACTER: *The Deschutes River is Oregon's most popular whitewater river, but this attention is focused on the runs around Maupin, Oregon, near the Columbia River Gorge. The Deschutes runs through the high desert of central Oregon and its bed is mostly rough volcanic rock. Sections range from mellow floats to Class 6 waterfalls with transitions between whitewater and flat, moving water.*

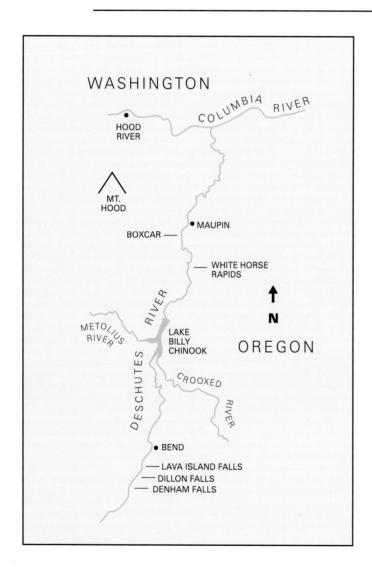

The Deschutes River offers paddlers of all abilities challenge and excitement. The river starts quietly on a high plateau among Cascade volcanoes, but as it tumbles down into the foothills, its drops become more dramatic. At times a Class 1 run may be punctuated by a limit-of-navigability waterfall. Needless to say, it's important to be aware of landmarks here so you can take out in time.

The most commonly run section of the Deschutes is near Maupin. The whitewater here is easily accessible Class 3 and the numbers for this section push close to 100,000 boaters each year. Trips range from half-day affairs to multi-day floats through the high desert. The flow on the Deschutes is remarkably consistent for a river in such a dry area and runs can be made year-round. It's best to avoid summer Saturdays, though, because the crowds come and cram the eddies around Maupin. Whitehorse and Boxcar rapids are probably the best known of the rapids in this run, but there's good play as well (and an annual whitewater rodeo). Opportunities for solitude and the river's most challenging whitewater can be found among the other less-used sections of the river, though arranging commercial trips on them won't be as easy and some of the land bordering the river is private and access is restricted.

Central Oregon's Deschutes River is one of the most popular rivers in the northwest United States, offering paddlers a wide range of challenging runs in the high desert.

Motu River, New Zealand

HEADWATERS: *Raukumara Range on the North Island of New Zealand*

LENGTH: *55 miles*

DIFFICULTY: *Class 4*

CHARACTER: *The Motu River is remote with challenging rapids and water levels that can vary widely with local rainfall.*

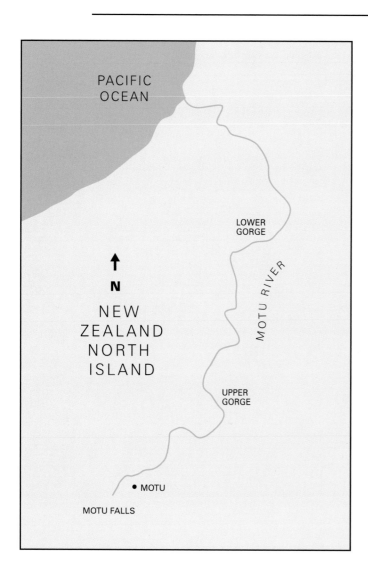

PACIFIC OCEAN

↑
N

NEW ZEALAND NORTH ISLAND

LOWER GORGE

MOTU RIVER

UPPER GORGE

• MOTU

MOTU FALLS

The Motu River is just one of many challenging whitewater rivers in New Zealand. First run in 1919, the river is remote and access is limited. Paddlers have been caught out on the river for days, waiting for isolated flooding to recede so they could continue down river through reasonable rapids.

The Motu was the first river protected by New Zealand for its wilderness and beauty and was saved from a dam project. It remains protected and lovely, offering paddlers a tough run through hard country and thick forest. Only a few roads penetrate the forest after the put-in and they are rough and not passable in all conditions. Once you put on the Motu, you can expect to stay there, no matter what trouble you might find.

New Zealand's whitewater industry has become popular in recent years with outfitters running rafting clients down steep rivers that were previously the domain of kayaks. The Motu offers similar, though slightly less dramatic, whitewater where the challenge lies as much in the remoteness of the trip as in the difficulty of the rapids.

New Zealand abounds with whitewater; the north island's Motu River offers a wilderness paddling experience.

Clothing

LIFE JACKETS

No matter how good a swimmer a padddler might be, he should always wear his personal flotation device (PFD,) or life jacket, on the river. PFDs help swimmers float higher in the water, giving them more opportunities to breathe. This is especially true in whitewater, where currents, waves, holes and even less dense aerated water can keep a swimmer down and out of breath. It's still possible to drown while floating through heavy water while wearing a life jacket, and it is no guarantee of safety. But without one, a swimmer is sunk.

Fit and flotation are key considerations when selecting a life jacket. At the most basic level, it must fit correctly—snugly—to stay on amid the powerful forces in a rapid. Quality lifejackets have

Even dogs need a little extra flotation. Size your dog's PFD to fit snugly yet allow him to swim.

sturdy adjustable buckles on the sides under the armpits to snug the PFD to the body. At the bottom of the jacket, is another buckle and strap intended to cinch the open bottom of the jacket close to the body. While a snug fit is a necessity, a comfortable fit will make the jacket feel less cumbersome.

New low-profile jackets cut for freedom of movement ride close to the body and you will barely know it's on. These models were designed mainly for twisting and reaching movements of kayaking and canoeing. Older-style, bigger PFDs will feel more bulky but still offer comfort with the added advantage of more flotation when faced with swimming big water rapids.

PFDs should be sized to the wearer. Children should wear child-sized life jackets that fit them snugly. Don't try to cinch an adult model down to fit. Children are naturally wiggly and their body shape may make it easy for them to slip out of the PFD in a rapid. Many children's PFDs come with crotch straps that run between the child's legs to keep the PFD from riding up over her head during a swim.

Dogs can also benefit from PFDs. Aerated water is less buoyant and because most dogs are so lean, even the best swimmers can get into trouble in rapids. The PFD will let a dog ride higher and paddle to safety.

The minimum required floatation for a Coast Guard-approved Type III PFD, the most common life-

Oar: **A one-bladed device used to row a boat. Used in pairs, one hand holds each oar and the rower uses leverage against the oar lock to pull or push against the water.**

OC-1: **An open whitewater canoe for one person.**

Life jackets, or PFDs, give paddlers an extra, vital edge when faced with swimming whitewater. Here a paddler surfs the Bio Bio in Chile.

Some PFDs are designed for rescue work with a quick-release harness that allows them to safely tie themselves to a rope and wade into the water to help a boater in trouble. Knives, tow tethers, carabiners and prussik loops are other necessary bits of rescue gear often carried on PFDs.

jacket worn on the river, is 15.5 pounds. This means it adds 15.5 pounds of lift to a floating body and is intended to keep the chin of a 160-pound swimmer out of the water. The Type III PFD is a swim vest and is not intended to keep unconscious swimmers upright in the water. The Type V PFD is commonly used by whitewater outfitters and is distinguishable by the flap of flotation attached to the collar behind the head. These vests usually have more flotation than the Type III PFDs and are intended to keep customers floating higher and in a better position to breathe while the outfitter works to rescue them.

Off-side: **The side of the boat opposite your dominant hand.**

On-side: **The side of the boat where your dominant hand feels most comfortable.**

In addition to the flotation a life jacket offers, it also keeps paddlers warm and offers some protection while swimming through rock infested whitewater and from falls on the bank. The inch or more of foam flotation next to the body holds in a lot of heat and makes a big difference on cold days and especially in cold water. The closer and better the fit, the warmer the life jacket will be.

The foam panels of the PFD also serve as armor against rocks and other bumps the river dishes out. It's not unusual (but is highly annoying) to be hit by an out of control kayaker while waiting in an eddy, and lifejacket foam is good protection against pointy bows and flying paddles. Slippery riverside rocks are a hazard on most rivers and the lifejacket also may cushion some of the blow from a fall while scrambling around at lunch. It's a good idea to wear a PFD any time you're on the river, whether in your boat or stopped to walk the bank and eat a snack or shoot pictures of your friends.

Some lifejackets come with quick-release safety harnesses designed to help in whitewater rescue.

The safety harness can be an invaluable aid, whether for performing tethered swimmer rescues or using the harness with a carabiner and shock-corded webbing as a tow system. Whatever the intended purpose, a rescue PFD should be worn only after a paddler has been trained to use it. It's vital to swim rapids and get a sense of the forces needed to release the buckle. These jackets can be worn without the safety belt until the paddler is properly trained in their use.

HELMETS

Whitewater is an unforgiving environment, and a helmet offers an extra margin of safety. Paddlers need all their faculties to negotiate the river and a blow to the head from a rock, a log, a boat or a paddle can leave a river runner dazed, or worse, unconscious and helpless. Kayakers, C1 paddlers and open canoeists strapped tightly to their saddles should always wear helmets, even in slow moving water, and rafters should always wear them in Class 3 or harder water. Children should always wear helmets. Since a helmet also offers protection from riverside slips and tumbles, all paddlers should consider wearing them whenever they are moving around in the whitewater environment, whether on the bank or in a boat.

Paddle: **A one- or two-bladed device used to paddle a canoe or kayak. A paddle is gripped with two hands and is pulled through the water using body twist.**

Playboat: **Any boat designed mainly for surfing and playing on river features.**

Speed of impact is less of a consideration with whitewater helmets than with bicycle or ski helmets because river runners rarely get going fast enough to need the shock absorbing capabilities of those helmets. Sometimes seen on the river, bicycle helmets are constructed to take one violent blow,

Ocoee River, Tennessee

HEADWATERS: *Appalachian Mountains of southeastern Tennessee*

LENGTH: *6 miles.*

DROP: *57 feet per mile*

DIFFICULTY: *Class 3+*

RENTALS AND GUIDED TRIPS:

CHARACTER: *The Ocoee is a pool drop river that packs a lot of action into a short space and has been a destination for Southeastern thrill seekers since paddlers won recreational releases in the '70s on this dam controlled river. It's a play-boater's mecca, full of friendly-but-fun holes and great surf waves. The river is crowded, however, and while commercial raft groups come in what sometimes seem like endless waves down the river, kayakers queue up in long lines to wait for a chance to surf the more popular features.*

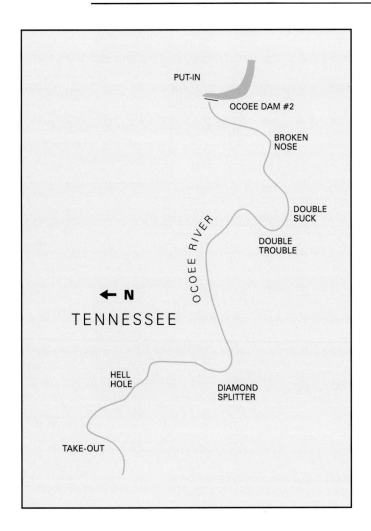

Few rivers have books written just to catalogue all of their play spots and the tricks you can try to do in them. But that's the Ocoee River, the Southeastern fun house of whitewater. From the must-make ferry at the put-in on the lower run through action-packed holes and waves along the its 6 miles, the Ocoee is a joy to paddle. For rafters there's a thrill and a splash in the face around every bend, and for kayakers and canoeists there are challenging-but-friendly features and excellent surfing. The downside to all this is that it's perhaps too much fun for too many people, and if solitude is what you want, don't go looking for it on the Ocoee on summer weekends.

The river is also home to the whitewater park built for the 1996 Olympics in Atlanta. The park is upriver several miles from the put-in on the lower section where the Forest Service narrowed the channel of the river to pump up releases from the dam. The result is a pushy, powerful course with a number of sticky holes. While they were playing with the riverbed, course designers added some artificial rocks to intensify the river's features, and further manipulation has built some rodeo-competition-worthy play holes.

The lower section has its share of classic features with names like Flipper, Tablesaw, Double Suck and Hell Hole. If you plan to play here, find a time to beat the crowds—weekday releases are good (call first to get the schedule) as are early and late in the day. Late put-ins may not be advisable, however, since the releases often end in the early evening and you might find yourself out on the river with no water. Parking is limited and the police there like to write tickets.

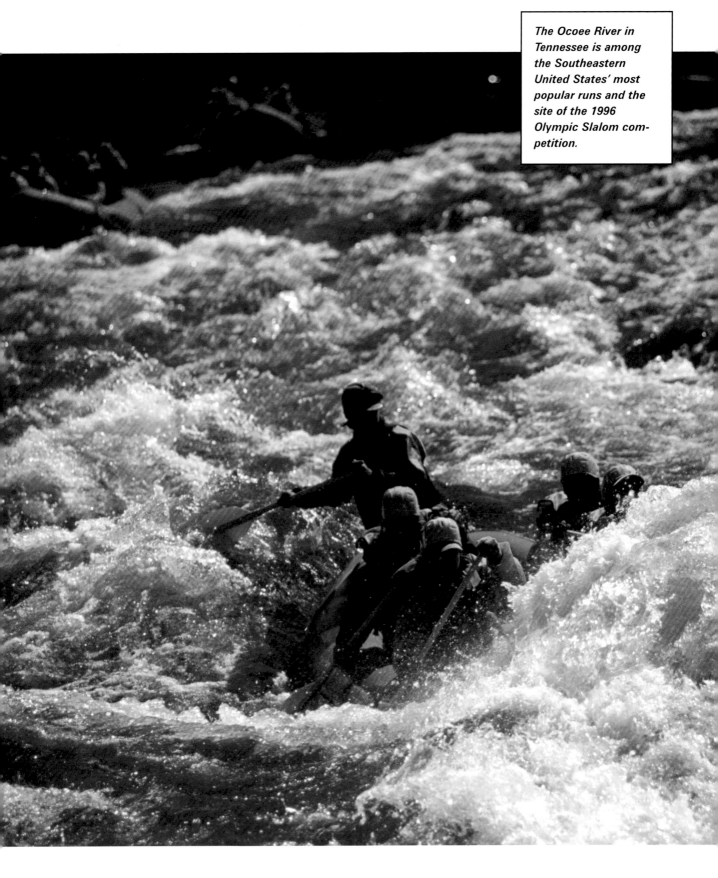

The Ocoee River in Tennessee is among the Southeastern United States' most popular runs and the site of the 1996 Olympic Slalom competition.

Rio Noguera Pallaresa, Spain

HEADWATERS: *Pyrenees Mountains west of Andorra*

LENGTH: *21 miles*

DIFFICULTY: *Class 2, 3, 4*

CHARACTER: *The Rio Noguera Pallaresa is a popular whitewater river running out of the Pyrenees Mountains on the border between Spain and France. Many of the runs are Class 3-4, but sections of harder and easier water allow paddlers to break the run up to fit their ability levels.*

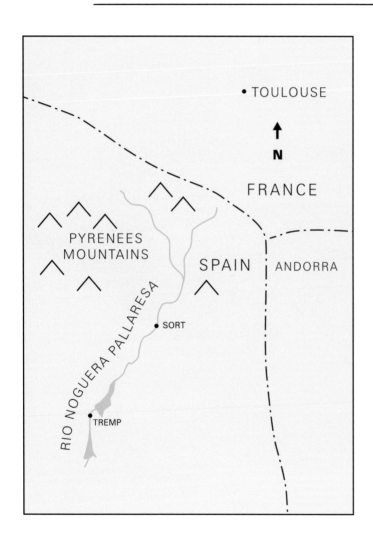

The Rio Noguera Pallaresa is at the center of a bustling hub of outdoor play in the Pyrenees Mountains. The whitewater is excellent, and the river has an annual whitewater festival. Commercial raft trips are popular. The river is about 150 miles northwest of Barcelona on the eastern end of the Pyrenees range near the Mediterranean Sea.

Access to the river is abundant and one local guide lists eleven different runs with most sections of Class 3 or Class 4 difficulty. The river starts in a narrow canyon and runs through it for the first eight miles. These upper sections are more difficult and range up to Class 4+ with a weir that is dangerous at some levels. The Class 2 section is below this and offers a run for boaters not ready for the river's more challenging rapids.

Tucked among 10,000-foot peaks, the Rio Noguera Pallaresa is just one of many whitewater opportunities in the area. A variety of rivers flow out of the mountains on both the Spanish and French sides of the border and the region offers a lot to explore. The Segre and the Rio Noguera Ribagorcana flow nearby and the Garonne, Salat and Ariege drain the French side of the range over the crest. It's a fun-loving place with plenty of opportunity for biking, hiking, caving and skiing if you want to take a day off from paddling.

The Pyrenees offer some gorgeous opportunities for paddlers of all levels. The rivers here wind through stunning alpine forests and arid foothills—and offer some of the most versatile white-water in Europe.

absorbing shock and sometimes breaking apart, making them a poor choice for the paddler who might have to swim a rapid with a crumbling helmet.

Whitewater helmets are constructed to take multiple hits and withstand the abuse of many swims, flips and errant bonks from low hanging branches and flailing paddles. While speeds in whitewater are low, the force of water pushing objects along in it is great, intensifying impacts with immovable rocks and logs. A good whitewater helmet must be able to withstand many of these low speed, high force hits. Even the best Kevlar-reinforced helmet will leave your ears ringing after a hard hit by an underwater rock.

Whitewater helmets are molded from plastic or constructed from fiberglass, carbon fiber or Kevlar cloth and resin. Plastic helmets often provide more head coverage than helmets constructed from resin and fiber and are usually less expensive, making them a good choice for outfitters, raft crews and paddlers seeking durability and lower cost.

Plastic helmets, especially those used by outfitters, may also be easier to adjust. Resin and fiber

Power face: **The face of a paddle blade that pushes against the water in most strokes.**

Rise: **The amount that a raft is upswept in the bow and stern. Rise can help a boat turn more quickly and ride over holes.**

helmets are generally made from tougher materials with funkier designs and paint jobs and are more expensive. Fit is usually a matter of the shape of the helmet and customizing the closed-cell foam that lines these helmets to a specific head. Resin and fiber helmets can be paddling fashion statement, personalized and unique, but if choosing such a helmet, a river runner should consider its application. Some of the more sleekly cut helmets may not cover enough of the head to make them the best choice for tricky and demanding whitewater when flips in sketchy places are common.

FIRST LAYER

Don't wear cotton on the river. It holds water, and turns into a heavy clammy mess that sucks heat out of your body. Cotton can leave you dangerously chilled, even in summer and even under other good insulating layers. Save the cotton t-shirt for the takeout, when it will feel great.

The best choice of fabric next to the skin is polypropylene, capilene or some other non-absorbent insulating material like wool. Polypro is the most common first layer on the river, and knitted in a wide range of weights and with a variety of cuts, is versatile for summer and winter. In summer a polypropylene t-shirt on warm water rivers will provide chafe

Rocker: **The amount that a canoe or kayak is upswept at the ends. Rocker lets a boat turn and resurface quickly but makes it harder to paddle in a straight line.**

protection from lifejackets and spraytops. Under a wetsuit, polypropylene adds another layer of warmth. Combined with heavier fleeces and other special insulating clothing, it is an efficient first layer in winter.

Polypro should fit close to the body, so avoid baggy cuts, and high collars may interfere with tight-necked paddling tops. Ranging in thickness from ultra thin silk-weight to cozy expedition weight, pieces of polypro can be mixed and matched to best suit the air and water temperature.

Wild rivers are earth's renegades, defying gravity, dancing to their own tunes, resisting the authority of humans, always chipping away, and eventually always winning.

—Richard Bangs, River Gods

Warm weather, warm water paddlers often wear short-sleeved splashtops over a layer of polypropylene. This combination will help keep a paddler's core warm but remain comfortable when the sun beats down

Dry tops and dry suits seal out water with latex gaskets around the extremities. Velcro closing neoprene cuffs help protect the more fragile latex.

Heavier fleeces also fit into this first-layer category and can be a very warm solution—though sometimes bulky—for people who just can't be warm enough. Try several different types and weights of tops and bottoms to see what works best for your needs. It's hard to have too much polypro and fleece.

Finally, for the sake of your paddling buddies and your own nose, keep polypropylene clean and dry. Stored damp for a few days in a paddling bag, it will develop an aroma strong enough to gas out everybody else in the bed of the pickup shuttling to the put-in. It's not a good sign if the dog nuzzles up close while you have to mouth-breathe.

WETSUITS

Allowing freedom of movement with a broad comfort range, close fitting neoprene wetsuits are a fundamental piece of paddling equipment. Outfitters issue them to customers paddling chilly rivers and for fall and spring trips in warmer climates. Private boaters rely on them because they are effective, inexpensive

and durable. Wetsuits are often one of the first pieces of gear new paddlers buy.

Neoprene, the rubber material wetsuits are made from, works by trapping a thin layer of water next to the skin and keeping that layer warm. Neoprene rubber has bubbles in it, like foam, that insulate and help slow the transfer of heat away from the body when immersed. Thicker neoprene is warmer, but may also restrict movement. Thin neoprene is stretchy and comfortable but may not be enough to keep a swimmer warm during an extended swim in cold water. Three-millimeter neoprene is probably the most common thickness for paddling wetsuits

Rowing frame: **The metal frame strapped to a raft that provides leverage and support for oars. It also tends to stiffen the boat, making it less likely to bend when it hits a river feature.**

Rudder: **Using a paddle blade to steer like the rudder of a ship.**

and strikes a good comfort-warmth balance.

For warmer-weather paddling or as an underlayer, thicknesses as small as .5 mm are available, sometimes with special surface treatments to increase comfort. Heavy-duty diving wetsuits are usually ill suited for the river because of the thickness of the material and the cut of the suit itself. Most whitewater wetsuits come in a "farmer john" cut that is sleeveless and collarless, allowing full movement of shoulders and head. The long sleeves, high necks and hoods of thick diving wetsuits may be too restrictive for the twisting and reaching demands of whitewater, though such features built into the thinnest whitewater wetsuits can be quite comfortable.

Fit is key to wetsuit effectiveness: the neoprene must hug close to the body, but not be so tight as to restrict movement or blood flow. Manufacturers offer a wide range of sizes for paddlers male and female, thin or stocky, and it's a good idea to try on several sizes and fine-tune the fit when buying or renting from an outfitter. Sagging spots are signs that you should try a smaller size, a wedgie when you reach for your toes means you probably need a wetsuit with a longer torso. That said, wetsuits do take a little getting used to—most of us don't wear rubber suits to the grocery store and they can feel a bit…close.

Paddlers can further customize wetsuit fit by wearing separate pieces of the full wetsuit. Neoprene shirts and vests are versatile and comfortable, neoprene shorts have a sleek fit that helps kayakers wiggle into their boats, and neoprene pants can be worn with a variety of tops as a warm solution for cold-weather paddling.

Thin polypropylene underwear works well under a wetsuit. Polypro tops will be essential under a farmer john to cover shoulders and arms with a nonabsorbent insulating layer, and polypro bottoms are good to wear under rental wetsuits.

SPLASHTOPS AND SHORTIES

Nylon splashtops are among the most pervasive pieces of paddling gear because they are effective, inexpensive and comfortable. They're standard issue to rafting customers in transitional seasons or on cold rivers and are a basic piece of paddling clothing for private boaters. Teamed with a wetsuit and enough polypropylene, splashtops can serve paddlers in many climates year round.

Splashtops aren't insulation. Usually made of thick nylon with a waterproof coating and sleeves and neck that hug tight to the body, they work by blocking evaporative heat loss from the wind and inhibiting the flow of water around the body when running rapids. They're not waterproof, but they work by keeping most water out. They work best when dealing with splashes of water (hence the name) but not so well when fully immersed, so splashtops are best suited for paddling rivers where the paddler won't likely be taking long swims in cold water. For kayakers, splashtops will keep a boater with a quick roll mostly dry. By slowing evaporation of water next to the skin, splashtops keep working even after a paddler has been immersed and returned to the air.

Shorty splashtops are a warm weather piece of gear designed to stem the chill of summer breezes on wet paddlers. Cut with short, tight-fitting sleeves, they work on the same principle as long sleeved tops, but allow more freedom of movement while still keeping the body's core protected from heat loss.

Splashtops come in a variety of styles with features and materials that make prices vary widely. The most inexpensive splashtops have elastic gusseted cuffs and necks that don't hug as close to the body as Velcro-closing neoprene cuffs and collars, but they will work well for paddlers running easier rivers high and dry on rafts and in canoes. Neoprene cuffs and collars are the next step up, and they will seal out a quick dunking or a long day of spray from crashing waves. Kayak specific splashtops have double tunnels, like their drytop cousins, intended to seal around the kayaker's neoprene skirt. Some splashtops, or semi-drytops, come with latex gaskets at the wrists and can be an effective solution

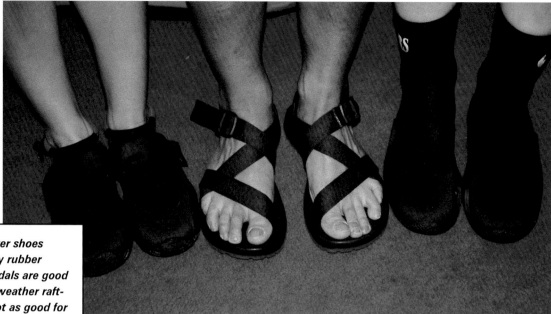

for a paddler uncomfortable with a drytop gasket on the neck but wanting a better seal around the wrists.

DRYTOPS

Drytops offer a significantly warmer and drier option for paddlers. With latex gaskets at the neck and wrists and a sealed waist, drytops are a standard for keeping paddlers, especially kayakers, warm and dry. The gaskets seal out water and the fabric top is seam sealed to make it completely waterproof, the result is a top that will withstand a day full of rolling and playing without leaking any appreciable water. This is important in cold water or in cold weather when the risk of hypothermia may be the most dangerous thing you face on the river.

Drytops have drawbacks, too. Because they're so sealed up, many can be too hot for warm weather river trips when you don't get very wet. This is especially true for kayakers and canoeists who spend a lot of time playing and sweating. A good drytop should keep the water out, but it also tends to keep water in. A good play session in warm

Slicy: **Whitewater playboats have thin bows and sterns that allow them to slice into the water, making moves like cartwheels easier.**

Stern: **The end of the boat behind you.**

weather might get you soaked from inside out. This problem has been solved somewhat by incorporating breathable fabric such as Gore-Tex into the drytop material. These tops are significantly more comfortable and can extend the season of the top. They're excellent for warm weather, cold water paddling when you want protection when you flip but want some relief, too, when you come back up. If you're going to spend the money on a drytop, shell out the extra $100 for breathable fabric. It makes a big difference and you'll wear the top more.

The gaskets on drytops can be a pain as well. They're rubber, fit tightly and eventually tear. When you buy a drytop, expect the gaskets to go eventually. Latex rubber breaks down over time in sunlight and in the conditions that paddlers use it—variably wet and dry, hot and cold. You can slow the aging process by regularly treating the gaskets with auto vinyl protectant like 303 or Armor-All, and it may add a few months or years to the life of your gaskets. The gaskets tend to break when paddlers are putting the top on or taking it off because this is when the gaskets take the most abuse. So try to be gentle when wiggling in or out of them and be careful with earrings and other jewelry that can snag on them. Most manufacturers don't warranty gaskets, but they're easily replaceable (with some glue and a good form) and don't cost too much.

Gaskets can also be uncomfortable. There's an unending debate among paddlers as to whether you should stretch the gaskets to make them bigger or trim them down. Needless to say, both sides make good arguments, and both options have drawbacks. Wearing your drytop frequently will do a lot to stretch out the gasket. Whether it's the rubber stretching or your neck becoming more comfortable

What makes a river so restful to people is that it doesn't have any doubt—it is sure to get where it is going, and it doesn't want to go anywhere else.

—Hal Boyle

with being constricted, drytop gaskets do get more comfortable with time. You should hesitate to make any rash cutting or stretching decisions before you've worn the drytop a few times. If you feel terminally red-faced with it on, then you might want to consider a cut or a stretch of the gasket. Just remember, it's made to fit tightly to keep water out, so cut or stretch conservatively.

DRYSUITS AND BIBS

Drysuits take the drytop concept even farther by making a full-body suit that keeps all water out. Drysuits may be a better choice than drytops for canoeists and rafters since those folks tend have their whole bodies exposed to the cold water or cold

T-grip: The grip at the top of a whitewater canoe paddle. It's shaped like a t to allow your fingers to wrap on it and get a more positive grip.

air throughout the river trip. Drysuits are great, too, for kayakers in cold weather or very cold water. They can get a bit hot, though, for kayakers when the weather turns warm.

Drysuits seal with gaskets at the neck, wrists and ankles (or incorporate latex or Gore-Tex booties so that the feet aren't exposed). A heavy-duty waterproof zipper usually cuts across the chest or back for entry and once the paddler puts it on and zips it tightly, no water should leak in. They're absolutely wonderful for people who tend to chill easily or for any boater in cold weather. An added bonus is that your first layer clothes shouldn't get wet, so changing at the put-in and takeout can be a much warmer affair.

Drysuits come in breathable materials as well, and this is the ultimate solution for paddlers who can afford them. Drysuits made of Gore-Tex and other materials can be worn in a broad range of temperatures and river conditions and are a good solution for anyone who wants a simple do-it-all kind of whitewater outer layer. Unfortunately, breathable drysuits cost nearly as much as a kayak or canoe, so they're out of range for many paddlers.

Bibs offer another alternative to the full-blown drysuit. Used with a drytop, bibs seal water out just like a drysuit and can be a handy solution for a paddler who owns a drytop and wants the extra warmth of a drysuit but doesn't want to spend the money to buy one. Bibs are hundreds of dollars cheaper than drysuits and can work just as well in combination with a drytop.

If you get a drysuit or bibs, consider carefully getting one with a relief zipper or a drop seat. It makes a huge difference when nature calls and is worth the extra cost when you're hopping around on the bank. Remember to zip up before you get back on the river or you'll have a lap-full of cold water.

Kayakers use neoprene skirts with big rubber bands that snap around the boat's cockpit, and there's a trick to putting them on and taking them off. The grab loop must always remain outside so that the paddler can remove the skirt. A kayaker stretches the skirt on from back to front; it can be a wrestling match at first, but with a little practice, he'll find it easy to do. To remove the skirt, he pulls the grab loop away and up to release the rubber band from its snug fit around the lip of the cockpit (called the combing).

SHOES

For comfort and safety, paddlers should wear appropriate footwear on the river. River shoes should grip well—even on wet slimy rocks. They should also protect your feet against rocks, uneven terrain and the rubbing of boat hulls. Again, what you wear on your feet will be determined largely by the kinds of rivers and boats you will paddle.

River sandals have grown popular in recent years and many people who never spend any time on the river own a pair. Most are comfortable, durable and provide decent traction, but they have limitations. For warm weather rafting and canoeing, they can be an excellent choice. They're also handy to stick in a kayak to supplement neoprene socks for extended walks on the bank or hikes to put-ins and take-outs.

Unfortunately, it can be hard to make some sandals fit properly during colder weather and water use. Neoprene socks worn under them can work, though the combination is bulky. They also don't work particularly well in kayaks. Most of the newer kayak designs don't allow much extra room for the thick foam soles of river sandals. Sandal designs vary, using a variety of buckles and Velcro adjustment straps. Designs are largely a matter of personal preference, though paddlers should be aware that Velcro and other hook-and-loop fasteners don't bind as well when wet, causing the sandals to fall off in a swim.

Neoprene socks and booties are another option for the whitewater paddler. They offer warmth, protection and come in a wide range of prices. Neoprene socks are warm, but they provide a minimum of protection and won't last long if worn out of the boat. They can extend the paddling season of a pair of sandals and may be the only thing that fits on the feet of kayakers wedged into ever-smaller boats. Neoprene booties are neoprene socks beefed up with thicker soles and neoprene. Booties usually have a side zipper to help with getting them on and taking them off. The warmest footwear for whitewater paddlers, some booties rival river shoes for support and protection, but the heaviest booties may be too bulky for smaller kayaks.

River shoes—shoes made specifically for river adventures—are sort of a cross between booties

Thwart: **The crosspieces in a canoe that run between the sides of the hull from gunnel to gunnel. They're usually made of wood and they help to make the boat stiff. Rafts have inflatable thwarts that may be removable and provide extra stability for the boat, keeping it from twisting and folding during rough rides.**

and sneakers. They offer the most protection for paddlers and often come with special "sticky" rubber designed to reduce slipping and sliding on the river bank. They are a good solution for paddlers who will be in rough terrain and may need to make difficult portages or hikes to and from the water. They're also great for an added margin of safety on any river, but some may be too bulky for big-footed kayakers in small boats.

Sneakers or old tennis shoes are a time worn tradition among river rats. A favorite and raggedy pair of Chuck Taylors or old Nikes can be great river shoes, but paddlers should remember that once relegated to the river, sneakers (like paddlers) will never be quite the same.

KAYAK SKIRTS

The kayak skirt is one of the essential pieces of gear you will need to head down the river. It's a simple device that hasn't changed much over the years—save for a few new materials and design tweaks. The skirt is worn around the waist and consists of a neoprene tube that you must step into and pull up over your hips. The neoprene tube should be snug to your body but not so tight that you can't breath and should extend up pretty high for maximum watertight-ness. For men, the top of the skirt will reach up to the bottom of the shoulder blades while women's skirts may not go quite so high up the body.

The bottom seam that connects the tube to the tutu-like neoprene deck is more important for fit or placement of the skirt tube. It should line up around the crest of your hip bone so that when you sit in the boat the deck lays flat around the cockpit of the boat. The deck is a broad oval of neoprene ringed by a giant rubber band called a rand. Some skirts use shock cord threaded through a sewn tube in the neoprene instead of a rand. The rand or shock cord is meant to snap around the protruding rim of the cockpit.

A good fit may take a little stretching. The skirt should fit snugly around the cockpit rim: not so loose that it implodes when loaded with water in a heavy rapid and not so tight that it's a struggle to remove if you have to swim. The rands and shock cords that manufacturers use for whitewater skirts are heavy and hard to stretch. You'll learn the tricks of putting them on with regular use (one of which is to use it regularly and stretch it out a bit). If you're riverside and struggling, try wetting the skirt—it will be easier to stretch over the cockpit rim.

The last piece of the skirt is the grab loop. This is the loop of webbing sewn in around the rand or shock cord at the front of the skirt. The grab loop is what you use to remove the skirt, whether you're getting out to take a lunch break or have to swim. It should be made to withstand years of pulling and tugging. Be wary of old used skirts and check the grab loop well on these: they have been known to break off. Some grab loops are just simple webbing while others add in a piece of plastic tubing or a small wiffle-ball golf ball so that it's easier to get a hold of when you're in trouble.

You should only use neoprene skirts for whitewater paddling. Nylon pool and touring skirts are fine for flat water where it's unlikely that you'll have waves crashing over your deck, but they won't hold up in whitewater. Pool skirts are a good idea if you plan to spend any time at the local pool learning to roll. The chlorine in most public pools will eat neoprene alive, so it's a good idea to use a pool skirt or wash your river skirt thoroughly after using it in the pool.

FLOAT BAGS

Float bags are nylon bags filled with air that many paddlers stuff into the empty spaces in their boats. Kayakers and canoeists often use float bags in their boats to displace water in case of a flip. They help a swamped boat ride higher in the water and that helps

to keep it from getting pinned. Since it also displaces quite a lot of water, the swamped boat is lighter and easier to manage. This makes rescue quicker and safer. Some boats don't have much flotation other than what you add to it, so it's a good idea to put extra in. Otherwise, your boat may sink for good.

Kayak float bags are shaped to fill the narrow space on either side of the stern wall and the tiny pockets beyond the foot pegs or bulkhead in the bow. Since the skirt is snapped tight to the boat, sealing out water, the float bags see little use until the kayaker goes for a swim. Then the float bags shine. They keep the kayak riding high in the water and make it easier to tow or bulldoze to shore. They also make the boat a good platform for the swimmer to hold onto in the event of a long swim in heavy water. In this case, the higher the boat rides in the water, the more air the paddler will get as he rides with it.

Canoe float bags serve an even more critical purpose, doing all that kayak float bags do and more. Open canoes have nothing to keep water out of them, so through the course of a rapid the boat will naturally take in water. Float bags displace this water, cutting the physical space that water can fill in the open boat. The result is that the boat will be much more maneuverable with float bags in heavy water than without.

> *Tube:* **Tubes give rafts their characteristic shape. Tubes are usually made of coated fabric with multiple chambers, so that the raft can maintain its shape and buoyancy if one is punctured. Tubes are also integral to the design of catarafts and inflatable kayaks, serving the same purpose.**

Helmet, PFD, sturdy river shoes and warm clothes will stay warm when wet. Once you're dressed appropriately for the whitewater environment, it's time to go paddle.

DURANCE RIVER, FRANCE

HEADWATERS: *The French Alps.*

LENGTH: *20 miles*

DIFFICULTY: *Class 2, 3*

CHARACTER: *The Durance draws paddlers from all around the world to its playful rapids and paddler-friendly atmosphere. There's a slalom course here as well and at times flood lights illuminate the river for night surfing.*

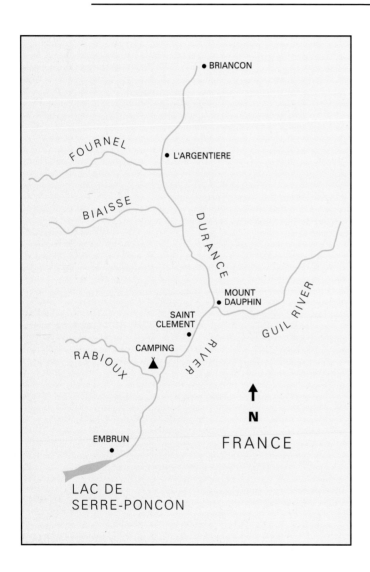

The Durance is the whitewater hub of France for paddlers from around the world. The most challenging rapids are Class 3 on the lower section, but paddlers also run the Class 2 upper section. The center of activity at the Durance is at the campground where the Rabioux joins the flow of the Durance. There's also a famous rapid here, Rabioux Rapid, whose big waves are legendary among Europe's whitewater enthusiasts. There are more difficult sections of the Durance, for the more adventurous, and the Class 3 to Class 5 Guil River runs into the Durance above the Rabioux. The Ubaye River enters farther downstream with three sections ranging from experts-only water to Class 3. Many other tributaries flow into these rivers, offering tighter, technical options for advanced and expert paddlers.

The Durance and its tributaries flow out of the Southern Alps with 10,000- to 11,000-foot peaks looming in the distance, and the various runs are spiced up with difficult gorges. The lower runs course through farmland, and the base for rafting operations in the area is at Embrun, where Lac de Serre-Poncon floods the Durance.

This area is a training site for whitewater slalom boaters with an artificial course at L'Argentiere. The Durance and its surrounding rivers offer everything from big water to high gradient, low volume Class 5. Paddlers should beware of unexpected dam releases, especially on the hard stuff as the difficulty level of many of the narrowest, most technical runs gets substantially higher with more water.

The Durance River is a hub of whitewater paddling in France. It also flows through gorgeous alpine settings.

PAYETTE RIVER, IDAHO

HEADWATERS: *Salmon Mountains, central Idaho*

LENGTH: *Day trips can be made on the north and south forks and on the main Payette river that vary from a few miles to 18- or 20-mile epics.*

DROP: *Sections range up to 100 feet per mile*

DIFFICULTY: *Class 2, 3, 4, 5+*

CHARACTER: *Paddlers can find just about anything they want to challenge themselves with on the branches of the Payette near Banks, from Class 2 runs for beginners to Class 5+ runs on the North Fork. There's even a mix of cold and warmish water here where the cold clear waters of the South Fork mix with the dam-drained agricultural sediment flow of the North Fork.*

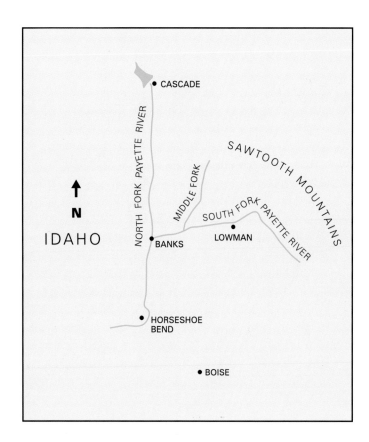

The complex of whitewater runs on the various flows of the Payette is centered on the town of Banks, Idaho about an hour and a half north of Boise. The rivers that meet here draw paddlers from around the world to challenge themselves in this Idaho whitewater paradise. The North Fork is the big draw for the best of the best, and its Class 5 rapids are scary, even from the road in the safety of your car. Some paddlers make this stretch a regular fling, but this is no place to dabble in extreme boating.

For the most talented boaters, the North Fork is a thrill, but for all others they should consider some of the less dramatic, but still challenging runs in the area. The South Fork offers several runs which are much more accessible to mere mortals, and the water here is colder and clearer. Commercial raft trips on the South Fork are challenging and worth the trip. For novices or those looking for an even more mellow paddle, the main Payette below Banks offers a few Class 3 rapids to keep things exciting. This section is generally friendly and is a great place to hone newfound skills.

Rafters take a break between rapids on the Payette River in Idaho. The Payette and its tributaries offer paddlers of all abilities thrilling whitewater in stunning central Idaho.

WATER

River Features

In a frictionless world with no obstacles, the river would flow as fast along the banks as it does in the channel, uniform from surface to bottom. Absent would be the tiny whirlpools that swirl along an eddy line or the pillows of water that stack up in front of rocks, bulging and sometimes breaking. There wouldn't be haystacks or brain waves, roostertails or pourovers. There wouldn't be placid pools or tricky lead-ins. Or hogbacks or keeper hydraulics or reasons to boof. No glassy waves, no playful holes. No white water.

But the river doesn't run in a

The mark of a successful man is one that has spent an entire day on the bank of a river without feeling guilty about it.

—Chinese proverb

frictionless environment. Instead it's a soup of fast and slow water, of rocks, logs and you. As the river tumbles on, a paddler needs to be aware of how it flows and how she can use those flows to find fun

Water flows downhill. Simple, right? Ask this paddler managing the holes and waves of this chaotic rapid.

and be safe. Understanding the river and learning how it moves are the first steps to learning how to paddle whitewater. Beginners thrash and flail because they don't have a feel for the forces at work in the water. Expert paddlers look effortless because they let the river do most of the work.

Feeling the river's energy is a thrilling and sometimes frightening experience. Paddlers play with a force that grinds river canyons out of solid granite over millions of years. That same force can, in an instant, in even mellow ripples, squeeze a boat flat to a rock, requiring a minor engineering miracle to free it. It's an even worse feeling when those forces work against you. Moving water is always more powerful than you think. The key to being safe and having fun is learning how that force works.

Floating a river is a study in relativity. If a paddler sits in her boat and lets the current catch it and carry her downstream, she will be moving relative to people and objects on the shoreline, the river bottom or other boats sitting in eddies. But if she reaches down into the flow of water surrounding her, she will notice that the water isn't moving around her hand. Relative to the flow she's in, she's not moving at all. She won't feel movement unless she picks another reference point—a friend she wants to wave to on the bank or rocks that appear to be whizzing by beneath her boat. So if this paddler is in a clear channel with a consistent flow of water and she just wants to float along, she'll be pretty stable. The tricky part comes when she has to paddle from the flow she's in to another flow or if the flow she's in is disrupted in some way by change in the depth of the river channel or a rock in her path. Such obstacles and changes are river features: eddies, waves, holes, rocks and logs.

THE V

Water moves more slowly near where it comes in contact with the bottom, the bank or the air. Friction from rocky, rough bottoms and irregular shorelines pulls on the flow. Wind pushes the water as well, rippling and slowing the surface layer. In the channel, the deepest, steepest part of the downstream flow, the water moves fastest, and objects in its flow tend to stay in it. The main channel, however,

The V points downstream. Aim for its point and you'll be in the deepest channel and likely headed for a clean, if not smooth, ride.

is often not at the middle of the river: it may lay a few feet off one bank or be ill-defined across a broad shoal of gravel. It might turn radically or fall and pool in a basin. On some rivers it runs under logs and rocks or through boulders like a sieve. Identifying and understanding how the channel flows is one of the first lessons a paddler must learn.

The channel is marked by a downstream "V", which is also called the "tongue" or the "slick." The tops of the legs of the V mark the widest upstream part of the channel and are defined by whatever is slowing or diverting the current, usually rocks. The downstream point of the V is the line that the fastest water in the channel is following. A perfect V formed

Big water: **High volume flows tend to spawn large and chaotic river features such as exploding waves, boiling eddies, dramatic eddy lines, whirlpools. Some rivers are big water runs all the time— the Zambezi or the Grand Canyon of the Colorado being two notable examples— but most rivers have the potential for big water features when flooding.**

Whitewater is a chaotic environment, but the water usually behaves predictably. Learning how to spot river features will help you to have fun and safely learn your limits.

Nantahala River, North Carolina

HEADWATERS: *Appalachian Mountains of western North Carolina*

LENGTH: *8 miles*

DROP: *35 feet per mile*

DIFFICULTY: *Class 2+*

CHARACTER: *The Nantahala is a dam-controlled river that runs most days in the summer and supports several hundred thousand paddlers each year. The bulk of this traffic comes from the numerous outfitters based in the Nantahala Gorge who rely on tourists visiting the area from all over the East Coast. Rapids tend to be more continuous, and as the water is drawn from the bottom of the dam, it's frigid year round, so dress warmly.*

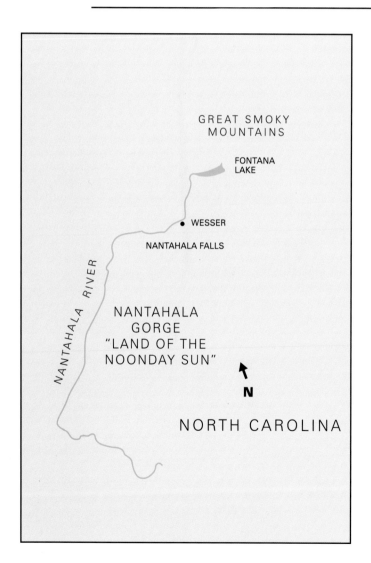

GREAT SMOKY MOUNTAINS

FONTANA LAKE

● WESSER

NANTAHALA FALLS

NANTAHALA RIVER

NANTAHALA GORGE "LAND OF THE NOONDAY SUN"

N

NORTH CAROLINA

The Nantahala River is a great place to learn to paddle whitewater and a great place to for seasoned paddlers to hone their skills. Several outfitters offer whitewater instruction and self-guided trips and because it's so accessible and so friendly, the river gets a lot of use. Popular weekends can get crowded, but the rapids are pretty mellow and the water moves quickly and spreads the people out.

The Nantahala ends with a bang at Nantahala Falls. Crowds of people fill a deck overlooking this low Class 3 rapid to watch the carnage, and for the unfortunate few who don't run it clean and find themselves swimming, the takeout is only a few hundred yards downstream. The end of the run is strung up with slalom gates and the Nantahala Outdoor Center at the takeout is a training center for national team slalom paddlers.

Runs on the Nantahala go pretty quickly, but be prepared for cold water, even in the summertime. The Cherokee named the river Nantahala—land of the noonday sun—because the gorge has steep walls and the sun only shines in it for a few hours a day. It can get pretty chilly down there near the cold water and out of the sun, even in the warm months, so dress appropriately for your trip.

The Nantahala River is a great place to learn, for experienced paddlers to hone their skills and for Olympians to train for world-class competition.

Rizzanese River, Corsica

HEADWATERS: *The Corsican highlands*

LENGTH: *17 miles*

DIFFICULTY: *Class 2, 3, 4, 5*

CHARACTER: *The Rizzanese River is a steep Corsican classic, featuring the island's most famous runnable drop, the 30-foot Big Falls.*

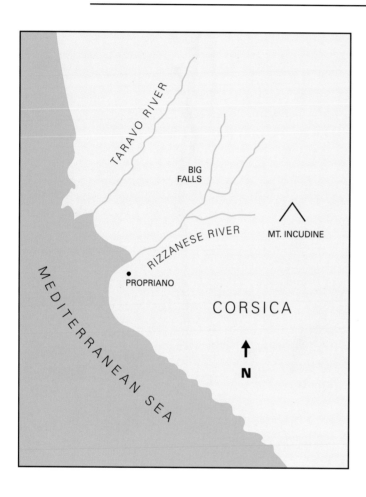

Corsica draws the best boaters from across Europe each year for the spring melt from its 9,000-foot highlands. The island nearly launches itself from the Mediterranean Sea with its tall granite mountains contained in an area that leaves little room for them to fall into the sea. It's a perfect vertical environment for paddlers who want to challenge themselves on what may be Europe's most tricky whitewater.

The Rizzanese River is one of the best known of the waterfall runs on Corsica, with its hairiest section pushing the limits of Class 5. Big Falls is a 30 footer, but there's plenty else here to keep even the best of the best busy.

Needless to say, this is mostly experts-only whitewater on the hardest sections, though there are mellower runs that are fun for a wide range of ability levels. Paddlers attempting the waterfall runs should scout, take all safety precautions and bring their sharp skills and best judgment to these creeks. They are dangerous and claim lives every year.

Paddlers from all over Europe head to the island of Corsica for the runoff from its abrupt mountains. The runs are steep with many waterfalls cascading off the rocky slopes.

in a deep unobstructed channel will be appear glassy down to the point, hence the alternate name "slick". Vs mark all the river's channels, and it's good practice to learn to spot the main channel and its alternate passages as you paddle down the river. (You can do the same with any flow. Look out the window on a rainy day as water flows down the street and pick out the Vs as if you were a mouse-sized river runner.)

On simple rapids, it's usually best to aim your boat for the point of the V and paddle or row through it pointed downstream. A series of waves will likely follow the V, but it's the deepest, clearest and safest passage through straightforward rapids. Longer rapids may have multiple V's that the paddler will need to find and line up on.

As rapids increase in difficulty, with obstructed passages and hazards in and across the main flow, a paddler may need to move across the channel, aim for a point other than the V or avoid the main chan-

nel altogether, picking an alternate channel with better, safer options. As a paddler looks at a rapid, she must consider the V, and whether where it points is where she wants to go.

Remember, once committed to the V, it can be difficult or impossible to get out of it. A body and boat in motion tends to stay in motion, and a poor choice of a channel can take you on an unpleasant and dangerous ride.

As spotting the V is a key to scouting a safe line through a rapid, paddlers can also use the momentum they will gain in the V to their advantage. By moving out into the current and using its energy, paddlers can execute dynamic moves that will carry

Boiling eddy: **An eddy filled with boiling water. Usually a big water feature or one where water is subjected to unusual pressure. A boiling eddy is usually not a friendly place to hang out and rest.**

them through trouble spots. Holes are often broken where the deepest part of the channel goes through them. And the momentum gained by hitching a ride down the fastest part of the channel may allow a paddler to launch her boat off a rock—a move called a boof—in order to clear nasty stuff below.

To learn more about the V, start looking for them as you paddle down the river. What options would each one give you? Throw sticks into the current and see where they go. Paddle or row into them and ride them out. See how it feels to paddle or row with the current, then turn and go against it. Experiment.

Pretty soon the river won't seem as baffling, pulling you and your boat in unexpected ways.

EDDIES

When water meets an obstacle, it finds the path of least resistance around it. Diverted, the bulk of the flow continues downstream forming one leg of the downstream V, but if there is space behind the obstacle, such as a rock standing alone in the current, flowing water will fill the void behind it and form an eddy.

An eddy line is the border between the downstream channel and the relatively slack flows in the eddy. Currents on the eddy line itself can be unpredictable and it's best to move decisively across them.

Eddies offer a place to hang out between moves. Here paddlers wait to surf a hole in the placid waters of the eddy next to it.

Usually an area of relative calm amid the seething chaos of a rapid, an eddy offer a chance to rest, a way to control speed and an opportunity to scout what's coming next. Learning to spot eddies, get in and out of them and then "hop" them—move from eddy to eddy down a rapid—is essential to whitewater boat control.

A paddler floating in the channel and lined up for the V will be pretty stable and moving as fast as the river will take her downstream. An eddy, on the other hand, is water that appears still even though water in the channel is moving fast beside it. In fact, that still water is actually flowing upstream, however slightly, in a cyclical pattern that feeds back into the main channel. These radically different flows, separated by sometimes only a few inches, present opportunity and anxiety for many beginning paddlers.

This separation, called the eddy line, is perhaps the greatest source of trouble for novice river runners. The eddy line is the boundary between the downstream flow of the main current and the slack or upstream flow of the eddy. It may be clearly defined as one of the legs of the downstream V and marked with small whirlpools or a seam in the water. The flow here actually sucks water to the bottom in a circular pattern much like a spring laid on its side and pointed downstream. This is funny water, a zone of seeming unpredictability between two contrasting

> **Boulder garden:** A type of rapid clogged with boulders. Passage is usually not straightforward and may take eddy hopping to run cleanly. Expect pourover holes and many quick moves, especially in steep boulder gardens.

flows. Eddy lines can be great fun to play on for advanced kayakers, canoeists and rafters, but they're no place to stop and rest. Beginners have trouble here because they are unprepared to deal with the opposing flows.

Eddy lines are sharpest, or most narrow, close to the object that forms them. This is the part of the eddy that paddlers look for when they are considering entering or leaving the eddy. The interface between the downstream flow and the pooled water in the eddy is only a few inches and it is the place in the eddy that is the most predictable for paddlers to cross. Downstream, the eddy line gets wider, mingling with the downstream flow to form an ill-defined region of boiling soup that pulls and pushes unpredictably. For beginning paddlers, it's no place to be: it flips kayakers and canoeists and holds rafters in a hard-to-control-the-raft limbo. The upstream limit of the eddy, the "top" of the eddy, is where paddlers want to make their moves.

Catching an eddy is rather like grabbing a light pole as you walk past and hanging on. Straight-line progress down the sidewalk is shifted to rotation: You grab on and turn around the light pole. So it is with a paddler approaching an eddy. Ideally, the paddler will cross the eddy line, lean into the turn and stop pointed upriver in the eddy. Trouble comes when the paddler is unprepared for the change in speed and direction. If he doesn't hit it right, he'll flip, or he'll miss the eddy, bouncing off the opposing flow of the eddy and spinning down the eddy line in unforgiving water. The same is true for leaving the eddy. A paddler must make a decisive move into the main flow, or he will face the same helpless feeling of spinning slowly down the eddy line, water sucking down on his boat.

When paddlers become comfortable with entering and exiting eddies, they can really start to use them to run rapids more efficiently. While the simplest rapids require a paddler to stay in the main channel lined up for the V, more demanding rapids often require a paddler to use eddies to make moves around obstacles or to find new, more clear channels. They also help to slow things down. Eddy hopping is a basic skill that when mastered on ever smaller eddies in ever more powerful water will

In spite of the durability of rock-walled canyons and the surging power of cataracting water, the wild river is a fragile thing— the most fragile portion of the wilderness country.
—Biologist John Craighead

Brain Wave: A monstrous wave that boils on top and looks a bit like a brain. It's a variant of the exploding wave.

Busy water: Busy water requires a lot of tight, quick technical moves. A waterfall with a technical lead in and followed by a steep boulder garden with no real eddies would be pretty busy water.

carry a paddler through Class 5 with relative safety. It can get busy out there, and whatever a paddler can do to break down rapids into individual moves will help make his paddling more efficient, fun and safe.

Eddies come in a variety of sizes and characters, from parking lot to needle thin and from placid to boiling. Parking-lot eddies can hold dozens of boats, and they're often a named feature frequented by paddlers above or below a significant drop. On a river with a lot of commercial raft traffic, they may be places for private boaters to avoid because of too much bumping and confusion. At the other end of the spectrum, a one-boat eddy is just that—one boat fits and that's all. Catching one-boat eddies can be tricky, they're small targets and a miss may leave the boater in a tricky spot. One-boat eddies are usually also places to enter and leave quickly because the paddlers following you down the river may need to use it too for a quick breather or scout of what's below.

For multiple-boat eddies next to play spots, a rough line may form in the eddy of paddlers waiting to ride a wave or a hole. These self-governing lines

Waves frequently form in the channel of a rapid, and when they get big, waves may break like waves in the ocean. Waves make for a thrilling ride for these rafters.

can get a bit hairy in trickier eddies, and it's important to remember your place in line if you want to surf. Cutting into line is bad form as is clobbering waiting boaters as you enter the eddy. River people are very friendly, however, and recognize that transgressions of etiquette happen sometimes especially with beginning boaters. (Just don't do it twice....)

Some multiple-boat eddies are pretty small, and if you're the first to enter, you may be the last to leave. If you don't want to lead through a particularly nasty stretch of rapid, it can be a handy trick to know. If you're an impatient person, don't eddy up.

Eddies vary in character as well as size. Most eddies are the slack water havens described above,

Chundered: **What a hole does to you when it "keeps" you in its recirculating current and you lose control. Characterized by a spontaneous cartwheeling, barrel rolling ride. To be chundered is to get a real thrashing. It has many regional variations—getting worked, munched, eaten and clobbered among them.**

but there are a few other types, too. Moving eddies are slow spots in the river formed by a subsurface obstruction, and the water continues to flow downstream—just not as fast as in the channel. Moving eddies can be handy for buying time or turning the boat, but they don't offer much chance for rest or more than a quick glance downstream. Boiling eddies are often formed in powerful, or "pushy," water, and hanging out in them, if you can get in them at all, tends to be more stressful than relaxing.

In "big water," high-volume whitewater rivers, whirlpools can also form where eddies should be. A whirlpool, like a boiling eddy, is likely to take a paddler on a ride. Such a feature is often called a terminal eddy. What looks like a nice eddy from the road scout 100 feet above may be an unfun choice to make at river level. Tipoffs to whirlpools are logs and other debris that keep going around and around.

Spotting and using eddies is key to skillful whitewater paddling, but think before you enter (or try to enter). From a safety standpoint, what's in and around an eddy is just as important as the eddy itself. Beware of logs that may lurk under the surface of the obstruction forming the eddy. Watch out for guard rocks in the eddy and on the eddy line that may prevent your boat from cleanly moving into the eddy. Be careful of the outflow of the eddy. What are the consequences if you miss it or find yourself slowly slipping out the bottom of the eddy backward? Undercut rocks and logs just below the eddy should make you think twice. The eddy may also have a strong upstream current that can pull you into unfriendly places. In short, scout carefully and think before you paddle.

WAVES

With channels and eddies, waves are among the most common river features. From riffles that lap at the sides of your boat to 15-foot exploding waves that cast shadows in their troughs, waves form when fast water slows down. Lone waves rise up behind shallow features at the bottom of the river, wave trains are formed when river gradient eases from rapid to pool and reaction waves push out laterally from hard rock channels. Water physically

piles up when it slows, forced abruptly out of the confines of a smooth channel. The result is a standing wave that behaves much like an ocean wave, except that it doesn't move. In the ocean the energy of the wave moves through stationary water, but in the river, the energy of the water piles to form the wave—the water moves but the wave doesn't. Like ocean waves, river waves come in a variety of forms: green or breaking, steep or stretched out.

The most common wave formation is the wave train, a series of waves formed in the river

Waves are also immense fun to surf, especially the big ones. Accomplished wave surfers can spin and cartwheel on a wave.

Holes can be a lot of fun to play in, if they're playful holes. Redsides is a popular surfing hole on the McKenzie River in Oregon.

channel as the gradient of the channel gets less steep. Wave trains generally start at the point of the V. In fact, the crest of one of the biggest waves in the series will often be the very tip of the V. Following it will be a number of waves lined up, and depending on the river's characteristics, the second or third wave may actually be the biggest. Farther downstream in the wave train, the waves get progressively smaller until they run out completely in a pool or the river drops again to form another channel and another series of waves.

Waves are also formed by single features in the river, usually a shallow rock that slows water in the channel. These lone waves can rear up in the middle of a rapid and, depending on the water flow, may break or be glassy and green. At some flows, usually the lowest water levels, a lone wave may also become a hole. In addition, a single out-of-place-

seeming wave in the middle of a run may be a pressure wave formed by a rock with water pouring over it. These "funny little waves" usually signal a nasty hole below and are good to avoid.

Water dragging along rock walls also forms waves laterally, and the result is a tricky wave that rises up and often breaks at an angle to the channel. So called "lateral waves" are common raft flippers, as the unprepared boater may hit them sideways. Lateral waves also tend to move boats across the channel spontaneously, "typewritering" them to a new and unexpected part of the river.

Waves size is determined by the river flow and by the feature that's causing the wave to form. High volume rivers tend to form bigger waves, stacking up 10- or 15-foot giants that may cause a too-slow boat to stall climbing out of them. Most river waves, however, are only a few inches to a few feet tall. A one- or two-foot wave can be great fun to surf and play on, and waves of that size can

> **Creek:** Any tight and narrow flow of water. Usually creeks are steeper than their neighboring rivers and often hold waterfalls, slides and technical passages that demand sharp skills. Creeks are also often remote and beautiful and their access can be arduous.

> **Curler:** *A* wave that curls like an ocean wave. It may be a small feature used to gain bearings while running a river or it might be something you can surf.

swamp open canoes and flip unwary canoeists and kayakers.

Waves offer a fun roller coaster ride through most rapids, but a few can cause problems. Again, lateral waves can be tricky because they tend to surf boats unexpectedly. So too can breaking waves and curlers. These waves have a bit of whitewater at their crests that can slow or stop a boater, causing her to fall back into the trough or catch an edge in the downstream flow and flip. Curlers often break on the decks of boats with a surprising plunging motion.

Some waves also surge and pulse and may not stay in exactly the same place over time, rising up unexpectedly. So it's important to look at a tricky feature, get a sense of its timing and plan for the worst. Really big waves, 10-footers or more, may require more forward momentum to climb out of than what passive floating provides.

On really big water, the biggest waves may explode periodically or appear to percolate on top. These haystacks, exploding waves and brain waves have nasty unpredictable properties. Suffice to say that running through them is a crapshoot and boaters—rafters, kayakers and canoeists alike—should be prepared for a good stuffing.

Wave surfing is a delight, and it's often one of the first things boaters try to master. Rafts, canoes and kayaks each can get a good surf on the right wave, and hanging there in the middle of the river as water rushes beneath is addictive. Surfing also gives

Picking your way through the maze of holes and waves in a tricky rapid gets easier as you learn to read the water.

boaters a chance to practice skills that will translate well to downstream travel.

In essence, a wave surf is a form of ferrying, a way to move across the river without going downstream, and learning to catch waves and ride them will go a long way toward being comfortable with this essential skill. Waves also teach padders boat control and balance that plain downstream paddling requires.

Good surfers can catch a wide variety of waves in tricky spots and then carve and spin and make the whole thing look easy. Novices should look for smaller predictable waves to learn the moves and just get comfortable with the sensation. Kayakers and canoeists can rock from edge to edge and rudder with their paddles and feel their boats respond,

Loisach River, Germany

HEADWATERS: *Zugspitz, Germany's highest peak, and the alpine region of southwestern Germany.*

LENGTH: *4 miles*

DIFFICULTY: *Class 4*

CHARACTER: *The Loisach is a low volume technical river best paddled between March and October. It is also the most popular whitewater run in a country where whitewater paddling has been established for a number of years and is growing in popularity. Small boats are recommended as the flows are about that of popularly paddled creeks in the U.S.*

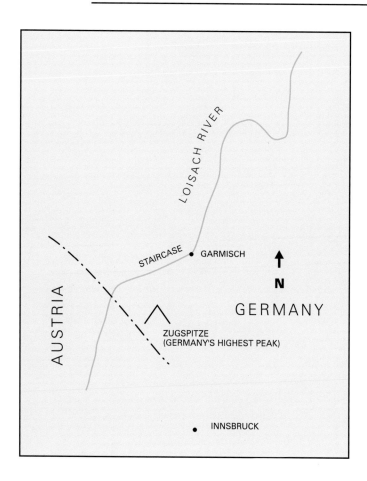

The Loisach collects its water from the flanks of the Zugspitz, Germany's highest peak, and the surrounding mountains. The area in southwestern Germany has long been popular among skiers, mountaineers, hikers and, more recently, whitewater paddlers. The put-in is near the town of Garmisch near the border with Austria, and the run that follows is tight, technical and continuous. The most difficult rapid is probably Staircase, a Class 4, but there are other challenges, not the least of which is the river's narrow bed. The Loisach is a natural slalom course, full of boulders and tricky moves. Eddies are small and choices few as paddlers bomb down it. Playing is less popular on this river and most paddlers tend to head downriver rather than try to surf the features in the river's gorge.

The gorge itself is narrow and forested, with civilization nearby (a road), but not frequently noticed by paddlers focused on the drops. Two footbridges cross the river and serve as landmarks for the run: the takeout is after the second footbridge. The flow is rain dependent and runs at about eight cumecs, or 350 cfs, a small, but exciting, river by any standard. The Loisach continues into Austria where the section features a low falls.

The Loisach River is a tight, low-volume whitewater run popular with wildwater canoe racers, like these paddlers locked in close competition.

Holes can completely swallow boats and paddlers and are the source of much river running mystique.

and rafters can experiment with weight placement and control.

The only problem with all this is that it's just too much fun. Start surfing and the next thing you know a couple of hours will pass, your arms will feel like noodles and you'll still have a river to run. No matter, you'll be smiling.

HOLES

Few things inspire more fear in novice boaters (and more than a few experienced boaters, too) than holes. Perhaps it's the reputation of some of the well-known nasties: Woodall Shoals on the Chattooga River comes to mind, or any low dam anywhere with too much water going over it. Maybe it's the names: Big Nasty, Greyhound Bus Stopper, Jaws, Maytag, Go Left and Die. Or the terminology: stopper, sticky, keeper, terminal. Holes, the big ones especially, have mystique. They are the punchlines of river stories ("…and then she just disappeared…") told and retold.

Holes really aren't much of a mystery. Just as waves are formed when fast water slows and bunches up, holes are a product of the same phenomenon. Falling water dramatically slows and forms a hole, the white frothing water rising and splashing upstream into the downstream flow. The most dramatic form may be the soup created at the bottom of a waterfall. The water hits the pool at the bottom and the moving energy of the water is translated into cyclical flow, tumbling and falling upon itself. Some people call them hydraulics for this plunging cycle while other river runners prefer more pragmatic washing-machine metaphors.

The problem with holes (and the fun of some of them) is that they tend to stop and hold floating objects. This spontaneous surf can be upsetting for the unindoctrinated in a friendly hole and downright intimidating for many paddlers stuck in one of the meatier ones.

Despite the wide variety of holes, they all have features that develop in varying intensity that a paddler should be aware of. First, the green water of the hole is the incoming flow that hasn't been aerated by the churning of the hole itself. This is a fast downstream flow and marks the upstream edge of the hole. The pile is the foamy backwash that paddlers spot first when they see a hole. This water is flowing upstream. The pile is generally white and chaotic, some appear more violent than others, and may surge or crash or throw foam into the air.

A violent-looking hole, however, doesn't necessarily mean it's nasty or terminal. In fact, many terminal holes formed by low dams and other regular features have insignificant-looking piles. The pile on such a hole may not even be particularly aerated and appear more like a fold in the water. This adds to the danger by making it easy to underestimate their power. The way water flows out of them is what

makes these holes so dangerous. Keeper holes are so named because they stick boats and bodies and keep them in the cyclical flow. The paddler remains upstream of the boil line, the part of the hole downstream from the pile where water either flows back into the hole or on down the river. The boil literally boils up behind the hole, a bulge in the surface. The boil is an important gauge of the relative stickiness of a hole because the farther away the boil is from the pile, the more dangerous the hole will be. A floating object will recirculate in the space between the boil and the green water.

To escape the hole at the surface, a paddler or swimmer must paddle up and over the boil, which can be difficult or impossible when the boil is more than a few feet from hole itself or is very tall. Escape in this case may have to be out one of the edges or through a break in the hole, from beneath the surface by catching deep downstream flows under the hole or with help from rescuers outside the hole.

Holes also have kick or current that tends to push a floating object across to the downstream end of it. Kick is most dramatic in holes that are formed on an angle to the downstream flow. The hole will tend to kick toward the downstream end of the hole because the water isn't recirculating perfectly

The first river you paddle runs through the rest of your life. It bubbles up in pools and eddies to remind you who you are.

—Lynn Noel

upstream. This downstream kick is usually a good thing, giving a paddler momentum toward a break in the hole that he can use to punch through. But this isn't always the case: holes can also kick a boat into the stickiest part of the hole or into obstructions such as logs and undercut rocks. Reading how a hole displaces or kicks objects is essential to running holes and getting out of them when stuck.

Hole forms depend on how the water flows into and out of them. Holes on high volume flows tend to be more trouble than holes in low volume flows.

> **Eddy:** A seemingly slack flow of water bounded by downstream current. Usually formed behind obstructions such as rocks, bridge pilings and bends in the river, eddies and moving from eddy to eddy, called eddy hopping, is an essential river running strategy.

They are dependent on a river's character, but they also change dramatically on one river between flood, normal flow and low water. A friendly play hole can turn nasty at high water or it could wash out. It's important to scout unfamiliar flows even on rivers that you feel comfortable with. A few inches on the river gauge can be the difference between a clean run and a good munching.

Flow, too, tends to vary across the river bed, and spotting the channel and what the main flow does when it hits the hole offers good insight about the relative safety of the hole. Frequently, the current in the channel, the most powerful downstream flow, will break the hole and allow a paddler passage. Such a break is called a seam, and it may be the best route through the hole. Sometimes the flow in the fastest part of the channel doesn't break the hole. The resulting maw is no place to go—it will be the strongest part of the hole. If a seam does form where the channel breaks through the hole, the hole will tend to kick toward that seam as it's the easiest route for water to move downstream. The channel may form a subtle V across the face of the hole, and spotting it and understanding how it works are fundamental to learning how to negotiate holes.

Rocks move around, sand and gravel get redeposited but generally holes stay where they are on a river because they usually are formed by the river bed itself. The shape of the river bed has a lot to do with the way holes form. A very steep gradient that piles into a flat part of the river will form a hole. Steep rivers and creeks that pool and drop tend to develop strong holes where the drops hit the pools. The stickiest holes tend to be formed by smooth-rock slides and steep runs that hit slack pools. The angle that the water hits the pool tends to push the boil far back from the hole, making escape difficult.

In such a case, a paddler will need plenty of momentum to punch through the hole or she will need to find a seam or an edge that she can aim for to dodge the grabbiest part.

Two specific features tend to form strong holes: pourovers and ledges. Pourovers are rocks with water pouring over their tops and ledges are long low abrupt drops in the river bed. Both of these are common river features with the potential to form strong hydraulics.

Pourovers can be tricky to spot from a boat in the middle of a rapid, but there are some clues. An unusual bulge or wave (a "funny little wave," as William Nealy calls it in his book *Kayak*,) in the middle of a rapid is a sure sign of a pourover. Froth spitting into the air and highly aerated downstream flow are further clues. Observe your surroundings, pourovers are common in boulder garden rapids and a paddler should be wary when her view of the rapid is obstructed.

While pourovers may hide in rapids, ledge holes form strong hydraulics at many different flows, but they are usually easier to pick out. Ledges will form long hydraulics and, depending on the height of the drop, may spray mist into the air below them. A paddler may need to find the lowest point on the horizon line of the ledge and expect that the channel pushes through the ledge at that point. If the channel doesn't break the hole, a paddler may need to aim high and hope to skip or "boof" off a tall feature that will give her boat some clearance over the hole. Running ledges blind is dicey so plan on scouting as they are often a hard-to-avoid feature.

Sticky holes are often formed by the most symmetrical geologic or manmade formations. Smooth-rock slides tend to make sticky holes because they spread the water out evenly over a wide area and then pile into a pool below. Regular smooth ledges do the same thing.

Low dams, weirs and some concrete fish ladders are the most treacherous river formations to be concerned about. They're usually engineered without river travel in mind. They are squared to the current and are designed to spread the flow evenly across the feature. Flows spill over them at low angles to the pool below, and the result is a hole with no kick,

Big holes may seem disorienting, especially if they hold on to you or your boat. It's important to stay loose and ride the hole rather than muscle out of it.

a boil set far back from the green water and no channel to break through the hole. Often, too, the water is sluiced between concrete walls, offering no edges where the paddler could escape. To compound the problem even more, manmade river obstructions tend to break down over time or may have intentionally been broken to restore a more natural flow to the river. The result is a jagged, steel-rebar-infested mess. Be wary of manmade river obstructions and give them a wide berth.

Funny Water: **Funny water is boiling unpredictable water that surges and sucks at a boat. Often a big water feature, funny water can make for an unstable feeling ride and is a notorious kayak and canoe flipper. To an extent, poorly formed eddy lines are examples of funny water.**

Despite the nasty potential of holes, most of them are fun to surf and paddle through. Like wave surfing, hole surfing is an addictive pasttime. Paddlers should start in small, friendly holes and feel how holes hold a boat. Kayakers and canoeists can feel what it's like to brace downstream in a hole while keeping their upstream edge out of the green water. Rafters can feel how weight shifts and high siding influence the behavior of the boat in the hole. Rides can be smooth but are typically violent, bucking paddlers in the pile and demanding precision balance. Practice hole riding is valuable for river running: it teaches the skills necessary to move in a hole and eventually escape it and gives confidence to paddlers who may find themselves stuck unexpectedly.

Gauley River, West Virginia

HEADWATERS: *Summersville Lake, West Virginia*

LENGTH: *28 miles*

DROP: *30 feet per mile*

DIFFICULTY: *Class 3, 4, 5*

CHARACTER: *The Gauley River is an annual pilgrimage for Eastern whitewater paddlers. Big, pushy rapids cut through tight passages, making the upper Gauley's biggest rapids Class 5 and turning the lower Gauley into a big water Class 3 play run. Rocks at the Gauley are undercut and swimmers should beware.*

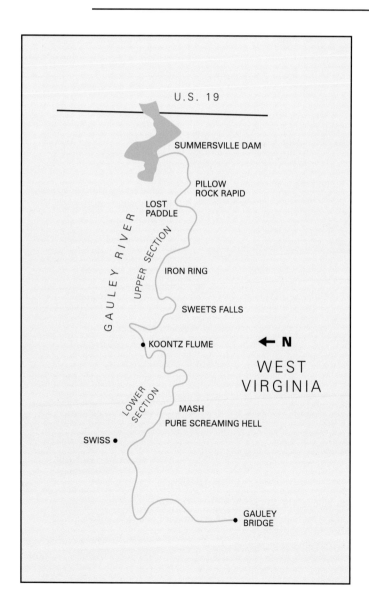

September is Gauley month for legions of East Coast paddlers. For September and a couple of weeks in October, the Gauley River runs on a weekend schedule, the water jetting out of three tubes at the bottom of Summersville Dam. The flow is consistently big and pushy, and though the river itself doesn't drop radically in the 28 miles of whitewater below the dam, the narrow gorge and dramatic rock formations kick up 100 major rapids in that distance.

The toughest part of the river comes in the first nine miles, the Class 4 and 5 upper Gauley. The Class 5 rapid Insignificant is anything but. Pillow follows with most of the river crashing into a huge rock outcrop. While flashy kayakers try to get their boats vertical on the rock, or visit the Room of Doom on top of the pillow, everybody else braces like crazy, wide-eyed and adrenaline jazzed. Lost Paddle is a long and technical Class 5 made even scarier by the undercut rocks that define its course. Iron Ring has a nasty hole and sharp rocks left over from another era when loggers tried to blast a channel through the drop so logs could float freely through. The run ends with Sweets Falls and a choice: run the meat of the hole or, for kayaks and canoes, a technical boof move off a rock outcrop on river left that dodges most of the scary stuff.

The lower Gauley is a great warm-up for the pushy run above. A dozen miles of Class 3 rapids are spiced up with a few Class 4s—Koontz Flume, Mash and Pure Screaming Hell—and some great play waves and holes to make a great run for those who want a less stressful taste of the Gauley. Because it's such a demanding run, outfitters on the upper Gauley run may require previous rafting experience among their customers, and the lower Gauley is a great place to become accustomed to big water rafting technique.

When the day on the river is done, Gauley paddlers don't usually go home. They take their river smiles to the nearby campgrounds where parties go on around campfires until late in the evening. The Gauley Festival is also scheduled for one of the release weekends, drawing paddlers from around the country to try the river by day and get wild at night. The festival is a reunion for many paddlers, who block off large chunks of time in September to head to the mountains of West Virginia for their annual dose of some of the East's biggest, most notorious whitewater.

Gauley season, the annual September dam releases to the Gauley River in West Virginia, draw paddlers from around the country to the carnival atmosphere of the river run and the parties that follow in the evening.

Hazards

ROCKS AND LOGS

While holes have a scary mystique, rocks and logs that obstruct a rapid are just scary. Sometimes rapids contain rocks and logs that don't divert the water in the channel. Instead the water flows between, around and under them. The river flows with tremendous force through its channel, and when the channel is obstructed by logs or rocks, the stakes of running through it are very high. Pinned boats are, at the least, difficult to retrieve, but when they're broached with someone still inside, it's a life-threatening situation.

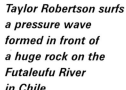

Taylor Robertson surfs a pressure wave formed in front of a huge rock on the Futaleufu River in Chile.

Rock seives and too-tight passages and slots are common on rivers with boulder-garden rapids and steep gorges. A paddler should know what's in the outflow of an intriguing-looking slot before running it. Many of these squeeze down too tightly for a boat to fit through, and others are too tight for even a swimmer to wiggle through. Getting stuck in such a spot is an emergency, and a paddler should work to rescue as quickly as possible—it may take help from fellow paddlers to get out and they'll need to move quickly.

Logs can present an additional problem in a slot. While the channel without the log obstructing it may

To trace the history of a river...is to trace the history of the soul, the history of the mind descending and arising in the body.

—Gretel Ehrlich

be a simple rapid, the log adds an element of danger that all boaters should heed. Simple moves around them can turn dicey quickly, and it's easy to underestimate the strokes you'll need to make a critical move above a log. In addition, logs with branches still attached—called strainers or sweepers—pose an even greater threat. Logs can be hard to spot if they're just under the surface in aerated water and paddlers should scout the outflow of rapids as well as the technical moves within for wood. When in doubt, walk. Logs are not to be taken lightly.

After scouting for a channel clear of rocks and logs, paddlers should also be alert to undercut rocks. Though dependent on the geology of a river, undercuts are a common river formation. Rocks may actual-

ly look like mushrooms in river courses susceptible to undercutting. The tricky part is that often the head of the mushroom shape is sticking out of the water while current flows underneath the rock. This may mean that the current works to push a paddler into and under such a rock.

To compound the problem, logs sometimes are lodged under the undercut, an extremely dangerous feature. Undercut rocks can be spotted by the behavior of the water around them. If water doesn't pile up on the face of a rock in the current, it is likely flowing beneath it and should be avoided. Undercut

Rocks may form a natural slalom course for paddlers to negotiate. Some rocks are undercut and present an additional hazard to paddlers who may be swept under them.

Grabby: **Any river feature that wants to hold a boat. Usually used in reference to holes.**

Green Water: **Un-aerated water. Usually used to describe the water coming into a hole or the face of a wave.**

Middle Fork Salmon River, Idaho

LENGTH: *96 miles*

DIFFICULTY: *Class 3+*

CHARACTER: *The Middle Fork Salmon River is a classic remote Western wilderness run. The rapids* are manageable at normal flows, but paddlers should be confident and skilled to run the river at higher levels. Strict permitting by the U.S. Forest Service allows only 10,000 people on the river each year.

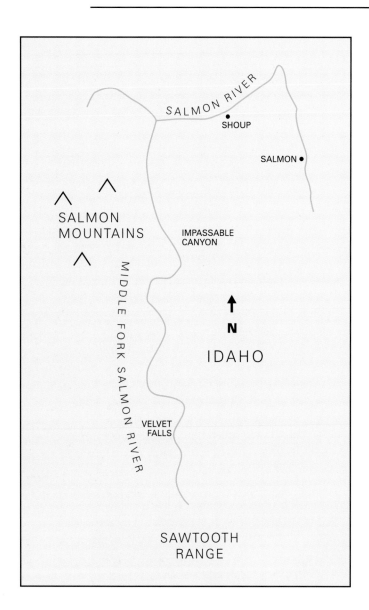

In 1968, the Middle Fork Salmon River was designated Wild and Scenic—one of the first rivers in the U.S. to come under such protection. That preservation has kept the river undeveloped as it crashes down out of the Sawtooths to meet the big water of the Main Salmon. The Middle Fork is strictly regulated by the Forest Service, and permits are awarded in a lottery system that prospective paddlers await anxiously. The river at summer flows is manageable for aggressive intermediate paddlers, but higher water and a more continuous nature in the spring demands more skill and experience from Middle Fork paddlers.

The high country of the Sawtooths offers spectacular scenery and the river thrills with its many rapids, but the Middle Fork holds an added bonus: hot springs. Natural hot springs well up at several points along the river, giving paddlers a chance to take a relaxing soak. Some of the springs are very hot and may need to be tempered with cold river water.

Rapids on the Middle Fork tend to be technical and tight, ranging from Velvet Falls, Class 4, five miles from the put-in, to hard the Class 3's of Impassable Canyon like Redsides and Weber. There are no roads into the area along the Middle Fork's 96 miles, so paddlers must be prepared to be self-sufficient and ready for any problems that may arise.

The Middle Fork Salmon River in Idaho is one of the western United States' classic runs. Remote, challenging whitewater offers river runners a multi-day trip into the heart of the northern Rocky Mountains.

> **Hole:** When water flows over an obstruction in the river, it often causes the surface water to reverse flow and move upstream, creating a hole.
>
> **Horizon line:** The farthest point downriver that you can see. If it's very close and you can only see treetops beyond, expect a steep slide or waterfall.

rocks will also form weak moving or boiling eddies in the area where the water passes beneath, so it's important when scouting a rapid to look for indistinct or poorly formed eddy lines behind rocks. They're good indicators of undercuts.

Some rock walls are undercut or form caves. Since flowing water forms the undercut, it's important to stay out of the flow that might take you into it. Caves can be very difficult for flipped boaters or swimmers to escape.

If caught on an obstruction, a paddler should lean into it. If he leans away, the current will catch the upstream edge of his kayak, canoe or raft and flip him. The result is a swimmer trapped underneath a pinned boat. It's a bad place to be. If he leans into the obstruction, he lifts the edge of his boat, and he can buy time to figure out a plan of escape. Though counter-intuitive, such a position can be very stable; in many cases the pressure of the water under the hull or floor of the boat will push it even higher out of the flow.

LEDGES AND FALLS

If all you hear is thundering water, if you feel a burst of adrenaline course through your body, if you look out over the river and all you can see below are treetops, it's a good sign that you've come upon a waterfall. Whether you're in a raft, kayak or canoe, you should catch an eddy soon.

Waterfalls and ledges represent the extreme end of river gradient and offer paddlers a chance to test their nerve and equipment. They're also good places to get out and walk around. At the very least, you should make it policy to get out and look, even at

the falls that you've run a hundred times. Rivers change, even hard granite waterfalls, and you never know if there's going to be a log at the bottom of the drop. Scout, just to be sure.

Ledges and waterfalls come in a variety of forms. Ledges are usually lower than waterfalls, the cutoff being somewhere around 6- to 8-feet high. While you may expect a vertical column of water running over these features, it is usually less so, especially on the lower drops. The momentum of the water shoots out away from the vertical rock face of a classic falls and into the pool, like holding a garden hose horizontally and watching the flow pour out in an arc from its end. This is especially true of falls at high water when a lot of water is squeezing through a small area (put your thumb over the end of a hose). In addition, falls are rarely so abrupt that they just drop off into a pool. Often there's a progressively steep lead-in that drops off vertically part way down.

While dramatic, many ledges and falls aren't that bad, and the tough paddling you'll do in running the falls will likely be negotiating the entrance and putting your boat in good position for the drop. You can't maneuver much in the air, so your setup is criti-

Boundaries don't protect rivers, people do.

—Brad Arrowsmith, landowner along the Niobrara National Scenic River, Nebraska

cal. When you're scouting, look for a clear path to the lip of the drop. Look closely. Are there any subtly hidden rocks that will knock you off course? Is the water deep enough near the lip so that you can get a few good paddle strokes in before you take the plunge?

In kayaks and canoes especially, you may need to find a place to boof or ski jump the drop by using a high spot on the lip—a nub, bump or the rock bordering the flow—to give your boat a little lift going over the edge. A boof will help you clear the nastiest parts of the hole with good momentum. A really

Waterfalls, like this one on Dry Meadow Creek in California, are a thrilling ride—if you've made sure the landing is clean and if you have the skill to put your boat where you need it to be.

Chutes are steep, narrow passages that offer little room for maneuvering and are prone to having logs, rocks and even boats and ropes stuck in them. Scout carefully.

good boof will land you in the eddy, but be careful about boofing tall drops into green water: in a kayak or canoe, you can squash your back on the landing.

Look for aerated water to land your boat in—it will cushion the fall—and try not to land perfectly flat on your hull. Creek boats are designed for boofs and landings and their highly rockered shapes will help to soften the landing, even if you land pretty flat. Canoes have good rocker as well, offering good boof and landing possibilities. Inflatables boof, too, though it's harder to get lift with them. You are almost guaranteed a soft landing at the bottom, though.

Another option for getting through the hole at the bottom—the option with the softest landing for kayaks—is to aim low on the horizon line and follow the flow down and into the hole, rather than to try to get lift. This may cause you to go deep under the hole and pop up on the boil, a move called a meltdown. Sometimes you'll meltdown when you didn't plan it, so hold your breath and wait for the buoyancy of your boat to return you to the surface. The drawback to melting down is that you go deep, and there might be something in there that you hit. Melting down is especially not a good idea on shallow creeks where you could hit bottom and perhaps vertically pin—get your boat lodged in the riverbed vertically. Melting down is ill-advised on waterfalls that don't have clean landing pools or in narrow slots and tight passages that could hold subsurface obstructions. This type of landing is risky because you may not be flushed out under the hole, and when you resurface, you'll be surfing.

Creek boats are probably the best kayaks for running the steepest drops. They're heavily rockered with blunt bows and sterns and are made for boofs and landings. Creek boats are shaped to resurface quickly after a vertical drop, even if you enter vertically, or pencil in. As an additional safety feature they are built with bulkheads to give your feet a solid platform to absorb the shock of the landing without slipping and wedging deep in the bow of the boat. Finally, the blunt bow and stern of a creek boat resists vertical pinning in drops and the heavier plastic resists being smashed.

Canoes operate on a similar principle as creek boats. Good whitewater canoes have a lot of rocker and blunt bows, and they tend to ride up and over the water rather than cut into it. For really steep drops, the canoe should fit you closely, or you may be separated from it upon landing if you don't hit the drop quite right. If you enter vertically in a canoe, you'll likely swamp it, so consider that when scouting the run. Will there be a critical move you need to make just below the falls with a boat full of water?

Rafts run vertical drops with mixed results. If the crew doesn't mind a swim, go for it, but be aware that a landing at the bottom of a steep drop will be abrupt and may fold the boat and disgorge the paddlers violently. Inflatables offer a well padded surface to land on, and that can be a less jarring advantage. The only problem with running really big drops in rafts and inflatable kayaks is that it can be hard to stay attached to the boat on the landing. Many high performance inflatables have thigh straps or foot cups to give paddlers extra purchase when the going gets vertical. Smaller rafts—two person R2s and little paddleable catarafts like the Shredder—do best in this kind of stuff, in fact in the hands of skilled paddlers they can run cleanly many of the steepest drops.

SLIDES

Slides are the waterfalls' not-so-vertical cousins. Water pours over a sloping rock face that drops steeply but not vertically, and the result for the whitewater paddler is a bobsled ride on a few inches of water and solid stone. On the biggest slides you may hit 35 miles per hour while dropping dozens of vertical feet. Imperfections in the rock will cause your boat to skip, and if you're unlucky, may knock you off line. Unfortunately, the small amount of water running over the rock face affords little purchase for your paddle and mid-run corrections are difficult. Because of this, it's critical to scout thoroughly and choose a clean line. The forces on you and your boat are about the same as on a vertical waterfall, but on a big slide there are more variables and you must evaluate them all the way through the hole at the bottom.

As with a waterfall, the entrance is the most critical of the moves you'll make. Make sure the approach is clean and that you'll be able to set up the angle you want and hold it. On your way down you'll want to stay loose and ride out any bumps in the rock: flipping is not an option, because you can't roll up when you're skidding along on your face. The holes at the bottom of slides can be downright nasty with boil lines pushed back far from the green water. As you hit the hole try to reach across it and pull yourself through with a few quick strokes. On big slides, you'll usually be going so fast that as long as you hit the hole pretty straight on and keep your nose up a bit you'll skip right over it. If you don't clear the hole, you'll likely have to reach deep in your bag of hole-escape tricks to get out. Slide holes are mean—and they don't give up easily once they've got you in their clutches.

CHUTES AND SLUICES

Chutes and sluices neck the river down into a tiny passage, creating pressure and powerful river features. Some chutes and sluices combine waterfalls, ledges or slides to add an extra technical element to vertical kayaking and canoeing. There's not a whole lot to running narrow passages except to say that you should always take a look at them before you drop off the edge. These are likely places for logs

Logs and other debris gets lodged in narrow passages. The line that was clean yesterday, may be terminal today. Scout carefully.

Kick: **A hole often has a current within it that tends to push a floating object laterally across its face. This kick can be useful for escaping a hole because it often leads where the current breaks the hole. Holes may also kick into their stickiest part, so beware and scout**

and other debris to get stuck, obstructions that may not have been there the last time you ran that feature cleanly. All boaters should be careful of undercut rocks lining the sides of the chute and kayakers should be aware that they may need to run the narrowest of these features with their paddles held lengthwise to the boat. Rafters may need help getting through from someone on the bank who can help tip the boat on edge to squeeze through the passage. Needless to say this is a tricky move.

Arkansas River, Colorado

HEADWATERS: *Sawatch Range of the Rocky Mountains west of Colorado Springs*

LENGTH: *104 miles*

DROP: *38 feet per mile average, but it varies widely from section to section*

DIFFICULTY: *Class 2, 3, 4, 5, 6*

CHARACTER: *The Arkansas draws the most commercial rafters of any river in the U.S. and any, probably, in the world. Put-ins and take-outs are highly developed and the river is managed to run thousands of paddlers through its tight gorges and fantastic whitewater. Brown's Canyon, a 20-mile run of Class 2 and 3 water, draws the most people. The river's most famous, more difficult stretches are Royal Gorge and The Numbers.*

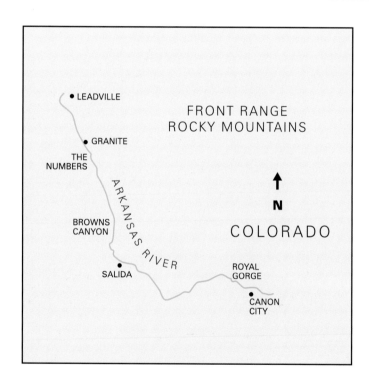

The Arkansas is big whitewater business, with more than 250,000 commercial paddlers annually. Most come for are the thrilling-but-forgiving rapids of Browns Canyon and views of 14,000-foot Rocky Mountain peaks. The run can be pushy with a complex boulder garden that's no place for novices to paddle blindly. Despite the vast number of visitors, the river can offer solitude or at least the feeling of getting away from development. Steep canyon walls have impeded development and the road doesn't follow the river for the whole way.

More than 60 outfitters run trips on the river and for those seeking a guided trip—advisable for those unfamiliar with the river—nearby Salida, Buena Vista and Colorado Springs offer plenty of rafting company choices. More advanced and adventurous boaters may want to try Royal Gorge or The Numbers, featuring Class 4, 5 and 6 rapids. Royal Gorge's sun-blocking 1,500-foot vertical walls have the potential to intimidate even before you put on. It's mostly Class 4 but Sunshine Falls, Class 5, pushes the limits. Higher on the river, The Numbers is even-more-intense Class 4 and Granite Canyon and Pine Creek are steep, continuous whitewater with a portage and the potential to be Class 6 at higher flows.

The Arkansas River sees the most commercial river traffic of any in the United States, but solitude can be found within its canyon walls among the wide range of runs available on the river.

River Spey, Scotland

HEADWATERS: *The Cairngorms in the highlands of northeast Scotland.*

LENGTH: *Ballindalloch to the Tandhu Distillery is about 5 miles. Eighty miles of the river is runnable.*

DIFFICULTY: *Class 2*

CHARACTER: *The River Spey is a good introduction to much of the challenging whitewater in the United Kingdom. A mellow river that's rated Class 2, it's good for any level of paddler with surf waves that novices can enjoy and easy access. There are scheduled times for fishing on the river that paddlers should respect.*

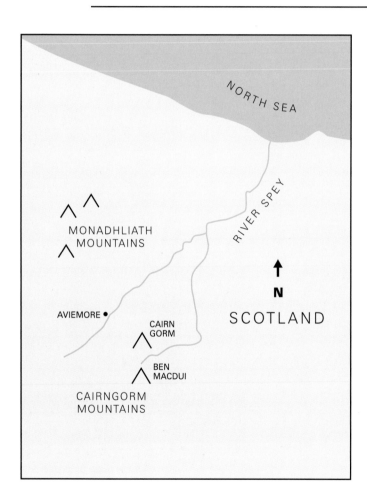

The River Spey tumbles out of the Scottish Highlands among the most rugged mountains of the British Isles. It offers a trip suitable for novices trying their sea legs and more advanced paddlers sharpening their moves for steeper waters of Scotland, England and Wales.

The river has specific days and times when it's open to paddlers—salmon fishermen get access during the alternate times—so it's best to check locally before putting on and always respect other river users.

The river has the added advantage of having a distillery at its take-out in Knockando. You can warm your chilled river blood with a "wee dram" of some of the world's finest single malt whiskies. On the Spey, the sights are as thrilling as the river itself and stunning landscapes make the region a vacation spot for all of the UK.

On the river, look for challenging rapids at the confluence with the River Avon and at Blacks Boat Rapid, both short Class 2 runs with waves and good opportunities for play and practice. At high flows on the Spey, the river remains manageable, according to locals, but paddlers should be wary of tricky eddy lines and funny water. The run is suitable for most boats and paddlers and is a good training ground for beginners and groups.

The River Spey offers accessible whitewater in the stunning Scottish Highlands. After a run, paddlers take out in Knockando, the site of several of Scotland's famous scotch distilleries.

Kern River, California

HEADWATERS: *Sierra Nevada of California*

LENGTH: *50 miles*

DROP: *Most sections are about 30 feet per mile*

DIFFICULTY: *Class 3, 4, 5*

CHARACTER: *The Kern River is only a few hours from Los Angeles and thus is a popular river playground in the Sierra. Designated as Wild and Scenic, the Kern drains the area around Mt. Whitney, the highest mountain in the lower 48 states of the U.S. The runs here are accessible to a wide range of paddlers and numerous outfitters provide a variety of options for potential paddlers.*

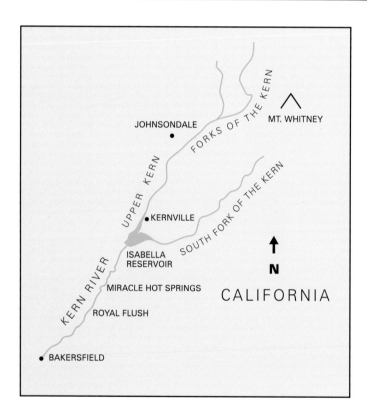

The Spanish called the Kern the Rio Bravo when they first ventured into California because they had so much difficulty getting across it. The Kern River is the heart of Southern California boating even though it doesn't draw as many paddlers as the American River drainage to the north.

There's plenty of possibility for escape from the pressures of urban California on the Kern and its tributaries, among them multi-day trips that are strictly rationed by the Forest Service. The whitewater home base is in Kernville, where an annual whitewater festival in the early spring kicks off the western whitewater rodeo tour.

The options for running the Kern are varied, and trips can be easily tailored for group size and ability level. About 40,000 boaters a year pay to paddle the Kern so the crowds don't get as intense as on other much more popular rivers in the U.S.

Whatever your ability, keep an eye out for hazards. There are a few recommended portages among the rapids of the Kern, and high water can be particularly dangerous here. The Kern feels the effects of manipulation by dams and irrigation projects however, with flows on some sections coinciding with the irrigation season for farms.

Only a few hours from Los Angeles, the Kern River is the hub of Southern California whitewater.

TECHNIQUE

The Body

Be loose, the kayak instructor says, watching beginners nervously lined up in their boats like ducks behind her. Whitewater moves in three dimensions, and finding your sea legs, your sense of balance in the fluid river environment, is the first step in learning to paddle. A paddler stiff with fear or inflexibility will quickly flip over or fall out of the boat, so it's important to work up to more challenging water and practice regularly on water that seems easy. Time in your boat in the water, even pool or lake water, is invaluable to giving you good body sense. Even pros and Olympians spend time on flat water honing their moves.

Good technique requires paddlers to do things their bodies might not be used to and coordinate those moves with other members of the team. It gets easier with practice as this crew shows while digging into the Lochsa River in Idaho.

There's a river somewhere that flows through the lives of everyone.
—Roberta Flack

Body position, movement and flexibility are fundamental to proper whitewater technique. It's unfortunate that paddlers use paddles and oars because it often makes them focus too much on their hands and arms when they should be learning better movement with their torsos, hips and heads. Using your body rather than your arms to move downriver will make you a more effective, fluid and safe boater.

Before you head into the hard rapids, you should

try to stretch and be loose. Before you head to the rapids at all, you should get a sense of paddling straight and the feel of the boat as it turns and you lean. Stretch, twist and remind your body of the motions you will ask it to make on the river. Finally, relax and think positive thoughts: focusing on the bad stuff is sort of a self-fulfilling prophecy. As kayaking wit William Nealy put it: "The time spent staring at a nasty hole is directly proportional to the time you'll spend getting trashed in it."

ARMS AND HANDS

Hands and arms offer convenient hooks for holding your paddle or oars. If they're really tired at the end of the day, then your technique is likely flawed. Arms should be bent slightly when holding a paddle, and you should maintain that bend throughout most of the movements. When rowing, you will keep that same slight bend through the most powerful part of the stroke, but the arms will need to bend more when you pull the paddles out of the water. With a kayak paddle, your hands should feel the indexing on the shaft and be aligned so that the knuckles on the control hand (usually your dominant hand) line up with the top edge of the paddle blade. The control hand holds the paddle shaft and doesn't allow it to rotate, while the off hand holds loosely and lets the paddle shaft rotate during the stroke to accommodate the paddle's feather. Canoe paddlers hold the paddle shaft similarly, but there's no rotation because there's only one blade and the t-grip handle. Rowers may accidentally feather the paddle in the water, turning it so that the thin edge slices through the water rather than the face catching it. It will take some practice before you can subconsciously pull the oars and get a solid bite of water with the blade each time. You should cultivate a "just enough" grip on the paddle or oar, meaning you should use just enough squeeze to keep the paddle

> **360:** To spin a boat in a complete circle. Also called a spin or flat spin. Two spins in a row are sometimes called 720s, but after that the arithmetic is usually beyond most spin dizzy paddlers.

Use your head. Good technique starts with a good attitude and good judgment.

from rotating in your hands but no more. White knuckles will lead to blood blisters and carpal tunnel syndrome.

Excessively bent arms or elbows that collapse are a sure sign of trying to muscle a stroke. Your biceps really shouldn't have much to do as you paddle down the river, and collapsed-arm strokes also may set up a paddler for injury by stressing the shoulder.

SHOULDERS

The shoulders are vulnerable in whitewater paddling, especially for canoeists and kayakers. Paddlers can do a lot to reduce the risk to this very complex and mobile joint. Because shoulders have such a wide range of motion, they offer many possibilities for you to stress them. The arms and the torso should always move together to reduce the amount of movement to the shoulder during paddle strokes.

Reaching strokes and collapsing arms tend to move the upper arm into a position near the limit of the shoulder's mobility and all it takes at this point is an ill-timed flip to put the shoulder under dangerous stress. You should always avoid raising your hands over your head while running rivers. Some paddlers instinctively run steep drops with their paddle raised over their heads, but if they fall over when they hit the bottom of the drop they can severely stress—read, dislocate—their shoulders. It's also about as unstable a position as you can put yourself in. Run steep drops with your paddle low near your waist. If you fear it hitting you in the teeth when you land and the water pushes it up, try paddling through the drop and timing the last stroke so that you reach across the hole and plant it on the boil line. A good draw stroke in this position will keep the paddle out of your face, and it'll also give you a little extra momentum through the hole.

It's a good idea to incorporate some kind of shoulder stretch into your paddling warm-up, even

Forget the arms—the torso is the power-house of whitewater paddling. These canoeists rotate their torsos to make effective paddle strokes.

Backstroke: **Any stroke done against the direction of travel. They can stop or slow a boat if done on both sides or turn the boat if done on one side only. Also called back paddling.**

if it's just taking a few minutes of mellow strokes at the put in. Tight and tense shoulders are ripe for injury. Take care of them.

TORSO

The torso is the paddler's engine. The complex network of stomach, oblique and back muscles that form the body's trunk are the source of a paddler's strength, movement and balance on the river. The torso leans the boat, drives the paddle and oar strokes, twists to turn and snaps to right a flipped boat. Learning to use the torso properly is the key to paddling effectively.

Posture plays a big role in this. You should sit up straight in a position that's neutral from front to back and side to side. The spine should be straight but

Hands and arms are convenient hooks for managing the oars. Use your body to power the strokes.

not rigid. Kayakers and canoeists can feel how the torso can bend and move to influence the movement of the boat. If you lean forward, you weight the bow and the boat "trims" low at the front. This might be an effective move if you want to engage the edge of the boat to turn into an eddy or if you want to sink the bow in a hole to get an ender or cartwheel. If you lean back, you sink the stern,

handy if you want to stern squirt or quickly lower your center of gravity. Leaning back also compromises some control of the boat. It may feel stable because you've lowered your center of gravity, but it also moves your center of gravity to the trailing surface of the boat. It's a bit like trying to steer a bicycle while doing a wheelie.

Front and back leans have more subtle influence on boat behavior, but side-to-side movement will have a profound effect on the boat's behavior. A lean lifts one edge and sinks another, and depending on the flow of water around the boat, the lean will allow water to slip easily underneath or catch the edge and drive it down. Sideways leans engage the oblique muscles on the sides of the torso. These muscles are not commonly used to the extent that paddlers do, and in your first days of paddling they will likely be tired and sore. They will also grow more

Bombproof: **A one hundred percent, absolute, combat-tested river skill or piece of equipment. A bombproof roll means you roll up when you need to and (almost) never have to swim. Bombproof gear doesn't break (right). A variant, "bomber," is another synonym for river reliability. My van is bomber dude—did you see me boof that rock on the takeout road?**

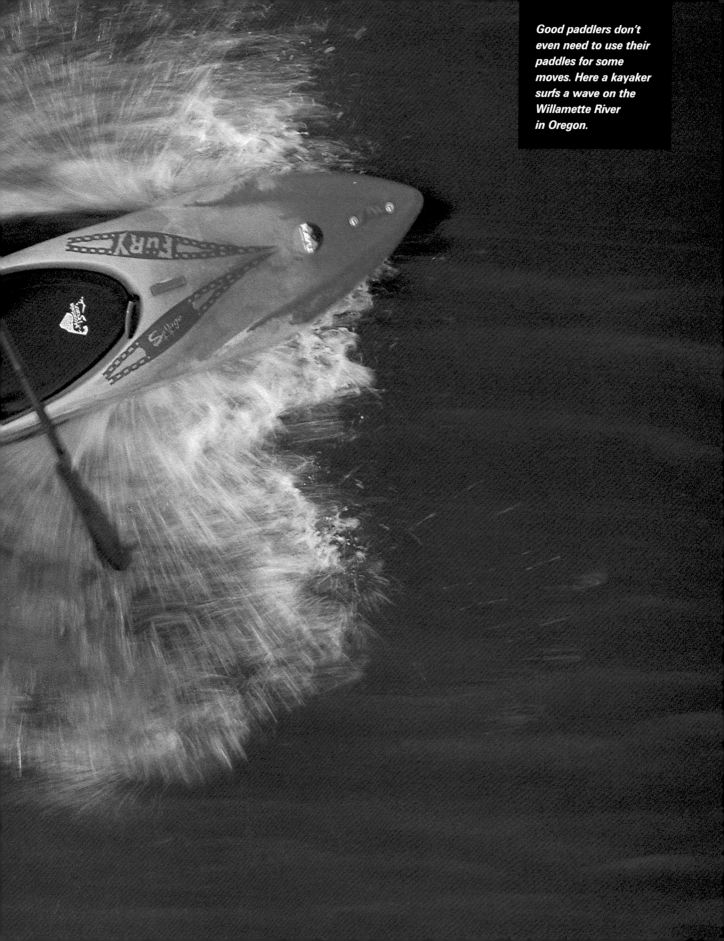

Good paddlers don't even need to use their paddles for some moves. Here a kayaker surfs a wave on the Willamette River in Oregon.

> **Boof:** To skip a boat off a rock to get lift (or air). Boofs are named for the sound a boat's hull makes when it lands in the water below—boof! like a bass drum. It's a useful move for avoiding nasty holes or other unfriendly features in the main channel of a drop. Done correctly, a boof will land a paddler clear of the hole below the drop and usually in the eddy. Care should be taken on especially tall drops not to land flat, however, because you can hurt your back.

flexible as you use them and their movements will become easier.

Finally the movement of the torso dictates the movement of the boat. You should learn to move your paddle to the position it needs to be in by turning and twisting your torso and never overreaching with the arms. At first this may be difficult, as many people don't regularly use their bodies in the way that paddlers do. But flexibility will come, and those movements that were once out of reach will become fluid and smooth.

HIPS AND LEGS

The hips and legs work with the torso to turn, lean and rotate kayaks and canoes. Rafters use them for power when rowing. What canoeists and kayakers commonly refer to as a hip snap, the upward lifting motion of the hip used to bring the boat level, comes mostly from the torso. The hip, however, translates the movement to the boat, and so it's useful to think of snapping the hip when actually it's the muscles of the trunk that are doing most of the work.

Though the legs don't have much room to move in kayaks and canoes, they can do a lot with subtle pressure and counter pressure on thigh braces and straps. A good fit in the boat is important as is a focus on what parts of your legs will be most effective to use. Generally the legs should be relaxed in the boat, but engaged with pressure up into the thigh braces for control. In a kayak, the feet should be loosely braced against the bulkhead or the foot pegs. In this position, you can lift a knee into the thigh braces to help rotate the boat during a lean or in the hip snap of a roll. You can also apply upward pressure to the knees to subtly affect the trim of the boat when surfing and playing. In a canoe, you're kneeling with your legs folded underneath you, so there's little room for movement. Fit is still critical, though, for comfort and performance. You should be able to fit snugly under the thigh braces so you'll be able to roll and manage rough water. Tightness, however, can lead to crampy feet, ankles and legs. Again it's a balance.

Rowers in a raft use their legs differently than kayakers and canoeists. They still serve to help brace and hold a the rower in the boat, but the legs can also give a lot of extra power to the oar stroke. By extending the legs in the pull phase of the stroke

> *. . . the time has also come to identify and preserve free-flowing stretches of our great rivers before growth and development make the beauty of the unspoiled waterway a memory.*
>
> *—President Lyndon Johnson's Message on Natural Beauty*

(when the oar pulls against the water to provide momentum), rowers use the big muscles of the legs to drive the oars. Paddle rafters use their legs and feet to a lesser extent, bracing against the tubes of the boat to hold themselves in in rough water and execute solid paddle strokes.

HEAD

The head is heavy. Sitting at the highest point over the water line, its position has a surprisingly profound influence on your boat's performance and the effectiveness of your moves. It also holds your brain, which is both good and bad. It's good because it learns the moves, imbues you with the desire to surf a wave and helps you hold the job you need to pay

While you're busy doing all the things you need to do to improve your paddling technique, don't forget to look up. The river is a beautiful place. Take it in like this scene on the Nantahala River in North Carolina.

for your boat. It's bad because it wants air and will do almost anything to get it and it may be reluctant to do what it perceives as risky or dangerous (though this is a good feature too, sometimes). A paddler may run into trouble with his head in the roll, when, searching for air in a stressful situation, it bobs up out of the water to ruin a perfectly good set-up and hip snap. The head might also be trouble in the brace, resisting the need to drop toward the water while it heads for high ground and pushes your long-suffering body down into the water. It wants air, after all, and these moves just don't seem right. But the difficult truth of paddling is that the head must lead the charge into most of the moves, and teaching it to do so, to execute the counterintuitive, may be a long process.

So why doesn't it work to lift your head? While you're reading this, drop your ear to your shoulder. Feel what it does to your body. Your neck does most of the work, but you'll probably also feel the muscles of your side compress a bit too, raising the hip. It's similar to grabbing the tip of a fishing rod and bending it. The rod doesn't just bend at the tip but

> *Brace:* **A type of paddle stroke used to add stability or keep from tipping over. What looks like a slap of the paddle on the surface of the water is really accomplished with a flick of the head and snap of the hips.**

absorbs the force along its length so that even a small twitch at the tip bends the rod, even if slightly, all the way to the handle. Your spine behaves similarly: movement at one end is absorbed along its length. So when you drop your head into a brace, you tend to lift the hip on that side and keep the boat upright. When you lift your head up, you push the hip you want to snap out of the water deeper under and lift

the opposite hip even higher. When you do this, you're helping the boat flip, so take one more big breath, because you're going under.

Your head is also pretty dense relative to the rest of your body, it packs a lot of bone and brain into a little space. Put on a helmet and you add even more weight to this small package so that the heaviest and weakest part of your body is now its highest point. When you lift your head, you're altering your center of gravity to a point deeper in the water with most of your body, and the muscles you need to get upright, underneath it. In its search for air, your head has climbed atop your body—literally like a rat on a sinking ship. When you keep your head down in the brace and the roll, your center of gravity is nearer the surface of the water and your body can easily get over it to move you upright. Now you can breathe.

Just dropping the head can do a lot for stability on the river. Called a head dink, the move is incorporated into the brace but can be done without a paddle with surprising effect. If you see a feature that might cause you trouble, drop your head into it and its flipping power will be substantially reduced because you've lowered your center of gravity and moved it into a more stable down-river position. If lowering center of gravity is so important, why don't we just hug the deck all the way down the rapid? A low center of gravity, by itself, isn't so useful, but the ability to move your center of gravity is fundamental to safe and fun river running. It's in the head dink, the brace and the admonition to "be loose." Anyway, if you just hugged the deck all the way down the river, you wouldn't be able to see what was coming.

EYES

Where you look will be where you go. Vision is an oft-overlooked part of learning whitewater. Good vision is tricky and elusive, like looking at those silhouette pictures of two people looking at each other and seeing either the faces or something that looks like a candlestick. It's hard to see both at the same time, and so, too, it is with the river. It's hard to see both the danger and path through it in the same instant. Ignoring danger is risky, but focusing on it is risky as well. Stare hard at a nasty river feature and it's bound to suck you in and wallop you. Stare hard at the wafer-thin line through it, and you'll likely run it clean (if you have the skills, if you spotted the rest of the line and made a good judgement call, if the river gods have been appeased and haven't sicced a school of rabid salmon on you to bat you with their tails and knock you off course).

Combat roll: **To complete a roll in real river conditions. A combat roll is a necessary step for kayakers and canoeists looking to safely run Class 3 and harder water.**

Draw: **A draw stroke pulls the boat to the paddle.**

Spotting the line and then seeing it through the rapid are skills you can practice anywhere on the river. First, train yourself to look farther down river than you think you should. Don't look at your hands or at the bow of your boat or even at the upcoming wave. Your subconscious and your body have already figured out the nearby river features and anything that you do consciously will probably mess you up. You will learn this the first time you try to rescue a buddy who's swimming. You'll probably find you run a rapid with little effort when you're chasing a swimming friend because you focus on the friend and look where he's going and don't obsess about the myriad waves, rocks and holes in front of your boat that would ordinarily give you trouble. So as you run the river, always work to extend your vision down river and trust your body to react smoothly.

The other vision trick is to always look where you want to go. Rivet your eyes on the spot you want to be, however improbable it may seem from the middle of the rapid, and you will likely get there. This will be an important skill when you learn to ferry across the river. By picking a spot on the bank and focusing on it, you will make the corrections you need to in your boat without looking at it. Look away and you'll find you drift off course. If you want to stop, look downstream and find an eddy and paddle to it, focusing on the eddy and not on the fast and slow water between, the hole below it or the nasty eddy line protecting it. Looking to the spot where you want to be will force you to paddle through trouble.

New River, West Virginia

HEADWATERS: *Appalachian Mountains of western North Carolina*

LENGTH: *14 miles*

DROP: *15 feet per mile*

DIFFICULTY: *Class 4*

CHARACTER: *The New River is big water. Wide and high volume, the river runs through three states before it plunges into the New River Gorge, or Grand Canyon of the East as it's sometimes known. Expect big waves and big holes on your trip down the New but few technical moves. It asks boaters to hang on through heavy water and make a few long ferries and river-wide moves.*

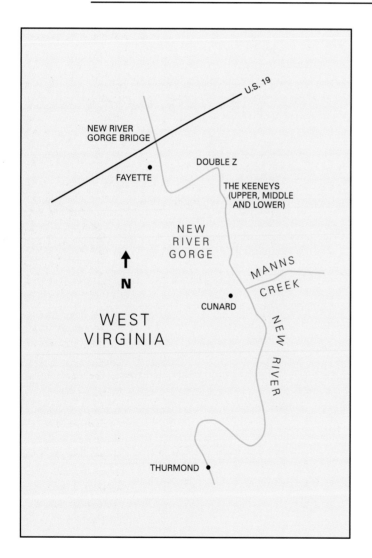

The New River is an eastern classic. Its shallow drop belies the intensity of its rapids, especially at higher flows. At decent flows, it holds all the big water features an eastern boater will fantasize about—big waves and holes, whirlpools and powerful eddy lines. The New runs year round and is in close proximity to the Gauley River, the other West Virginia whitewater mecca.

Rafts running the New tend to be bigger boats than most of the ones run down eastern streams. You'll even see oar-rig rafts plying the waters here: the new is that big. On popular summer weekends the New can be quite full of raft customers and private boaters alike, and paddlers may have to take turns and exercise some courtesy as they approach rapids. Boats especially seem to pile up in the Keeneys rapids where three drops fall in a succession of boat-swallowing waves and holes.

The New is a long run through beautiful scenery, though the water quality is generally poor, and if you run it at its highest flows expect to share the eddies with a lot of debris—wood, refrigerators, that sort of thing. The New does drain three states after all. At the end of the run, you will spot the highest arch bridge in the world spanning the gorge, but other than that, road access is limited. An active railroad track runs alongside the river, providing some access throughout its length.

The New River is a geologic marvel, one of the oldest rivers in the world, and is a lot of fun for whitewater paddlers as well. Features tend to be big—giant waves, monster holes, wide channels—by the time the river reaches the popular section known as the Grand Canyon of the East.

Zambezi River, Zimbabwe/Zambia

HEADWATERS: *Lake Victoria*

LENGTH: *75 miles*

DIFFICULTY: *Class 4, 5*

CHARACTER: *The Zambezi is one of the world's big water paddling marvels, with giant holes and waves, surging and boiling eddies and nasty whirlpools ready to snatch the unwary. The runs start just below Victoria Falls—a 300-foot-tall, mile-wide drop that locals call "the smoke that thunders"—and doesn't let up through the Botoka Gorge's Class 4 and 5 rapids.*

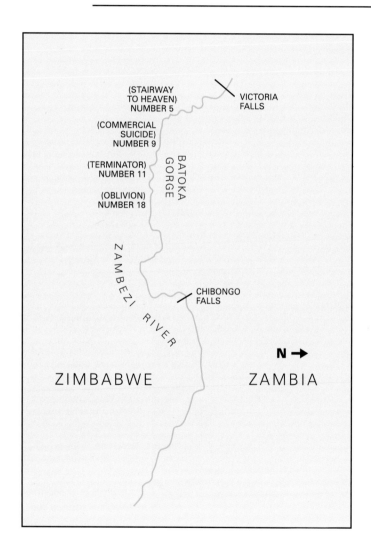

The Zambezi was first run in 1981. In recent years, it has become a whitewater-paddling phenomenon. There's nothing else like it. Big, powerful water rushes through a vertical-walled basalt canyon and drops over ledges and through constrictions to kick up Maui-size waves and holes that look bottomless. To add to the mystique, the rapids don't have names, just numbers (though a few have a secondary name). Local paddlers there make the play look easy on features such as No. 11, a wave with a tube like a well-formed ocean break, and No. 12B, a long wave with holes and green sections that the world's best paddlers shred to pieces.

This is a river that will clobber an eight-person paddle raft, standing it on end and flinging passengers into the torrent or grabbing and holding it while it picks off high-siding paddlers one by one. High water brings its own new challenges and some rapids just aren't run during the rainy season. For such powerful water, the Zambezi is actually pretty forgiving. The river is warm and most of the rapids have pretty good pools to collect the inevitable yard sales that come when paddlers get munched in rapids like No. 18—Oblivion. Much beyond this point on the Zambezi, some hungry wildlife becomes more prevalent on the river: crocodiles and hippos may make problems for kayakers.

The Zambezi River's monster whitewater features draw paddlers from around the world. The Batoki Gorge downstream from Victoria Falls is among the biggest of the big water runs in the world.

Rowing and Paddling

RAFT ROWING STROKES

Rafters have turned the rowboat's backward aiming stroke around so that they can face the rapids they're entering, rather than crash into them blindly. Since rafts are so large with innate momentum, rarely do they need much forward speed beyond what the river gives the boat to punch holes and breaking waves. Instead the rowing frame orientation favors strokes that move against the current—ferrying, especially—rather than with it, a set-up that's important understand when planning strategy for running a rapid.

The basic backward rowing stroke is essentially the same as that used in a rowboat. Like the whitewater strokes of kayaks and canoes, the backstroke is done with the body. Brace your feet against the bar of the platform attached to the frame and use your legs and torso to complete the stroke. Using your arms, place the oars in the water and return them to position for a new stroke after one is complete. Start by reaching out straight from your chest so that your arms are nearly straight, dig the oar blades into the water. Engage the oar blades and draw back using the muscles of the torso and thighs to drive the stroke. As the stroke finishes, your hands should be at the sides of your chest and your arms bent. Lift the oar blades out of the water and return them to the start for another stroke.

The opposite of the backstroke is the push stroke. It isn't as strong as the backstroke, but it's useful when you need to add a little extra bit of

Sometimes the river takes all hands to manage. Here the rower gets a little help from paddling crew members.

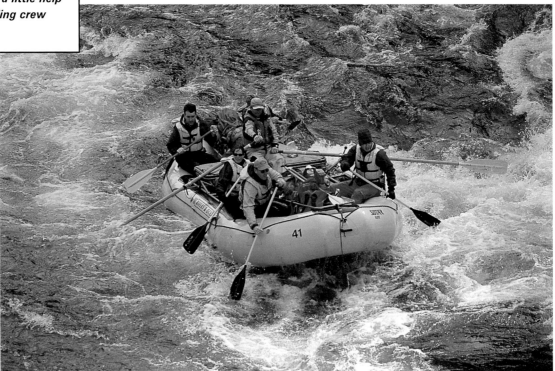

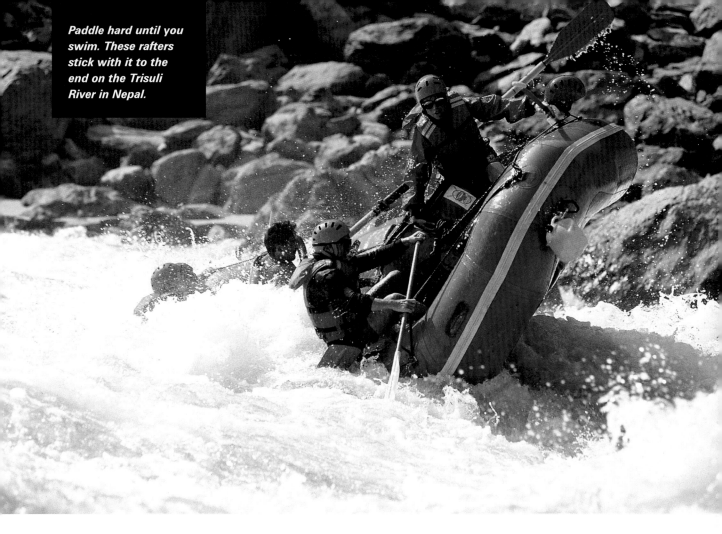

In the world there is nothing more submissive and weak than water. Yet for attacking that which is hard and strong nothing can surpass it.
— Lao-Tzu, Chinese philosopher (6th century B.C.)

momentum to a move. It is essentially the same stroke as the backstroke but it starts with the handles near the chest, and the rower pushes forward when the oar blades are engaged in the water. The stroke ends in the reach position of the backstroke.

Turning Strokes

As you row down the river you will notice that the boat starts to turn if your strokes are unbalanced. If you apply this imbalance further, you will have a turning stroke. Apply force to one oar and see how the boat turns in a slow arc. Backstrokes move the boat in the opposite direction from push strokes if using one oar. Try using both oars in combination to spin the boat. If you push on one oar and backstroke with the other at the same time, the boat will spin around with you as the axis. This combination of strokes is effective for making quick moves and changes of direction on the river.

Shipping the Oars

Shipping isn't really a stroke, but it is a good way to protect your oars so that you can take strokes later in the day. When you bring the oars completely over the boat, either by laying the blades on the tubes in front or behind you or by sliding the oars into the boat to physically shorten them, you are shipping them. It's a handy technique for tight rocky passages

Proper strokes will help you to punch through boat-swallowing holes and come out the other side unscathed.

> **Duffeck:** A type of kayak stroke in which the paddler plants the paddle in a different flow than the one she's in and uses the power of the river to turn the boat and pull it into that new flow.
>
> **Eskimo Roll:** The technique kayakers and canoeists use to right flipped boats while staying in them.

when the oars might smash on the rocks as they pass by. It also keeps the oar handles from punching or sweeping into you, clobbering you in the middle of a tricky move. Learning to ship your oars quickly will save you and your oars much abuse.

RAFT PADDLE STROKES

Forward Stroke

Paddle strokes for rafters include a few simple strokes similar to those basic kayak and canoe strokes. The key to paddle raft maneuvering is to use these few simple strokes in combinations that turn, stall, slip the current and power through river features. The simplest of all is the forward stroke. Sit far enough out on the tube so you can reach the water but not so far that you'll fall out of the raft in a rapid. Reach forward and plant the paddle vertically in the water. Using body twist rather than arm strength, pull the paddle back toward you. When it reaches your hip, lift the paddle out of the water and repeat the stroke. The key to good forward strokes is in the body: think of drawing the boat and you toward the paddle, rather than the paddle back toward you. If you're firmly braced in the boat, you will do just that, and in the process, take an efficient stroke.

Backstroke

The back stroke is the opposite of the forward stroke, and again you use body twist rather than arm strength to do it. Plant the paddle behind your hip, keep it vertical to the water and push it forward. Keep the strokes fairly short and rely on those first few inches of the stroke to supply the power you need to make the move.

Sweep Stroke

The sweep is a turning stroke that can be an effective rafting stroke if used from the stern or bow of the boat. Raft captains use the sweep extensively to guide the boat through rapids. The sweep varies from the forward stroke in that the paddle shaft is held closer to horizontal and the blade works out away from the boat. Plant the blade in the water and twist your body to move the boat to the paddle blade. You likely won't feel the boat move toward the blade much because rafts are so big and heavy, but it's an important distinction, one that will get you using your strong body more than your weak little arms to do the stroke. Many paddle captains use longer paddles to give them more effective sweeps from their high perch on the stern.

Draw Stroke

The draw is a forward stroke done out to the side of the boat that pulls the boat to the power face of the blade. It's a good stroke for moving the raft laterally, or slipping it. Plant the paddle vertically out from your hip with the power face of the blade aiming toward you. Draw the stroke into the boat (or the boat into the stroke). Done alone it won't have much effect, but in coordination with the rest of the crew on the side of the boat, it can be a quick way to get somewhere else. It can also be a good way for a stern or bow paddler to move that part of the boat laterally.

Pry Stroke

The pry is the draw's opposite and can be used to turn the boat or, in coordination with other paddlers, slip it across the water. The pry starts next to the boat and using the raft tube as a fulcrum, you pry the water away from the boat, driving the t-grip of the paddle to your hip and pushing out with your hand on the shaft. For a stern paddler, the pry has a ruddering effect that is useful for steering the boat subtly through rapids. Used in combination with the draw stroke (e.g. left side paddlers draw, right side paddlers pry) it can add a boost to a sideslip move in the current.

CAPTAIN AND CREW

It's the paddle captain's job to coordinate the raft crew's strokes as they go down the river. A good

captain and responsive crew can make for an enjoyable, crisply executed ride through demanding rapids. But with a difficult crew, as any commercial raft guide can attest, raft captaining can also be a day spent flirting with chaos. It's the raft captain's job to take command. She should be firm, but also remember that whitewater rafting is not the British Navy. No matter her disposition, however, it's the paddler's job as a member of the crew to follow her direction without hesitation.

That direction boils down to a few simple commands. Right forward tells the paddlers on the right side of the raft to take forward strokes. Right back tells them to take backstrokes. Left forward and left back follows this model. Stop means everybody should stop paddling and let the raft drift. The captain will combine commands to correct course, execute turns and make ferries. Right forward alone makes the boat turn to the left; right forward, left back will tend to spin the boat to the left; and right forward, right forward, left forward will turn the boat left and straighten it.

While this is going on, the raft captain is using sweep and pry strokes to more subtly maneuver the boat. She may pry or sweep to correct a few overzealous paddlers on one side of the raft. Or use those strokes to hold a ferry angle while the crew paddles back or forward in unison.

It's important for crew members to do what the captain says when she says it. While gross slacking or outright mutiny is rare, it can be maddening for an over-enthusiastic crew member to throw in a few correction strokes of his own. This may make the captain have to correct twice and confuses the

South Fork of the American River, California

HEADWATERS: *Sierra Nevada west of Lake Tahoe*

LENGTH: *20 miles total, but it can be broken into day trips*

DROP: *23 feet per mile*

DIFFICULTY: *Class 3*

CHARACTER: *The Chili Bar section of the South Fork of the American is California's most popular whitewater river and can get crowded in the summer. Flowing out of the Sierra Nevada, several dams interrupt the flow of the river but also provide more consistent year-round boating. The rapids are challenging-but-friendly Class 3 at normal summer flows.*

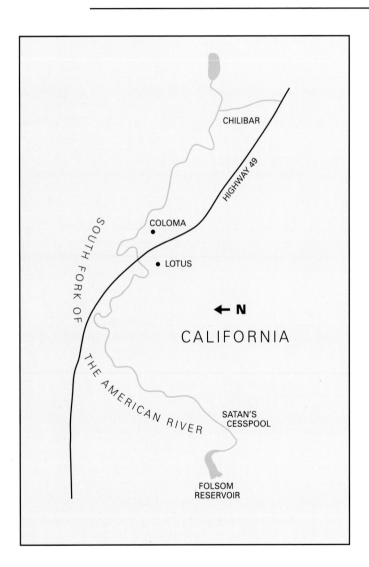

Chili Bar is synonymous with whitewater in California, drawing more than 100,000 boaters each year to this fun ride out of the Sierra Nevada. The American River is also gold rush country, where a few nuggets found in 1848 infected the many who would be known as '49ers with gold fever.

The South Fork is north and east of Sacramento and the San Francisco Bay Area and so serves a large population base. Combine spectacular Sierra scenery in the steep slopes of the river's canyon with consistent flows and the river is a natural draw. It can be hard to find places to play among the commercial rafts on busy summer weekends, so boaters looking for solitude should try weekday runs. Or if you're up to it, look for more challenging water on the nearby North and Middle forks of the river with Class 4 and 5 rapids.

Rafters can find many outfitters serving the river from the town of Placerville, and private boaters can choose from among several access points between the dam at Chili Bar and Salmon Falls where the waters of Folsom Reservoir back up. Expect Class 3 water throughout the run with Troublemaker and Satan's Cesspool among the notables that push the limits of many intermediate boaters. The South Fork Gorge stacks up a number of more challenging pool-drop rapids on the run just before the take-out at Salmon Falls.

boat's movement through the rapid. The captain should try to mix paddlers by ability, enthusiasm and experience and may need to shuffle them once she's seen what they can do. Finally, remember she's not really shouting at you because she's mad or your boat is facing a crisis, she's just trying to be heard above the river.

KAYAK STROKES

Forward Stroke

Making your kayak go in a straight line is tougher than it would seem. To attempt a straight-ahead course, a paddler uses the forward stroke. While it is a simple stroke, it can be the most maddening for novice kayakers to do effectively because slight variations in reach, twist, boat lean and force can make the kayak leave its intended straight-line path. The resulting spin out can be frustrating. Spending time in the boat, whether on moving or flat water, will go a long way toward effective forward control. With practice, a paddler will find her sea legs, and straight-ahead paddling won't take a second thought.

The forward stroke is accomplished with the body, while the hands and arms are just conveniences for holding the paddle and putting it in the water in the right place. The work comes from the torso. A good forward stroke requires you to sit up straight

There is no rushing a river. When you go there, you go at the pace of the water and that pace ties you into a flow that is older than life on this planet. Acceptance of that pace, even for a day, changes us, reminds us of other rhythms beyond the sound of our own heartbeats.

—Jeff Rennicke, River Days: Travels on Western Rivers, A Collection of Essays

Ferry angle: **The angle at which a boat needs to be to the current to move laterally across it without being swept downstream.**

Ferry: **Moving laterally across a river without going downstream. Ferrying works on the principle of river ferries connected to cables. By altering the angle of the boat, the paddler can use the river's power to move the boat across it.**

and balance in the center of the boat. Reach forward to your toes with the blade of the paddle and sink it into the water. The paddle shaft should be perpendicular to the surface of the water, and as you draw the blade back toward you, it should remain close to the side of the boat. Your body will twist to accomplish the stroke while your arms remain slightly bent. When the paddle blade reaches your hip, the stroke is complete. Pull the blade out of the water and reach to engage the blade of your opposing hand to repeat the process. Repeat the stroke from toes to hip with a vertical paddle, twisting the torso to provide propulsion. Find a rhythm or cadence to these strokes and train your body to remember it.

Short forward strokes are better than long ones because long strokes tend to breed bad habits that make the boat spin off course. A paddler can accelerate more quickly with a balanced flurry of short forward strokes than she can with fewer big "muscle" strokes. Longer strokes tend to make a paddler use her arms more because the body can only twist so far, and using the arms to give the paddle a little extra oomph is a waste. Your biceps are small, weak muscles compared to the muscles of the stomach, sides and lower back. Efficient paddling comes from the torso with a smooth cadence, so paddle from your belly button rather than from a point between your hands. At the end of a long paddling day, your arms shouldn't be tired.

Sweep Stroke

The sweep stroke is the basic turning stroke for kayakers. Like the forward stroke, it is accomplished

The sweep stroke turns the boat around its center point. The paddler uses torso twist to make an effective stroke. Here the bow of the boat is moving counterclockwise while the stroke is moving clockwise.

with a twist of the torso rather than a pull of the arms. With the sweep, the body is the pivot point around which the ends of the boat move. A skilled paddler should be able to spin his boat around this point without drifting.

Place your paddle parallel to the surface of the water and dip the blade in near your side so that the shaft is only slightly angled from the horizontal plane of the water. With the blade in the water, try to move the end of the boat to the paddle by twisting your body. Avoid moving the paddle blade to the end of the boat using your arms. Done correctly, your arms should remain slightly bent as your body moves the boat underneath you. Practice to develop flexibility and the ability to sweep from bow to stern with just a body twist.

Sweeps can be done backward or forward, in increments or as broad movements meant to radically change course. The paddle blade moves with the direction of travel in a forward sweep: done on the right side of the boat it will turn the bow left. A back sweep means that the paddle blade moves against the direction of travel: done on the right side of the

boat it will turn the bow right. Back sweeps tend to make the boat move more dynamically, but they also tend to slow forward momentum, and if used to steer exclusively, lead to a less fluid, stop-start motion in the water. Many novices rely too heavily on the back sweep because it feels like the boat responds more quickly with it and when dragged in the water against forward momentum, it feels more solid. But like many paddling maneuvers, sweeps are a bit counterintuitive. The back sweep,

Head dink: A flick of the head used to change a paddlers center of gravity when she's off balance.

J-lean: When you lean a kayak or canoe and keep your center of gravity over the top of it, your body makes a shape like a j. The j-lean is useful in surfing holes and for learning the effects of leans in holes.

The key to bracing is using your body. Drop your head into the side you're falling to and lift your hip. On this high brace, the paddler uses little force on his paddle blade to right his boat.

Bracing

Whitewater happens in three dimensions, and braces are the strokes that help paddlers control their vertical movement. At their most basic, they keep kayakers from flipping. They also combine nearly all the elements of a roll and are key to learning it. In their more advanced form, braces can be used to surf holes, cartwheel and play.

When you dip your paddle in the water, you are subtly bracing. Dipping the paddle in the water lowers your center of gravity and makes you more stable. If you add a forward or backward stroke, you will feel even more stable. When the paddle moves against the water it encounters resistance, a firm or

while an effective stroke that makes the paddler feel as if he's accomplishing something, is often used to correct problems with paddling technique that started several strokes before.

hard feeling to the paddler. This resistance is the platform off which you can find stability and right yourself if off balance.

Bracing strokes are specifically designed to right the paddler when she finds herself out of balance. Forward or backward strokes may help in some instances, but more commonly a paddler needs to use an actual brace stroke to get out of trouble. The brace is accomplished by placing the face of the paddle on the surface of the water and using the resistance of the water when you push down to regain your balance. Hold the paddle as you would for a sweep stroke but rotate your wrist and arm so that the blade lies flat on the surface of the water. If your knuckles aim toward the sky, you are high bracing. If you point your knuckles down, you are low bracing. Lean toward the blade that's in the water and start to fall over. As you start to lose balance, hip snap to the side you're bracing and drop your head toward the blade, using the resistance of the water to right yourself. This is another of whitewater's counterintuitive moves: when falling over the paddler actually moves parts of her body into the fall (among them the part that least wants to get wet— the head). At first the brace may come off as a slap, but as you practice, your body will become more supple and relaxed when falling over, and you won't have to slap at the water to brace. Practice on both sides, both high and low bracing.

Becoming adept at using a brace to stay upright is essential to safe river running in a kayak. Your comfort, skill level and what's convenient will dictate whether you use a high or low brace. High braces initially will feel more solid, but they tend to make a paddler over commit to the brace and may contribute to bad habits among some paddlers of leaning on their blades in holes and going through rapids. Bracing also can be risky if done incorrectly, and the paddler reaches out or up too far. Remember never to bring your hand higher than

Lean: Tipping the boat on edge in the water. Learning how to lean effectively in whitewater is a fundamental skill.

*Eventually, all things merge into
one, and a river runs through it. The
river was cut by the world's great
flood and runs over rocks from the
basement of time. On some of the
rocks are timeless raindrops. Under
the rocks are the words, and some
of the words are theirs.*

I am haunted by waters.
—Norman Maclean,
A River Runs Through It

your head—it's easy to overstress the shoulder
when falling into an overextended brace. The low
brace avoids this by limiting the reach of the brace—
it's physically difficult to move the paddle into a dangerous position from a low brace. The drawback to a
low brace is that may not feel as solid as a high
brace and requires better, smoother technique to be
effective. A paddler's center of gravity will be more
on top of the boat with a low brace, requiring more
refined balance and boat control, but the payoff will
be in the fluidity of her paddling. Low braces also
are integral in more advanced surfing moves and
may help set up for quicker rolls.

Braces may feel risky to practice because you flirt
with flipping over. That's good. Teaching your body to
manage risk, do the counterintuitive and stay fluid
will go a long way toward skilled river running.

Rudder Strokes

An outgrowth of the sweep is a rudder stroke.
Rudders use the paddle blade to steer like the rudder on a ship or airplane. The easiest rudder works
near the side of the boat toward the stern, and it's
essentially the last bit of the sweep stroke near the
stern. The paddle shaft is nearly horizontal and the
blade is vertical in the water. By moving the blade
slightly, the boat will turn if it is moving relative to
the water and not lose speed if the rudder is held
with only a slight angle off the direction of travel.

Stern rudders can be used on either side and they're
good for correcting the boat's course without losing
much momentum. Practice and get the feel of ruddering: a right rudder will bring the bow right, a left
rudder will bring the bow left. Since the rudder is
done behind the paddler's center of gravity, it's a
pretty comfortable stroke to do with little risk of flipping. Be careful of putting the rudder too deep in the
water because the edge of the paddle blade can
catch between rocks and stick, ripping the paddle
out of your hand and likely flipping you.

Bow rudders are a more advanced stroke, and
are similar to the start of the forward stroke. The
paddle shaft is held perpendicular to the water and

> **Mystery move:** Skilled paddlers in low vol-
> ume boats can use the river's currents,
> usually on strong eddy lines, to make
> their boats corkscrew down into the
> water. A really good mystery move makes
> the paddler completely disappear.

the blade enters between the toes and the knee.
Like the stern rudder, the blade slices through the
water nearly parallel to the direction of travel. Slight
changes in the angle of the blade will change the
boat's course. This move works in front of the paddler's center of gravity and if done incorrectly, can
lead to the boater running over his paddle and flipping. For beginners, it's a bit risky to do in strong
current or when the boat's moving fast. For more
advanced boaters, it's a valuable stroke, allowing
subtle adjustments to the boat's course in a body
position that offers many options for boat control.

Duffeck Stroke

The duffeck is an advanced stroke that allows snappy and controlled eddy turns. Like the bow rudder, it
looks a lot like the beginning of a forward stroke: the
paddle shaft is perpendicular to the surface of the
water and the blade enters between the toes and
the knee. With proper momentum, angle and boat
lean (see Eddy Turns), all the paddler has to do as
she approaches the eddy line is reach across and
plant the paddle in the eddy with the leading edge

Futaleufu River, Chile

HEADWATERS: *Cordillera de los Andes of Argentina*

LENGTH: *23 miles*

DROP: *Up to 50 feet per mile*

DIFFICULTY: *Class 5*

CHARACTER: *Clear water and high flows crash through a pool-drop river course that's among the prime paddling destinations in the world. The Futaleufu River is hard to reach, pristine and intense. For paddlers with the skills, it's a trip of a lifetime.*

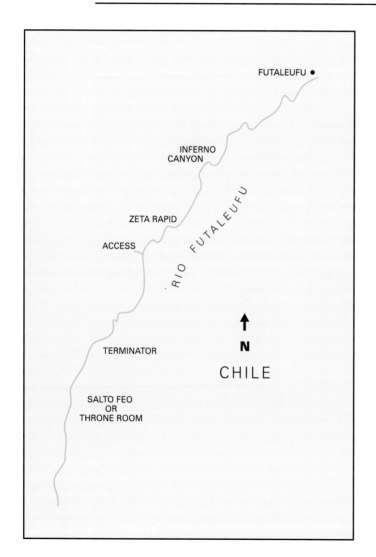

The Futaleufu is one of the most remarkable whitewater rivers in the world, boasting crystal clear water, powerful rapids and unmatched scenery. The river starts in Argentina, fed by the glaciers of the Andes, and crosses the border into southern Chile where the whitewater sections of river are. Futaleufu, a small town several miles from the border with Argentina, is the base for river runners here. The Futaleufu is a gem, but it's also threatened with damming like the Bío-Bío River, its Chilean whitewater cousin, many of whose rapids were inundated in the last decade. The Fu remains untouched and untrammeled still, and there's an international effort to stop plans for the dam on this incredible river. Showing the viability of tourism to the area, with whitewater a key component, is important to trying to preserve the river, say those fighting to save the Fu.

The rapids are intense. Zeta, Salto Feo and Terminator are the biggies, but the river has plenty of other Class 5 rapids to contend with as well. The holes are big, the currents are strong and this is not a river to be taken lightly. Kayakers will need to be in top form and use good judgement in assessing one's own skills to run these mighty rapids. Outfitters will likely ask for specific experience that you've had and judge your competency to paddle the Fu accordingly.

The Futaleufu River in Chile is a marvel of clear water and demanding rapids set among the rugged peaks of Patagonia. The river is threatened by a proposed hydroelectric dam.

Canoeists crossover to make strokes opposite the side of their dominant hand. It can feel a little awkward at first, but it's much quicker than switching hands with the paddle.

of the blade angled away from the boat. From here, all she has to do is hang on and the water will do the work. The effect is much like grabbing a pole as you walk past and hanging on: you and your boat will swing around your paddle and into the eddy.

The duffeck works the same way when leaving the eddy. The paddler approaches the eddy line with proper momentum, angle and lean and reaches across it into the downstream flow so she can catch the current on the face of her paddle. She will feel the boat accelerate quickly to the speed of the current, making a strong, solid eddy turn.

CANOE STROKES

Forward Strokes

The basic forward stroke gives the canoe the forward momentum necessary to complete many river moves. Skilled application of it is a matter of using good form and body positioning that will translate well to the other strokes and to your overall feel of the river.

Peel-out: **To exit an eddy using an eddy turn.**

Pencil: **To enter the water vertically off a steep drop. If you pencil into shallow water, you will hit bottom. Ouch.**

Kneeling in the canoe in the water, sit up with your back straight and look up and ahead. Reach out and plant the paddle blade as far forward as you can with the paddle shaft perpendicular to the water. Draw the blade back toward the hip, maintaining the vertical paddle close to the side of the boat. This movement should be accomplished with the body rather than the arms. Reach forward and twist with each stroke. Try to move your body toward the paddle rather than your paddle back to your body. Avoid taking strokes that are too long because the farther back you go the less efficient your paddle stroke will be. You can feel this as the resistance on the paddle eases through the stroke. Practice the forward stroke and concentrate on good form, feeling how it affects the boat. The boat shouldn't bob as you take your forward strokes—this is a sign that you have too much forward and backward motion in your body and not enough twist. Your arms should not drift out away from the boat during the stroke—this lapse in form mimics a turning stroke that will make it difficult to correct. If your arms bend too much at the elbows during the stroke, it's a sign that you're using too much arm and not enough body in your paddling. Remember—reach and twist.

Correction Strokes

It will be hard not to notice that paddling with forward strokes only on one side of the boat makes the canoe turn in circles. Canoeists use correction strokes to maintain a straight course, and the most common and simple correction stroke is the stern pry.

The stern pry comes at the end of the forward stroke. Rotate the paddle as it passes the hip so that the thumb on the hand holding the T-grip aims toward the sky. This will orient the blade so it slices like a rudder in the water. Use the gunnel of the boat as a fulcrum and pry out. The amount of pry you use will determine how much correction you apply to the boat. Usually only a few inches of movement will suffice, subtle movement that won't drag and hinder forward progress. With a little bit of correction every few strokes and a lot of practice to get the rhythm right, you will be able to hold a straight course. Try to keep the paddle against the gunnel and don't over-correct, both movements risk slowing the boat and pushing it radically off course

The J-stroke is a more subtle correction stroke. It too finishes the forward stroke, but instead of rotating the paddle so the thumb points to the sky as in the pry, rotate the thumb down so that it points toward the water. The paddle blade should be slicing through the water, again, like a rudder, but you won't have as much room to move the blade outward and overcorrect. The paddle shaft should stay close to the gunnel.

The stern pry is a correction stroke used to keep the canoe moving in a straight line. It should finish with the paddle blade nearly parallel to the boat and with the paddle shaft working as a lever against the gunnel.

Crossover strokes

Another option for straight-ahead paddling, especially for accelerating quickly, is the crossover stroke. After taking a standard forward stroke, lift the paddle out of the water and without changing grip reach across the bow of the boat and plant the paddle on the opposite side. As in the forward stroke, keep the paddle shaft vertical to the water and pull against it using body twist rather than arm strength. This stroke will feel awkward at first, but as you get more flexible it will become easier and quicker. It can be used to counter the drift from the forward stroke while offering some forward momentum, but it's usually most effective done only a few at a time. A good combination of forward and crossover strokes will get you the controlled forward momentum you need to make river moves. Try a forward stroke, followed by two crossovers and then another forward stroke, and see what it does to the canoe.

Steering

As you practice trying to go straight ahead, you might find that the concept of actually trying to turn a little absurd. "Isn't my boat already doing that?" you ask as a few uncorrected forward strokes cause you to veer off course. Turning strokes are important to quick river maneuvering, however, and their value will become much more apparent as you get the feel of your canoe. The forward stroke, uncorrected, may be the most simple turning stroke. To add more turn however, try the sweep stroke, the forward stroke's horizontal cousin. To sweep, put the paddle out to the side of the boat at a shallow horizontal angle and plant it so the blade is vertical in the water. Now twist your body to bring the stern of the boat toward the blade. This is a forward sweep. If you bring your bow toward the paddle blade, you will be performing a back sweep. Note how the boat spins around with you as the axis.

Crossover draw strokes will help you to sharply turn on your off side. These may feel like a bit of a contortion but they become more comfortable as you practice and paddle more. The crossover draw requires you to reach to your off side and plant the paddle out to your side rather than forward as in the forward stroke. The power face of the blade should be aimed toward your hip and the paddle shaft should be vertical to the water. If you are moving at all, expect the boat to turn sharply as you plant the paddle. Hang on and pivot around this point, following up with whatever combination of stokes you need to execute the next move.

> **Push stroke:** Pushing against oars rather than pulling them.
>
> **Ride:** The amount of time spent surfing or playing on a feature.

Braces

Braces help keep you upright when you start to tip over or offer stability though marginal water. A brace uses the paddle flat against the water as a way to reorient your body so that you can pull the boat under you. They are similar to the kayak braces in body position and body sense, but since canoe paddles are different from kayak paddles, hand positions are a little bit different. First, you must remember that your focus should not be so much on the paddle in the brace as in good body position. Dropping the head and compressing the muscles along the side of the torso to the side you're bracing, the hip snap and head dink, will bring the boat underneath you better than anything you can do with your hands. Practice making those snapping moves to each side of the boat. Holding the paddle, try a high brace by aiming the knuckles on your T-grip hand to the sky and holding the paddle shaft with the other hand like you're hanging on a chin-up bar: this will put the power face of the paddle blade flat on the water. Keep the paddle low—the T-grip hand should stay under your chin throughout the move—if you let it drift higher, it puts your shoulder in a vulnerable position. Try tipping the boat slightly and pushing your body against this brace with the hip snap and head dink. Be more daring and lean farther, really snap the hips and drop the head and feel how the boat rights itself. If you lean too much out on the paddle, you risk not being able to complete the move and flipping (or needing to brace again). The high brace is a powerful stroke that, done correctly, can keep you out of a lot of trouble.

The low brace applies the same concepts as the high brace but it requires the paddler to rotate his wrists and use the opposite side of the paddle blade. Aim the knuckles of the T-grip hand and the paddle-shaft hand down and hold the paddle nearly horizontal. The power face of the paddle blade should be aimed at the sky and the blade itself should be flat to the water. Try using the paddle in this position to support the head dink and hip snap. It may feel less powerful than the high brace, but it's a good brace because it keeps the paddle lower and puts your shoulder at less risk and it will keep you from leaning too much on your paddle in the brace.

Sculling

Sculling is a versatile stroke combination that you can use to brace, turn and move laterally. The sculling stroke works at the side of the boat and the paddle doesn't leave the water through its entire movement. Planting the paddle vertically in the water a little bit forward of where you kneel, aim the power face of the paddle blade toward you and pull it a few inches toward the boat. The boat will rotate toward the paddle blade when you do this and to counter that rotation and use the scull to slip laterally, finish that short draw stroke and slice the paddle blade through the water to a point just behind you and out away from the canoe. Plant the paddle at the same distance as the starting point of your original draw stroke. To do this, twist your body so that your shoulders are facing toward the side of the boat. Draw that stroke in a few inches to the side of

the boat and feel the canoe rotate toward it. When you finish, slice the paddle to the starting point of the first draw stroke and repeat.

The paddle should be making an hourglass shape in the water, and done briskly, you should be able to sideslip the boat. As in all paddle strokes, the movement really comes from the torso and hips: you should be moving the canoe to the paddle rather than the paddle to the canoe. Sculling works for sideslipping, but it can also be an effective brace as well—one that can be maintained indefinitely. For the bracing scull, you might want to hold the paddle more horizontal to the water. Relax and trust your scull to maintain a lean you set in the water. Try snapping off of it to right yourself. Finally, sculling can be used to turn the boat by applying it more in front of you or behind you. Reaching out forward and sculling will tend to draw the bow toward the scull and turn the boat into the side of the sculling. Reaching out behind will tend to turn the boat away from the sculling. Practice the scull to get more smooth with it and try orienting the paddle differently and feel what this stroke does to the boat. Become proficient with it and make it a reliable whitewater paddling tool—its versatility will pay off.

A cool head and smooth, efficient paddle strokes will help you dodge the nasty stuff that the river throws at you. Here a kayaker skirts a large hole.

Youghiogheny River, Maryland/Pennsylvania

HEADWATERS: *The river starts in western Maryland and flows into southwestern Pennsylvania*

LENGTH: *The lower Youghiogheny run is 7 1/2 miles. The upper Youghiogheny run is 10 miles and the top Youghiogheny run is 6 miles.*

DROP: *Parts of the upper sections reach 100 feet per mile with about a 50-foot-per-mile average gradient. The first mile of the popular lower section is in the 50-foot-per-mile range but the river flattens out after that.*

DIFFICULTY: *Class 3, 4, 5*

CHARACTER: *This is one of the most popular rivers on the East Coast and requires a permit for private boaters to run during peak times. There are plenty of seats in commercial rafts and on inflatable kayak trips, however. The upper section is demanding Class 5 water served by several outfitters and the lower is Class 3 and served by many rafting companies. The river is dam controlled and so flows are relatively consistent throughout the summer.*

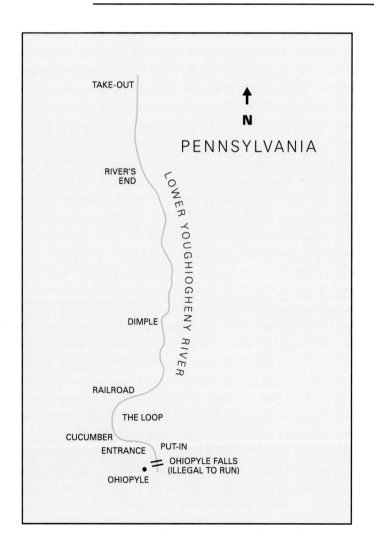

This popular tongue-twister of a river, shortened by those-in-the-know to the Yough (Yok), is one of the most crowded runs on the East Coast in the summertime. Access is limited during the summer on the lower Youghiogheny, but even on the most crowded weekends it's possible to get a launch time if you wake up early and sign up for it. You can skip that and buy a seat in a raft with six others who are there for the same exciting run as you. Most of the action is packed in the first mile with Entrance, Cucumber and Railroad rapids stacked up in quick succession (and a few other smaller rapids to keep it interesting between the bigger drops). Floating below the railroad bridge, you will find a lovely undeveloped run spiced up with several challenging rapids. The crowds also have a chance to spread out more in the lower part of the run and you might, maybe, get a piece of the river to yourself.

The upper Yough is a classic Eastern Class 5 run where some of the best boaters in the country have cut their teeth. Several outfitters run trips on it, too, so it can be experienced by those who may not have the skills to get down it by themselves. If you're a private boater and you want to run the upper Yough, make sure your skills are in order and find someone to show you the lines. It's long, tricky, demanding whitewater that offers little room for error.

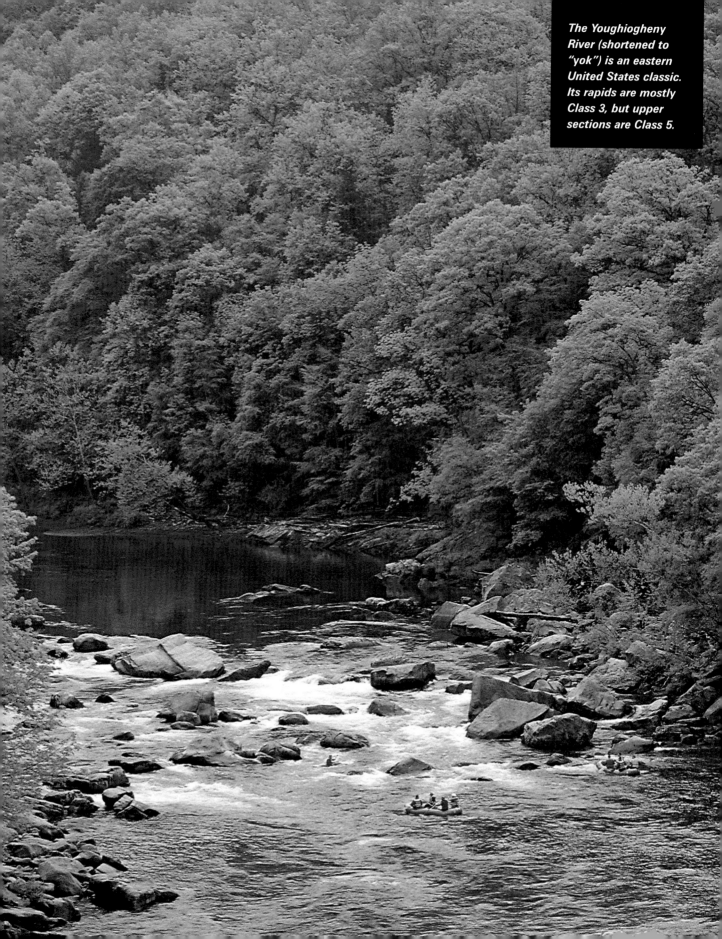

The Youghiogheny River (shortened to "yok") is an eastern United States classic. Its rapids are mostly Class 3, but upper sections are Class 5.

The Moves

Put your paddle and oar strokes together with your new-found sense of balance and movement, and you're ready to make the moves that will get you safely and smoothly down the rapid. Learning these moves will give you control in the rapid and the ability to break down difficult stretches of water into simpler movements. Especially in the beginning, there will seem to be a lot going on around you, but teaching yourself to make controlled moves through the rapid will slow things down and give you a chance to learn how the river works. Using the river's energy to help you move through it is the highest form of smooth and efficient paddling, and eddy turns, ferrying and surfing will let you tap into that energy.

EDDY TURNS

Eddies give paddlers an opportunity to stop, breathe and look at what's ahead on the river. Good paddlers learn to use eddies to break rapids apart, slow their descent and bring some control to a chaotic environment. Eddy hopping, moving through a rapid from eddy to eddy, is a great strategy for running almost any rapid. It's also great practice on easy rapids to pick out all the eddies you can see and try to move in and out of each one of them.

To catch eddies, and then get out of them, you need to learn the eddy turn. A well-executed eddy turn uses the river's energy to cross the tricky water of the eddy line, the boundary between fast and slow water, with control. The movement, like all paddling movements, is not about strength. Instead it

> *Meltdown:* **When a paddler runs through a hole and completely disappears, she has melted down. She's actually caught the downstream current under the hole and taken it for a ride.**

He thought his happiness was complete when, as he meandered aimlessly along, suddenly he stood by the edge of a full-fed river. Never in his life had he seen a river before—this sleek, sinuous, full-bodied animal, chasing and chuckling, gripping things with a gurgle and leaving them with a laugh, to fling itself on fresh playmates that shook themselves free, and were caught and held again.

—Kenneth Grahame,
The Wind in the Willows

demands good body and boat position and well timed application of basic paddle and oar strokes.

Eddy turns can be broken into three elements. First, a paddler needs momentum to get his boat across the eddy line. Going downstream into an eddy, momentum is easy to maintain because the river is doing all the work as the paddler floats along with the current. To maintain momentum across the eddy line as the paddler moves from fast to slow water, he will need to reach across the eddy line and with a few forward strokes, pull himself into the eddy. The paddle and oar strokes should continue through the eddy line: don't stop at the eddy line, take your paddle or oar out of the water and hope that you've paddled or rowed enough to carry you across it. Again, this isn't about strong strokes but rather well-timed and placed ones that are smooth

Eddy turns are fundamental to whitewater boat control. The paddler in the first figure is moving from the eddy into the current, peeling out. The flows are actually moving in opposite directions, separated by the unpredictable water of the eddy line. As he approaches the eddy line, he must have enough speed to cross into the downstream flow, he should have set an angle of about 45 degrees to the eddy line and he should lean downstream to allow the fast water in the channel to slip underneath his boat more freely. Done right, an eddy turn or peel out accelerates the paddler to the speed of the current within the space of just a few paddle strokes.

and easy—the river is doing the work here and you are just adding a little to maintain momentum. To illustrate the forces involved, kayakers who have learned to use the duffeck stroke eliminate those extra forward strokes and rely on timing and boat position to pull themselves into the eddy without, seemingly, taking a stroke. Advanced canoeists use a similar plant-and-carve technique with forward, draw and crossover strokes.

Leaving the eddy, "peeling-out," requires similar momentum, but since you are moving from slow- to fast-moving water you will likely need to add a few more strokes to the movement. The key again is to paddle through the move and don't stop at the eddy line. As you approach the eddy line, reach across it and pull yourself through with a well-timed stroke.

For more stability and to remind yourself to paddle through the eddy line, continue paddling as the current catches your boat and carries you downstream. If you're in an oar-rig raft, drive through the eddy line and continue to stroke as the current catches the boat.

Eddy turns are more than momentum—in fact the key to doing them well is not in the paddle strokes or the momentum you maintain, but the position of the boat in the water, the lean and angle you apply to it. Lean is one of the harder concepts for beginning canoe and kayak paddlers to grasp and improper lean causes a lot of flips, but take heart, it becomes second nature quickly. Leaning the boat requires the paddler to weight one edge of it, dropping the hip to the side of the lean and lifting the other side. In flat water, the paddler will be balanced over the boat with it rotated under him—this is called a J-lean because the body makes the shape of a J with the head as the dot.

On moving water, the balance point will shift as the current pushes on the boat, and in an eddy turn, the paddler will lean into the turn, a feeling similar to leaning into a turn on a bicycle or on skis. This means that when the paddler leaves the eddy, he must lean downstream and lift his upstream edge to the oncoming current. This lean allows water to slip under the hull of the boat without catching the upstream edge and causing a flip, and it puts the body in a more stable position as the boat accelerates to the speed of the current.

When you peel out of an eddy you almost can't lean too much—more lean will cause the boat to accelerate more quickly to the speed of the current and require a more radical body position for stability. You can, however, lean too little, and you will feel it when you do. If the current doesn't flip you, the stern of the boat will feel like it's being sucked down

into the current and you will be in a sickeningly unstable position. Relax, ride it out and lean more next time. If you hold the lean too long, you'll feel that as well, though it's not as dramatic. As the boat picks up speed, your body position will shift from the dynamic lean of the turning bicycle to the flat-water J-lean. Lean during the transition from slow to fast and ease off as you start to move downstream.

Leaning upon entering the eddy is the same drill. You will lean into the turn, so if it's an eddy on river right, you will lean to the right as you cross the eddy line. Though it seems counterintuitive, sink the upstream edge of the boat and lift the downstream one. The water in the eddy isn't moving but you are, and the change in speeds (rather like stepping off an escalator) might flip you when the slow water of the eddy meets the downstream edge of your boat. This radical slow-down flips beginning paddlers regularly, and they'll inevitably come up sputtering, "I run the rapids fine but flip in the pools. I just don't understand it." Lean.

With rafts, lean is less critical on most rivers because the boats are so wide and stable, though it can help to un-weight the upstream tube to allow water to slip under it. On big water, the force of the current can grab the tube of the boat and suck it down enough to topple paddlers into the water. When dealing with any eddy, rafters should try to shift their weight to the tube away from the change in current. When entering an eddy, shift upstream. When exiting an eddy, shift downstream.

You have good momentum and you have proper lean, so now you just have to put your boat in the right place. The third element of the eddy turn is finding the correct angle for the boat to cross the eddy line. Canoes and kayaks cross the eddy line at about a 45-degree angle in order to do an effective eddy turn. Remember it's a 45-degree angle to the eddy line, not to the general direction of the downstream flow. Rafts should use a shallower, less aggressive angle so that the bigger boat can move completely out into the flow before it's caught by the current.

Currents bend and twist, even within a broad flow, and you need to be able to spot an eddy line and how it's oriented to the flow you're in to be able

to set up your boat effectively for an eddy turn or peel-out. That optimum angle oriented to the current will tend to pull the boat across a flow when the boat is moving either slower or faster than the flow. If the angle is too much upstream, the boat will slowly cross the eddy line, lose momentum and likely not make it into the main, stable flow. If the boat is too perpendicular to the eddy line, the current will tend to push the nose downstream, deflecting the boat and leaving the paddler sitting awkwardly in the eddy line. Done correctly, the angled boat will be pulled out into the heart of the main flow and accelerate quickly to the speed of the current, avoiding the difficult soup of the eddy line.

The eddy turn or peel-out puts these three elements together: momentum, lean and angle. Getting it right will take practice, so find a mellow, but well-defined, eddy line and work on moving in and out of it. Aim high on the eddy line where it's most sharply defined. Feel how the current works on the boat. When you get the peel-out right, it's a thrill. The current grabs the boat with the paddler in solid position

and accelerates it, leaving a little trail of bubbles in the boat's wake. When you make snappy eddy turns into eddies, it's an equal thrill. You land and stick, ready for the next move.

FERRYING

When paddlers want to move laterally across the river without going downstream, they ferry, a move that incorporates the same concepts as the eddy turn and peel-out but to a different degree for a different effect. The principle of ferrying is the same as that used by old motorless river ferries. The idea is that by placing your boat at an angle to the current and maintaining its position, the river will move you laterally by the same interplay of high and low pressure that give lift to an airplane wing. Old river ferries maintained position by hooking into a cable or rope strung across the river; whitewater boaters have paddles and oars that they can use to break free of the downstream flow. Again, though, the

Ferrying requires a paddler to maintain boat angle across a channel of water. A well-done ferry moves the boater across the river without slipping downstream. It takes practice to manage in heavy water.

move requires little strength, depending more on boat placement, feel of the river and smooth paddle strokes.

The angle of the boat, its ferry angle, is the key to effective lateral movement. A 45-degree angle to the current is best for canoes and kayaks because it strikes a balance between presenting a low profile to the downstream current while giving enough boat edge to the current to create the wing-like effect of the ferry. As in the eddy turn, rafts may want to take a more conservative angle than 45 degrees.

Most boats ferry with the bow pointed upstream, but you can apply the principle with the bow pointed downstream as well—it just may be a little more awkward. Pointed too much upstream, the boat will move slowly across the current, requiring more paddling effort. On a long ferry you'll be out there a long time creeping slowly toward the

opposite bank if your ferry angle is too conservative. Aim too much downstream and the river will catch the boat along its length, pull it along with it and turning the move into more of a peel-out. Remember: set the ferry angle relative to the current.

Proper angle is one part of the equation, but boaters also must maintain a smooth paddle or oar stroke through the move. For canoeists and kayakers, sweep strokes will likely feel most comfortable in this move. These strokes allow you to easily change the angle of the boat, and if the same stroke is used on both sides of the boat—a right forward sweep followed by a left forward sweep—they give enough against-the-current propulsion for a smooth ferry. Oar rig rafts will need to use combinations of backstrokes with one- or two-oar turning strokes. Smooth, regular strokes are critical. On the river, you may be out there ferrying for a long time if you have to move all the way across the river in a big rapid, and big powerful strokes are more likely to upset the careful balance you've set with your ferry. Develop a cadence or rhythm and stick to it as you cross. Kayakers and canoeists should avoid using back strokes to turn the boat quickly. These strokes will destroy all the work you've done by instantly carrying you downstream, and you'll have to start the whole ferrying process again.

With correct angle and a smooth paddle stroke the ferry move is nearly complete, with one exception: the ferry requires proper lean to the boat to make it most efficient. Paddlers should impart a slight downstream lean to the boat as they cross. Whereas it's difficult to lean too much with a peel-out, a radical lean in the ferry won't be very efficient because the edge that you've sunk into the water will drag in the downstream current. A little bit of downstream lean, however, keeps the upstream edge from catching in the current and offers the flatter surface of the bottom of your boat for the water to slip underneath. It's also easier to hold a little bit of lean for a long ferry.

A few final things to remember with the ferry are less related to specific technique and more to learning to feel the river. Remember that the river current rarely flows at the same speed across a broad channel and patches of fast and slow water will have a dramatic effect on the angle of your boat. Learn to spot where these changes will occur in the flow—the backwash of a small hole, shallow water, the edges of the fast water—and make adjustments as you encounter them. Teach yourself to fix your eyes on the spot across the river that you want to reach and keep looking at it. Avoid breaking your gaze in a difficult ferry and especially don't look downstream. Your boat will go where your eyes do.

STEERING THROUGH A RAPID

Seeing the way through the rapid is essential to running it, and any moves you make in a rapid should start on the bank. Look at the river from different angles and approaches: some paddlers go so far as to wade out a bit into the river to get a sense of how to line up. Look also for landmarks and water features you can use in the rapid to make sure you're on course—a small curling wave right at the lip of a drop, a tree downstream that you can line up on, the rock that forms the eddy you want to catch. It can get busy out there, so focus on how the rapid flows and try to imprint it on your brain. Try to visualize what the rapid's features will do to your boat. Will a big lateral wave require a brace? Can you catch that eddy? Will the hole stop you, and if it does, what's below it that could cause trouble? What hazards must you avoid?

Now that you've spotted the tricky parts of the rapid, think about a strategy for handling them. If the current will push your boat into a hazard, then you should look for an eddy to catch above it to try to move around the problem. A ferry works well to move through a ledgy rapid with slots through the ledges that aren't lined up. A dynamic peel-out may be required to give your boat momentum to clear an obstacle or punch a hole.

Sometimes the strategy is to do little as you move down river and wait to make a move when you need to. The less-is-more strategy is prudent for most rapids. Rarely will you paddle full-steam-ahead down a rapid: forward speed will make you feel stable but will make it hard to set up for lateral movements like ferries and eddy turns.

Once you're in the rapid, you may feel disoriented or that things are moving faster than you can deal with them. At these times relax and remember the landmarks you spotted during your scout. Focus on where you need to go and let your chaotic surroundings slip away. The more rapids you run, the more the rapids will seem to slow down as you get used to all the irrelevant boiling and frothing water that has no effect on your boat. Smile, too. Tense, scowling boaters flip frequently. Whitewater is fun, remember? Happy boaters float higher, and someone may be taking your picture.

WAVE SURFING

Surfing a river wave can be one of the most sublime moments of whitewater paddling. While it may

Playing is one of the best ways to build river skills and boat control.

seem like pure play, surfing is useful for paddlers to learn. At its most basic level, wave surfing is a form of ferrying. You get on the wave in the same way you start a ferry, by setting an angle to the downstream current and paddling out into it. When you're on the wave, use the power of the river against the hull or tubes of your boat to move laterally. Your boat will hang in the current on a well-formed wave with little paddling and the bow pointing directly upstream.

Change the angle to the right or left, feel the boat move that way and change the angle to bring it back again: this is called carving on the wave. Rudder strokes will help keep you on the wave by creating less drag, but you may also need to add a flurry of upstream strokes if you feel yourself slipping off the back of the wave. Here too, big muscle strokes are more hindrance than help and tend to overextend your body and push your boat into places you don't want to be.

You can use a wave surf to ferry quickly and effortlessly across the river, and even if you don't completely catch the wave, the little extra momentum from it can be a big help in tough ferries. Learn to spot waves you can use for this and set up your ferries to run through their troughs. Now you're using the river and not fighting against it.

HOLE SURFING

Hole surfing, like wave surfing, isn't just about play. As a practical matter of river running, you can expect to get stuck in holes from time to time, and knowing what to do to get out of them is a skill you should plan to master. Like waves, you can use holes on the river. Friendly holes can be handy for ferrying and speed control as well as a convenient place to land in, like in an eddy, and scout what's downstream (in the friendly ones). The key to basic hole surfing is learning to keep your edge up out of the oncoming flow—the green water—and using a downstream brace to restore your balance. For rafting, you will need to learn to high-side, or shift the boat's passengers to the highest tube. High-siding will keep the raft from flipping in most holes, but in strong ones that tend to spin the raft, the high-side can turn into a hamster-on-a-wheel runaround as you try to keep everybody on the highest tube.

Most boats will naturally fit in a hole sideways, and riding a hole this way is called side-surfing. Some older high-volume kayaks and canoes will tend to stick a little more firmly in holes that newer, smaller boats find friendly. Easy-to-spin little boats offer a surfing advantage over older, bigger, high-volume boats, but a paddler in them must be ready to shift her lean and switch her brace as the boat comes around. While these boats may feel a little unpredictable for the new hole rider, in the end they will teach valuable skills and make your paddling more fluid.

Those spinning characteristics are especially nice when you find yourself surfing a hole that isn't particularly friendly: you're stuck and the way out isn't obvious. The first thing to remember in hole riding is to stay loose. Holes can feel violent and can buck

Surf: To hang on a wave or stick in a hole and ride it. Surfing is a great way to hone skills for river running and learn the fundamentals of boat control. It's also a lot of fun. In fact, surfing and playboating is a whole subculture of whitewater paddling, with international competitions and an ever growing list of moves to perfect.

and toss a boat around—that's why whitewater surfing competitions are called rodeos—and the only way to hang on and keep control is to remain loose.

Next, you should look for an escape. When you scouted the rapid, you might have spotted the break in the hole that you wanted to hit, or, even better, you may have identified how the hole kicks or displaces objects along its length. If you find that the hole kicks to its edge and you can get out that way, brace or rudder the boat so that you can ride the kick out. If you can paddle to the place where the hole

Waves and holes are fun whitewater destinations unto themselves. The best ones, like Trestle Hole on the Deschutes River, have big eddies that hold a lot of paddlers waiting to surf.

Ottawa River, Ontario/Quebec

HEADWATERS: *Laurentian Highlands of northern Canada*

LENGTH: *10 miles for the most common run*

DIFFICULTY: *Class 4*

CHARACTER: *The Ottawa River drains a huge area of northeastern Canada and is a big water river. Much of the river is mellow moving water, but the commonly run whitewater section less than two hours from Ottawa offers world-class whitewater.*

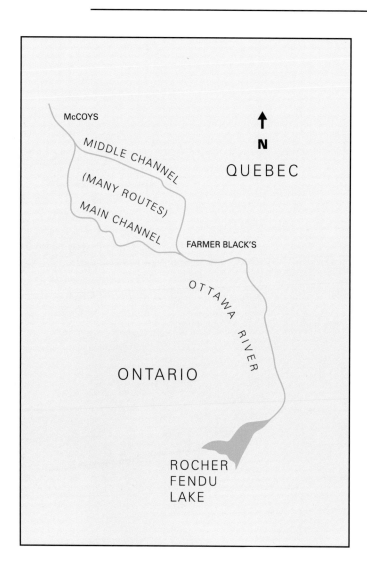

The Ottawa River is a center for Eastern Canadian whitewater paddling with its huge river features and many play spots. It's the most popular commercial whitewater river in Canada, running about 40,000 customers through rapids like Coliseum and Dog Leg. Play boaters can find many inviting river features to surf and show off their stuff in the sticky holes of McCoys. Farmer Black's is also a popular play spot with a big wave and hole combination sure to please the playful.

Paddlers should expect big water on the Ottawa and have the skills to match it. Holes and rapids generally are friendly, but there's enough funny water on the river to give the tense and tippy a bad day. Commercial trips are also a good option for learning the river's moves. The Ottawa forms the border between French-speaking Quebec and English Ontario and some of the rapids and river features carry French names such as the Rocher Fendu, a popular run on the Ottawa. Outfitters and services can be found in Beachburg, Ontario.

The Ottawa River is a big river that's braided with many channels in the whitewater section. It's possible to paddle the same section of river several times and not do the same complete run twice.

bow into the oncoming flow and letting it stand you on end. The deep downstream current will tend to push you out past the boil. If that fails, you'll likely be in position for a tried-and-true upside-down hole escape. While flipped over, reach out with your paddle from your set-up and down into the downstream flow that moves under the hole. Hang on tight and let that flow pull you and your boat out. Roll up after the roaring stops.

As a last, last resort, consider swimming out. For a few holes, this may be the only way out, but it's risky to separate from your boat. Most of the time you're body will catch a piece of the downstream flow and pop up out of the hole, but if it's a strong, well-formed hole, it may keep you for a few recirculations. If you find yourself swimming and being recirculated, remember the rules of surfing the hole: change your shape and the hole will likely kick you out. Tuck into a ball or spread your arms and legs wide. Time your breaths for when you resurface on each recirculation and look for a rope. Finally, if all else fails, take a big breath and swim into the green water, letting it drive you down and out underneath the hole. Don't give up.

PLAY

Intentional hole and wave surfing comprise the bulk of what river runners call play. They don't mean to imply that paddling down river isn't fun and in itself play, but like all things on the river, play is a relative term. For everybody on the bank, back in the office or stuck in traffic, whitewater is play. For river runners, play means stopping at a river feature and exploring what it has to offer, sometimes for hours at a time. Some kayakers and canoeists take the idea even farther and don't run downriver much at all, preferring instead to drive their boats to spot on the river where they will spend the day playing. This is called destination boating, and river runners who do it start and end their river trip in the same spot.

What could possibly be so fun about one hole or wave? Isn't the thrill of whitewater the feeling of crashing down through a rapid, playing on the margins of comfort and control? For many it is, but play takes all of the skill needed to run down the rapid and applies it to the energy the river exerts on one

Sometimes the only way into the river is to slide off a rock and take the plunge, what kayakers call a seal launch. Sometimes kayakers seal launch just for fun, like these boaters on the Futaleufu River in Chile.

breaks, try to surf the hole there, it may kick you out. Again edges of the hole are good escapes because the upstream stick of a hole is less strong near its edge and you might catch the downstream flow there.

If moving your boat around in the hole doesn't get you out, you will have to be more creative. This is where all that hole-surfing practice will help you. If you're stuck, the hole probably has an affinity for holding floating objects similar in shape to your boat. If so, try to change the shape of the boat relative to the hole. Spin. In a kayak or canoe, you can ender out of the hole by driving your spot. When you're playing, you feel speed, the thrill of learning what you can do and the splash of water in your face. In fact, in many play spots these sensations are intensified, and play can be a great way to build on the basic skills of river running and make you a better boater.

Whitewater has blossomed in the past decade: boats have been refined and paddlers have pushed the limits of what once was considered out of the question. Small flat-bottomed kayaks, short edgy canoes and rafts specialized for tight moves have all led the charge in making whitewater a more playful sport. New moves appear regularly on the whitewater competition circuit, but they are all based on the fundamentals of paddling that any beginner learns. Play is experimentation with body twist and lean, with edging the boat and with new combinations of old skills. All of this will give you a sense of how your boat performs across a wide variety of rapids. Finally, play will give you the confidence to be comfortable on the river and have fun.

KAYAK ROLL

The roll—also known as the eskimo roll—is the crux of many new kayakers' learning curves. The roll confounds many. Some people learn it in the pool and lose it on the river and then find it again. Some paddlers struggle in maybe-I'll-be-able-to-roll purgatory for several years, while a few learn it the first time they try it and never lose it again. Whatever the case, it's worth learning to do correctly. The ability to flip over and then get back up without swimming is an essential safety skill in Class 3 or harder whitewater. Because swimming is tiring and time consuming, a solid roll will also make paddling trips more fun. It's usually more safe in your boat than out of it.

The best way to learn to roll is with personal instruction. Books can help prepare you for what you'll do in the boat and we will describe it here, but competent instruction is the best way to learn the

roll. Often it takes an instructor putting your hands in the right place and moving you through the roll sequence for you to feel it. Make the investment in roll instruction early in your paddling career—take a class or bribe a skilled friend to help you at the pool. Avoiding focused instruction and roll practice will only make it harder to do when you need it to be second nature. Some people get the roll in just a few tries while for others it may take many practice sessions to train the body to roll. Stick with it and don't get frustrated.

The roll seems a slight-of-hand movement, requiring timing, coordination and relaxation underwater. But it's also a simple thing, combining a few basic paddling skills to achieve what for many is a mystifying result. The roll is a brace set from underneath the kayak. It uses resistance from a paddle moving through the water to set up a paddler for an effective hip snap. You should not use your paddle to physically pull yourself up and out of the water, but rather use it to keep your body near the surface so that your hip snap will move your center of gravity from underneath the boat to on top of it. Again, it's a counterintuitive move: the head, the part of the body that most wants to be out of the water, should be the last part to come out of the water in the roll.

Two types of rolls are commonly taught in the United States: the C-to-C roll and the sweep roll. Each has its adherents and disciples: some say the C-to-C is easier to teach and gives the paddler more protection underwater, others say the sweep is better in big water and quicker. Both rolls are equally effective for righting a flipped kayaker and the choice of which one you learn is a matter of your instructor's preference more than anything. Once you learn one technique, you can branch out and learn others—the skills from one roll translate directly to the other rolls.

Both rolls require similar set-ups, the body position you return to every time you flip. The set-up helps to make sense of chaos by having a consistent position to return to despite disorienting conditions. When you flip, Lean forward and try to put your head on the front deck of your boat. Hold the paddle as you do when you take a draw stroke—knuckles of the control hand align with the top of the paddle blade—and

Kayakers roll to return themselves to the surface after a flip. The key is to use your body to snap upright and keep your head down. Note how the paddler's head stays at the surface of the water through almost the whole sequence. He finishes with his head resting on his shoulder.

rotate your body and move the paddle so that it's parallel to the length of the boat with your hands near the water line. The paddle blade of the control hand should be pointed toward the bow of the boat. This is a protected position that will let you gather yourself before starting the roll. The paddle blade of the control hand must be flat relative to the surface of the water. To do this, you should bend the wrist of your control hand toward your forearm to move the blade into position rather than rotate the paddle in your hand. Finally, once in set-up position and flipped over, reach toward the surface and get the paddle out of the water. Now you're ready to roll.

The C-to-C roll is so named for the shapes a paddler's body assumes while doing the roll. It starts with the spine making a "C"—head dropped toward hip—on one side and finishing with a "C" on the other side. Try sitting in a chair and making the movement. Sit upright and look straight ahead. Drop your head toward your hip, compressing the muscles on the side of your torso that you're dropping your head to and stretching the muscles of your torso on the other side. Do the same thing to the opposite side and you have the core of the movement: your body will act like a whip to bring yourself upright when you are flipped in your kayak.

So from the set-up, you need to bend your body toward the surface of the water, compressing the muscles on the set-up side of the torso and stretching the ones opposite. This is the first "C". You then move the paddle from the set-up so that the paddle shaft is perpendicular to the length of the boat, the control hand is out to the side of the boat and the off hand is out of the water on the hull. The paddle blade must be flat to the surface of the water. In this position, your brace is set. From here, you snap from one "C" to the opposite "C," remembering to keep your head down to the very end. Finish the roll by keeping your head pinned to your shoulder.

The sweep roll uses all of the same principles as the C-to-C roll but applies them to a different paddle movement. The sweep roll starts from the set-up, but instead of moving the paddle to a position perpendicular to the length of the boat, the sweep roll engages the paddle at the start of the movement. So instead of a brace, use a sweep stroke to brace against and body twist and hip snap to right yourself. The sweep starts at the set-up and the torso twists to move the paddle blade of the control hand across the surface. The hips snap and the head stays dropped to the shoulder. The roll finishes with the sweep stroke passing the hip, and the head stays down to the end.

Beginning rollers often fail for two reasons. Either they lift their head at some point in the movement in a conscious or subconscious effort to get air, or their paddle dives and fails to keep the paddler's body in a good position to hip snap. The lifted-head problem is simple to diagnose, simple in theory to fix but requires practice to overcome.

Remember to keep your head pinned to your shoulder to the very end of the roll. If you're able to get a gasp of air at any time during your roll, you're probably lifting your head. The diving paddle problem is a bit more complex and usually is a result of poor set-up. The blade of the control hand must remain flat on the surface. If its leading edge dips even slightly, the paddle will bite into the water and dive. For rollers with exceedingly good form, this shouldn't be much of a problem, but for beginners facing a list of techniques that they have to figure out how to coordinate, it can be trouble. Keeping the wrist bent in the set-up and through the motion often solves the diving paddle problem. You should also remember to break the surface of the water with your control hand in the set-up. If you don't, it's hard to orient your paddle correctly for the roll.

Having a pool roll is one thing, but translating it to the river is the next challenge. Flips on the river happen unexpectedly and come with a small jolt of adrenaline and a face full of cold water. To compound the problem, the water moves at different speeds around the boat, and some currents may, for a time, inhibit rolling. That's why a roll after an unexpected flip in a rapid on the river is called a combat roll. Combat rolls require no different technique, but persistence, patience and a cool head will pay off when learning them. Your first combat roll will be twice as thrilling as your first pool roll: it's the roll that gives you confidence to explore the river in relative safety.

One key to combat rolling is to learn to be an opportunist. Because you and your boat will likely be going at a different speed from the water surrounding you when you flip, sometimes it's good to pause during the set-up to let the water catch you and move you at its speed. Doing this will make the water surrounding the boat more like flat water because relative to you it won't be moving. It'll be less likely that currents will do strange things to you, your paddle or your boat.

Typewriter: **To be displaced laterally across a river channel like the carriage return on a typewriter.**

Once you've learned the roll on the on-side or control side (with the right hand for most), you should very shortly try to learn the off-side roll. Many paddlers put this off. If learning the on-side roll was awkward, the off-side can feel like an advanced yoga position. Paddlers must go through the stress of relearning the roll and it just seems like too much of a hassle. But neglecting the off-side roll for too long will likely make you favor the on-side too much, even when conditions require you to use an off-side roll. You will also miss out on some important advantages to being able to roll on both sides. Missing a roll to one side puts the paddler in set-up position for the other side and provides rocking momentum that may help right you. The on-side to off-side roll is a handy, bombproof combination in tricky water. Missing a roll to one side likely means that there's funny water there (an eddy line perhaps) that probably won't be a problem on the other side of the boat. Finally, the off-side roll gives the paddler an extra boost of confidence by giving him another tool to use to solve a paddling problem before his air runs out and he must swim.

CANOE ROLL AND SELF-RESCUE

With a kayak, self-rescue is an either-or proposition. Either roll, or swim. This is not so with canoes. It's possible to roll a canoe, of course, and modern playboat designs make this a reliable option. But canoes with plenty of flotation will also allow you to climb back in them after a short swim. Both techniques require practice to get them right.

First, to re-enter a flipped canoe, right it by swimming underneath a gunnel and pushing up hard. This will rotate the boat upright. Next, from the side of the canoe, reach across it to the opposite gunnel and scissor-kick to give yourself lift to slide into the boat. The move is a lot like hoisting yourself out onto a low dock or the edge of a swimming pool, except that the boat moves and bobs around.

Try to move the boat under you as much as you try to haul yourself in. If you just grab the gunnel nearest you and try to pull yourself up, you'll succeed in sinking that edge of the canoe and flipping it. Once you're in the boat stay low, get situated back in the saddle and bail out the excess water. You're ready to head down the river.

To avoid swimming altogether, practice the roll. The roll is done with the body rather than the paddle and your focus should be on a good hip snap and keeping your head down through the move. Tandem boaters can roll as well with the right coordination. If your canoe doesn't have float bags to keep most of the water out and a saddle with thigh straps to hold you in, you won't be rolling.

The roll is essentially a deep brace, so deep, in fact, that you're doing it from underneath the boat. Practice first by setting a brace and falling over. The paddle should be flat on the surface of the water, perpendicular to the long axis of the boat and your head should be near your T-grip hand. If you have flipped so that your brace is set up on the right, you should start by contracting the muscles of the left side of your body to reach your body and head toward the surface of the water. This is the first "C" of the C-to-C roll. At this point the paddle serves to keep your body in good position near the surface of the water, and you should not be pulling down on it. In a decisive motion, begin the roll by snapping the body from one "C" to the opposite "C." Relax the left side muscles, contract the right side of the torso and drop your ear to your shoulder. The paddle serves only to keep your body's surface position, so again avoid trying to pull yourself up on it. To finish the hip snap, drive the right knee (for a right-side roll) up to the surface to rotate the boat under you. Your head should stay down through the move and you should finish by sweeping your body from a low forward lean over the right gunnel to the left gunnel. This will maintain the rotational momentum of the boat until you are completely on top of it. Practice this roll until you get the feel of the dynamics of it. It's not a muscle move and should feel effortless, so easy that it's almost a surprise that you've righted yourself with so little effort.

Once you become proficient at the deep brace roll, try rolling from the set-up position. This will be

Self rescue in an inflatable kayak is simple, but there's a trick to wiggling in. Reach across the boat and grab the opposite tube before climbing aboard, otherwise you'll flip the boat onto your head.

the way you want to roll on the river because the beginning of the roll requires you to find a way to consistently orient yourself to the water. You won't always fall over on a brace, and the canoe roll set-up, like the kayak roll set-up, helps you figure out where your are in a chaotic environment. Holding the paddle as you would for a forward draw or a high brace, rotate the paddle as if you were doing a low brace so that your knuckles aim down. Bring the paddle blade across toward the bow of the boat and place your T-grip hand in front of your belly button. The paddle should now be pointed toward the bow and the knuckles of both hands should be pointed down as if you were doing a low brace on your front float bag. Lean forward and tuck into a small package to avoid the rocks that you will be sweeping past when you're flipped over in the rapid. Now you're set up and ready for the combat canoe roll. To roll from this position, move from the tuck to the brace with your paddle on the surface of the water and go through the hip snap sequence. Remember to keep your head down through the move, or else you won't quite make it up.

INFLATABLE KAYAK SELF-RESCUE

Self-rescue in an inflatable kayak would seem to be a simple matter of just jumping back in the boat. It is, but because of your position in the water and the design of the boat, there's a trick to it. By just grabbing the tube of the boat nearest you and trying to

hoist yourself in, you'll likely just flip the boat on top of you. To proficiently re-enter an inflatable kayak you need to counterbalance your body and keep the IK from flipping as you try to slide in. Once you get the feel of it, you should be able to self-rescue pretty quickly, even in rapids.

If you flip in your inflatable kayak, try to hang on to your paddle and move upstream of your boat. If the boat is flipped over, swim under the tube nearest you and push up quickly to right the boat. With the IK floating upright, you now must get in position to pull yourself back in the boat. Swim up to the edge of the boat near the middle and reach across the tubes with the hand that holds the paddle. The paddle should be across the boat from you and parallel to the length of the boat in this set-up position. Now with your paddle arm draped across the two tubes, scissor-kick your legs to get lift and pull the boat under yourself while holding the paddle arm across the boat as you slide in. Stay low once you're in the boat, especially in rapids, because it's easy to fall out again while you are trying to get situated. Find your seat, settle in and get ready for the next move.

Fraser River, British Columbia

HEADWATERS: *Western slope of the Canadian Rocky Mountains*

LENGTH: *28 miles*

DIFFICULTY: *Class 4+*

CHARACTER: *The Fraser is the home of the giant river feature: massive amounts of water neck through a small passage around Hells Gate to form whitewater unlike anything you'll see elsewhere in North America.*

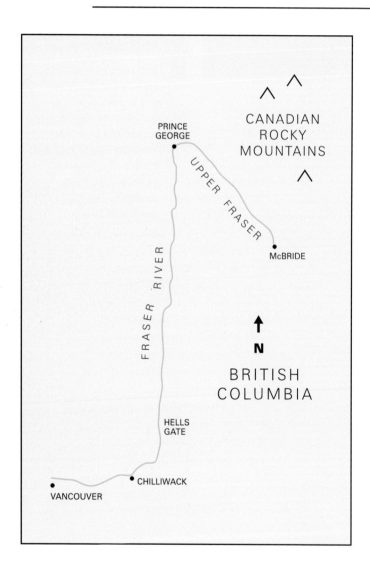

The Fraser River is the fire hose and Hells Gate is the nozzle. Big water, big boats and big country make the river an oddity among whitewater rivers of North America. For paddlers used to home flows of 1,000 to 3,000 cfs on most of the commonly run whitewater rivers in this hemisphere, the Fraser will seem Biblical in proportion, pushing a hundred times that amount of water through a passage as narrow as 70 feet at Hells Gate. The result is whitewater that is usually paddled…er…powered through on J-rig rafts in the 30-foot range.

The river is rated as a Class 4 but its scope will be different than what many have experienced. Whirlpools and boils redefine the concept of funny water, and smaller boats may have trouble crossing the powerful eddy fences formed on this river. Swimmers would be unhappy, indeed, to get tumbled through one of these features.

The upper runs of the Fraser in the Rockies hundreds of miles away offer challenging paddling on a river much different in character. Whitewater on the upper Fraser is between Moose Lake and Tete Jaune Cache, and the river runs are broken into Class 3 and Class 5 sections where the Fraser pushes through tight volcanic canyons west of Jasper National Park.

The river is recovering from manipulation of its course in the last century. The Fraser remains free-flowing, but blasting for a railroad during the gold rush of the early 1900s necked Hells Gate down to its present 70 feet, which made an impassable barrier for millions of spawning salmon headed upstream. The Fraser is the longest free-flowing river in North America, running 700 miles from the Rockies to its outlet at Vancouver.

The Fraser River in British Columbia holds some giant rapids. The river weaves through nearly half of the province before reaching the Pacific Ocean at Vancouver.

SAFETY AND RESCUE

Swimming

Giant lateral waves rear up and flip rafts. Canoes swamp, list and slowly disgorge their paddlers. Kayaks stick in holes and turn spontaneous cartwheels until their paddlers, out of breath, pull their spray skirts. No matter what their skill level in whitewater or the boat they paddle or row, eventually, all paddlers swim.

Rarely do paddlers get to choose where they swim. There are likely spots—holes and waves, rocks, eddy lines—but the swim itself is nearly always a surprise. However, its duration and its danger are at least partly under the control of the swimmer.

DEFENSIVE SWIMMING

For travelling and playing on moving water, basic swimming skills are a must. The more confident a paddler is out of his boat, the

The best laid plans often go awry. Swimming whitewater is another skill worth practicing so you're prepared when trouble strikes as it has for this raft crew trying to reassemble after a flip.

Road Scout: **To inspect rapids from the road. Expect them to be a lot bigger on the river than they looked from your car.**

more confident he will be in it. Paddlers should know basic strokes—the crawl and sidestroke, in particular—and be comfortable with breathing control. All of this will give him confidence to be on the water and remain calm when things don't go quite as expected.

So you're out of your boat. Whitewater is a hostile environment. Currents can dunk you deep below the surface and rocks rear up in your path, so paddlers need a defensive position in which they can float through rapids in relative safety. When the water is above knee-deep, the so called "swimmer's position" is the safest way to negotiate rapids. Point

Who hears the rippling of rivers will not utterly despair of anything.
—Henry David Thoreau

your feet downstream to fend off obstacles and keep your toes to the surface, floating on your back and sculling with your arms while following the contours of the surface currents.

It is critical to keep your feet at the surface in any moving water more than knee deep because feet and legs can be wedged in rocks on the bottom, and you can be entrapped and pushed over by the force of the current. It is difficult, if not impossible, to escape such an entrapment without assistance, even in shallow water, and foot entrapments are a leading cause of whitewater fatalities.

Don't stand up in moving water above your knees! Swim, even across places where you know you can stand. It may feel foolish to be swimming through shallow water, but the bottom of the river is a slippery and unforgiving place.

From the swimmer's position, paddlers can get their bearings and work toward saving themselves. It's important for swimmers to be aware of river features as they come upon them and take a big breath before they pass through. Instead of sitting up to get a better view downstream, put your chin to your chest and look downstream that way. Sitting up will force your butt deeper in the water, making it more vulnerable to rocks.

In heavy water you will need to time your breathing between waves as you ride low in the water and tend to punch through the crests of waves. Turn your head to the side to breathe to avoid spray and reduce the amount of water you aspirate while riding out the rapid. For long rapids, proper breathing techniques are important—you can aspirate a lot of water during a long swim and risk drowning despite floating at the surface of the water.

There is one case where the swimmer's position might not be the best thing: if you find yourself swimming approaching a waterfall, slide or other steep drop, pull your knees to your chest and tuck into a ball. This way, you'll bounce a little at the bottom of the drop—instead of auguring in feet first and

possible getting your extremities tangled in rocks or debris at the bottom. Protect your head and go with the flow—you'll resurface downstream from the drop.

Holes or hydraulics present further problems for the swimmer. The downstream flow of water through a hole or hydraulic may be several feet below the surface of the water, even in a small hole. In well formed, powerful hydraulics, the downstream flow may be at the bottom of the river. When floating through a hole, a swimmer may be carried deep under water for a long time. Because the foaming and frothing whitewater nearer the surface of a hole on the downstream side is actually flowing upstream, it's possible for swimmers to be caught in holes and recirculated. This washing-machine action can last indefinitely in powerful holes such as those formed by lowhead dams, low water bridges at high water, weirs and natural symmetrically formed ledges and slides.

The swimmer will be pulled beneath the water on the upstream side of the hole, carried some distance beneath the surface of the aerated backwash and pop up again near the boil line only to be carried back upstream for another cycle. Paddlers have many descriptive terms for such holes—"sticky" is a milder form of such a hydraulic, while paddlers should take care when adjectives like "terminal" and "keeper" are used to describe holes.

River runners get into swimmers position when they have have to swim whitewater. Aim your feet downstream and keep them at the surface to fend off obstructions and to keep them from being entrapped on the bottom. Use your arms to direct yourself around obstacles.

Everybody swims. When you know you're going over, take a big breath and stay cool. Move upstream of boats and try to hang on to your paddle. When you resurface, look for a safe place to swim to.

River etiquette dictates that you help out other boaters who are in trouble. This kayaker won't be able to do much to right the raft, but he can help collect gear and make sure swimmers get to shore safely.

Holes have an affinity for certain shapes, and swimmers caught in such holes should try to change their shape in the hole by either tucking tight into a ball or spreading their arms and legs out wide to try to catch downstream currents. Avoid the natural reaction to swim against the current and out the back of the hole; this is fruitlessly exhausting. Instead, use the river's natural power to escape.

If you are being recirculated, you should try to orient yourself by swimming to the light or following the bubbles to the surface. Look for a rope if a rescuer has been placed near the hole or find the natural break in the hole where the current is strong enough to push through the backwash. You can also try to swim aggressively into the upstream side of the hole, catch the downstream flow and hopefully

CFS: Cubic feet per second is the standard measure of flow of U.S. rivers. See also River Levels.

be carried down and out of the hole by the deep downstream currents. Keep your lifejacket on; you'll need it below the hole after you flush out. Few holes are so perfectly formed that there's no escape without assistance, so it's important to keep trying to find ways out. *Don't give up!*

SAVING YOUR GEAR

There's a narrow window of opportunity to collect gear when you first come out of the boat. Usually gear is within arm's reach or within a few strokes, but the longer you remain in the water without collecting gear the more likely it is to spread out. If you've fallen out of a raft, you are probably still pretty close to your boat, and your guide or fellow paddlers can drag you back topside quickly. In this case, it's a good idea to hang onto your gear—It saves time. Anyone who's ever spent hours searching the river, eddy to eddy, for a lost paddle, or worse, had to walk out because of a lost piece of gear, will hold on to gear much tighter on the next swim.

The first few moments in the water are the time to assess the situation. In easier water, a paddler should try to hold on to her gear if she can. It's time-consuming to collect loose gear and can be hard on boats and paddles to go floating ownerless down the river. There's nobody inside to keep them out of trouble, and kayaks and canoes can be pinned on difficult-to-reach midstream rocks. Hanging on to the boat also offers additional flotation that may be useful for riding out heavy water. Be careful, though, in violent wave trains, boats and paddles can beat up paddlers, and often it's best to let go and find rescue without the gear. If there's any question about getting to safety, ditch the gear. Boats and paddles designed for whitewater can take a lot of abuse. Sometimes it's a good idea to let go of the boat but hang on to the paddle. The paddle creates less drag on a swimmer's way downriver and can sometimes be harder to find. Boats, with proper flotation, ride high in the water and are easy to spot.

Swimming with gear can be awkward. Kayaks are fitted with grab loops and many whitewater canoes have grab loops and short sections of rope tied to the bow and stern called painters. Swimmers should try to hold the boat by the grab loop and the paddle in the same hand and use the free hand to sidestroke to safety. Stay upstream of the boat to avoid being pinned between a rock or log and the boat. If caught downstream of the boat, a swimmer should let go of it and move into a safer position upstream. If the boat is carrying the swimmer into trouble, she should let go and find safety without it.

Rafters have bigger problems. If the raft has flipped, swimmers should try to flip the raft back over if the rapid allows. Sometimes, especially in rough water, it's hard to flip it back over. It may be easier to climb up onto the floor of the upside down raft and paddle it to safety or to an easier place to right it. As with canoes and kayaks it's important not to be downstream of the raft, so give it a wide berth if you're downstream and won't be able to get back in any time soon. If the raft is caught in a hole with a recirculating swimmer, it's critical to get him back in the boat as quickly as possible. If the hole's recirculating cycle brings him to the surface under the raft, he won't be able to get air.

SWIMMING OUT OF TROUBLE

There comes a point as the swimmer is floating through a rapid that he should abandon the more passive position of the defensive swimmer and move aggressively to safety. Using the crawl or the sidestroke, swimmers can flip over and stroke for an eddy or for the bank. One of the most effective ways to move through current is to behave like the boat the swimmer's been separated from and use ferries and eddying techniques to find safety.

River Levels: **The amount of water in the river as measured by a gauge or personal experience. River levels in the U.S. are usually measured in cubic feet per second, by feet and inches on an established gauge, by a calculation derived from a downstream or nearby river's gauge, by a power company formula, and by eyeballing the river from the road at 40 mph while trying to avoid a head-on collision with a hay truck. High and low are the rough criteria of river levels. More specifically, gauges report actual data on the flow. A typical river usually flows between 1,000 and 3,000 cfs. Creeks may hold flows as low as 200 cfs and be runnable. Big water is often 10,000 cfs or more, but that's entirely dependent on the character of a riverbed. Some rivers are low at 10,000 cfs while others may be washing out the put-in bridge. Read guidebooks and check online with real time streamflow gauges and look at a lot of rivers to get a sense of what different flows look like. In the jargon of dam controlled rivers, a standard flow in the whitewater section may be a set number of "tubes" or turbines that the power company is running. It may also be expressed in megawatts or some other derivative of the river's energy. For safety, find out how many tubes, turbines or megawatts is fun, and how many is scary and how much the rain has had an effect on the flow. Calculations of the flow can be handy but are also highly variable and should be verified by personal inspection. Cumecs, cubic meters per second, are the metric counterpart of CFS.**

Flipping to your stomach, with your feet still pointed downstream, you can set a ferry angle and stroke upstream, moving laterally in the current to work around obstacles or to shore. You won't move as quickly or efficiently through the water as a boat so it's important to make moves early and decisively. Because they catch faster subsurface currents, swimmers generally float through moving water faster than the boats that are chasing them, so it's important to keep this in mind when seeking safety.

Catching eddies can be tricky for swimmers in heavy water because eddy lines can have strong downward currents that tend to suck swimmers beneath the surface and hold them in the chaotic water between the eddy and the main flow.

Swimmers, like boats, can literally bounce off eddylines if they don't approach them with good technique. A swimmer's speed and

Proper instruction helps to speed your river learning. Classes also stress safety skills.

Night and day the river flows. If time is the mind of space, the River is the soul of the desert. Brave boatmen come, they go, they die, the voyage flows on forever. We are all canyoneers. We are all passengers on this little mossy ship, this delicate dory sailing round the sun that humans call the earth. Joy, shipmates, joy.

—Edward Abbey, The Hidden Canyon; A River Journey

angle of approach are critical for crossing powerful eddylines or eddy fences.

As you approach the eddy, turn and try to hit it head first at its highest point, where the eddyline is sharply defined, stroking through the eddyline until you're completely out of the main flow. Your angle of approach should be about 45 degrees to the eddy-line—too shallow and you'll bounce off the eddyline, too perpendicular to the eddyline and you'll be spun off the eddyline and carried downstream. Some eddies, especially in heavy water, have significant current themselves and can carry swimmers back into holes or into nasty eddylines, so it's important to keep swimming until they've reached the safety of shore, a dry rock or slack water.

STRAINERS

Trees fallen in the water present further problems for swimmers that the defensive swimming position doesn't address. Currents move through, under and around trees, making them a particularly danger-ous river feature. Whether swim-ming or boating, trees in the water should be given a wide berth. They're a lot like icebergs: what's at the surface is just a small warn-ing of greater danger under water. Swimmers can be carried into strainers and caught among the branches, so it's important to swim aggressively over or through the branches if it's unavoidable.

Turn your head downstream from the swim-mer's position and stroke toward the tree, keeping your body aligned with the current and working to climb over the danger, or even up into the tree. If going under the trunk is unavoidable, swimmers must continue to move aggressively, pulling through the subsurface branches until they are free.

> *If you don't like the look of the rapid, walk around, what paddlers call a portage. Sometimes rafters can line their boats through trouble spots to avoid having to carry the heavy boats over difficult banks.*

Rogue River, Oregon

HEADWATERS: *Siskiyou Mountains of southern Oregon*

LENGTH: *35 miles from Grave Creek to Foster Bar*

DROP: *13 feet per mile*

DIFFICULTY: *Class 3+*

CHARACTER: *The Rogue is remote, stunningly beautiful and offers manageable rapids with a few real dangers. The river is nationally protected as Wild and Scenic and managed by a permit system conducted by lottery for the summer months. In fall, winter and most of spring, the crowds are gone and though permits are still required, they're not rationed. Trips usually run from 2 to 5 days.*

This classic Western run is great for paddlers looking to try a multi-day whitewater trip. Rogue runs are tradition among many rafters of the Northwest, and the river is a memorable outing for families, offering mostly Class 3 rapids, incredible camp sites and during some seasons, solitude among the steep mountains that define its course.

Two major drops punctuate the mostly forgiving rapids of the Rogue. The first one you will come upon will be Rainie Falls within the first few hours of the trip. There's a sneak route through a fish ladder on far river right. Some also choose the more challenging slots in the middle of the drop, but the river left falls and hole are big, powerful and meaty. Most people avoid it. Blossom Bar is the other major rapid on the run that claims a few boats on its left side. Many rafters and drift boaters misjudge a ferry move at the top of the rapid and wrap on a rock surrounded by heavy water in mid river. It's wise to scout this rapid thoroughly from the bluff above on river right, and anticipate the power of the rapid before it's too late.

Rogue runs are backcountry trips and paddlers should be prepared to be a long way from civilization. Some campsites have had bear problems, so food needs to be hung up at night at most sites. This river gets a lot of traffic, and only through minimum impact camping will it retain its wilderness character.

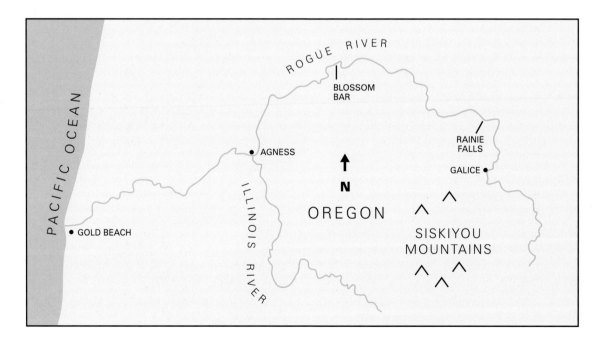

The Rogue River is a multiday trip in the heart of the Siskiyou Mountains of southern Oregon. The run features vertical gorges and exciting whitewater with spectacular camping and river life.

Rescue

RESCUE BOATERS

A quick rescue is usually the safest rescue. All paddlers in their boats on the river are potential rescue boaters and must be aware of their surroundings. Keep an eye on your buddies as they pass trouble spots and they should keep an eye on you. It is a paddler's responsibility to help a swimmer, even if she doesn't know him or is next in line to surf a great wave.

Once a rescue boater starts to help out, she will direct the swimmer through the course of the rescue, telling him which loop to grab and when. The rescue boater may direct a swimmer to let go of his gear if she needs to make an aggressive move to safety, and the paddler should follow all of the rescue boater's directions. It's important to keep communicating through the process, even if it's just to remind the swimmer to hang on or to kick.

The swimmer is the first priority in a rescue. Once the swimmer is in the process of being rescued, other rescue or safety boaters can work to get his gear. Paddles can be tossed javelin-style toward shore, or if the throw is too long, kayak paddles can be spooned with another kayak paddle (this only works if you have pretty big hands) and paddled to the bank or rescue eddy. Boats are a tougher to manage. Swamped kayaks aren't too bad for kayakers to bulldoze to shore, but canoes are heavier and rafts are even heavier and bulky. Whatever boat you're trying to get to shore, look downstream and find a reasonable rescue eddy. Encumbered by a swamped boat or flipped raft, the work will be slow, and it may take a lot of effort just to get a boat into the eddy on the edge of the river's horizon line.

But, if a rescue is leading you into danger, abandon it. Rescue boaters should do all they can to avoid becoming swimmers themselves. You won't be able to make the moves you may need to with a swimmer holding on to the back of your boat or two paddles in your hands, so if you need to, tell a swimmer to let go. You can stay nearby and offer encouragement and direction through the rapid and resume the rescue in the pool at the bottom.

ROPES AND THROW BAGS

Sometimes swimmers need extra help to get to safety, and throw ropes extend the rescuer's reach, increasing the margin of safety for paddlers running whitewater that demands quick and efficient rescue. While ropes can be effective rescue tools when

Scouting will help keep you out of trouble. Check rapids thoroughly before running them. Avoid running rapids blind: rivers change and the run you've paddled cleanly a dozen times may have a new log in it.

used properly, like any river technique, rope skills must be practiced to be safe. Swimmers risk entanglement in ropes, and ropes that rescuers lose control of can become twisted and wrapped around unseen underwater obstacles, adding entanglement danger for paddlers passing through that rapid in the future. Rescuers not adept at planning rescues, throwing ropes and retrieving swimmers may increase the danger to swimmers by their actions, so would-be rescuers should practice with their equipment and learn to think about how rescues can be accomplished before someone needs help.

Throw bags are the most common way of carrying rescue ropes on the river. Loose, coiled ropes are used sometimes, but they are harder to store and carry than throw bags, so most rescuers and swimmers nowadays will use bags in rope rescues. While the throw bag is convenient for first attempts at rescues, coiled rope throws should be practiced because good skills with loose ropes are essential to second and third attempts at rescues. It takes too long to restuff a rope bag to be effective for multiple throws during a rescue.

Throw bags come in a variety of sizes, and potential rescuers should consider how they will use the throw bag when they go to buy one. Most bags hold between 50 and 80 feet of rope of varying thickness and strength. Tiny waistbelt worn ropes might work on small creeks or for raft guides who need to quickly extend their reach just a few feet beyond their boats, but they won't do much good for longer throws and bank rescues on big rivers. If the rope will be used to pull pinned boats off rocks and logs, longer lengths of strong rope will be most useful. Finally, throw bags evolved as a convenient way to carry rope so rescues can be made quickly and efficiently. Convenience is the key: Don't buy a rope that you can't get to quickly in the boat you paddle or row. Eighty feet of line stuffed deep under the back deck of a kayak with lunch and a pair of sandals is only ballast if you can't reach it quickly.

The throw bag is only as good as the rope it contains. Most throw bags today hold synthetic ropes that float and also stretch a little under load. Floating ropes are spotted more easily by swimmers and reduce the amount of drag river current exerts on

them. Stretchy ropes, called dynamic ropes, reduce shock to rescuers and swimmers the same way climbing ropes stretch to absorb shock on a falling climber. Ropes vary in thickness and breaking strength, and the thickest ropes are not always the strongest. Polypropylene marine line 3/8-inch thick breaks at about 2,000 pounds, or about the same breaking strength as

Don't let the difficulty of the portage dissuade you from walking around. If you don't like the look of the rapid, don't run it.

Proper safety gear is important. If you're using ropes, a knife is essential to free entanglements.

STRATEGY AND THROWING

Scouting rapids should include more than just finding the "line" through a rapid. Good scouting involves considering trouble spots in the rapid, and what might happen to a paddler who becomes a swimmer. Should a rescuer with a rope be stationed next to a sticky hole to retrieve a boater? Where should potential rescuers stand so their throws will reach the swimmer? What are the hazards below the rapid that could cause a swimmer trouble? Just because a rescuer with a rope waits below a drop, does not mean she will be able to rescue a swimmer.

The swimmer needs to be aware of where rescue may come and how to get in position to make it work for him. The rescuer needs to consider her footing and her access to the river currents most likely to carry a swimmer past. She must be visible to the swimmer and be able to make eye contact so the swimmer understands that a rope is coming. Above all she must be practiced with rope rescues. The forces involved in pulling a swimmer to safety can be great, and rope throwers risk becoming swimmers themselves if they aren't prepared for the rescue.

The rescuer should consider the dangers below her as a swimmer swings to shore on the other end of a rope. Strainers and undercut rocks may lurk along the path the swimmer will follow to safety. Don't increase the danger to a swimmer by ill-conceived rescue plans.

Practice throwing your rope. There are a variety of ways to throw—overhand, underhand, possibly sidearm—and circumstances may dictate a certain type of throw, so it's a good idea to become familiar with each of them.

Underhand throws, while they don't have the power of the other two types of throws, might feel the most comfortable. The underhand toss requires proper timing, not power, to execute. Grasp the bag by its top, the loose fabric where the rope comes out of the bag, and swing it toward the target. Remember to keep your eyes on the swimmer, and if moving, account for the distance that he will float while the rope is in the air. Low, quick deliveries are more effective on windy days and probably leave a bit less slack line in the water.

more expensive ¼-inch Spectra line. More thin rope fits into a small bag, but it may be harder on a rescuer's hands under load. Again, consider the rope that will fit your application best. Rafters can carry a variety of ropes to solve different problems. Kayakers, limited by space, may have to make a compromise, trading comfort and added expense for a rope that's strong enough and long enough to fit a variety of rescue problems.

Ropes are lifelines, so take care of them. When using ropes on the river, rescuers should avoid stepping on them. Avoid letting them rub against rocks while under load. Restuffing rope bags is a tedious task, but rescuers should take care not to coil the rope and then place it in the bag. Run the rope over one shoulder to provide some drag and stuff the rope into the bag while you hold it in front of you. Held like this, the rope is unlikely to tangle on the next throw. Regularly inspect ropes to insure that they're still serviceable. Frayed or melted spots are bad signs. Mildew and mold can damage ropes, so store them where they can get air. Keep them out of direct sunlight. Finally, if a rope has been stressed significantly, consider replacing it.

Sidearm throws add power to the underhand toss, but they are less accurate for many throwers. They are handy, however, for throwing ropes around obstacles. Overhead brush may limit the overhand throw or there may not be enough room for the step and swing of the underhand toss.

Overhand throws are powerful, accurate and adaptable to a wide range of throwing positions. They require less space than the underhand toss since overhand throws can be made while sitting and are more accurate than sidearm throws. It's a good throw for wading rescuers as well because water at the rescuer's knees may interfere with the swing of the underhand toss. Many newer minimalist throwbags are stuffed so tightly with rope that they may be easier to hold and toss more like a football or a baseball than older-style loosely stuffed bags. Again, practice is key. If you expect to be throwing seated or over your rafting crew's heads, then practice making those kinds of throws.

RETRIEVING AND BELAYING

A successful rope rescue demands more than an accurate throw. Without proper preparation for retrieving the swimmer the rescuer risks losing him to the current, or worse, being pulled into the river herself and entangled in the rope. When a potential rescuer stations herself on the bank near a likely trouble spot, she needs to evaluate the place where she stands for good footing and a potential belay spot she can use

First try

Whatever kind of throw you use, there are a few basic elements to the first throw that you need to keep in mind. First the rescuer should hold the end of the rope in the hand she won't be throwing with and pull out enough slack to allow a full range of arm motion with the throw. Remember to hang on to the end of the rope: the throw won't do much good if you don't have control of the rope. She should make eye contact with the swimmer. If he's not ready for the rope, or not aware that it's coming, the throw will be much less effective. Yell, "Rope!" to get his attention and to let him know that you're throwing. The rescuer should account for the current and the swimmer's drift by leading him if necessary. She should maintain eye contact throughout the throw and be ready for the load on the rope when the swimmer grabs it.

Second try

If the first throw misses, then rescuers often have a brief window of opportunity for a second try. The rescuer should retrieve the rope by making loose coils that she collects in her throwing hand. Since the rope will have extended to its full length after the first throw, she should collect only enough coils for the distance she needs to throw and prepare to try again. The end of the rope attached to the bag will remain on shore. With coils in her throwing hand, she should hold the end of the rope (or perhaps the middle of it if the whole rope isn't necessary for the throw) with her opposite hand and make an underhand toss of the coils to the swimmer. The loose coils will unfurl in the air and reach the target. A third try or a throw to a second swimmer can be accomplished the same way. The whole process should take only seconds.

Short throws

Sometimes the swimmer is only a few feet out of reach, and a quick short throw is the best option for retrieving him. In this case, throwing the whole rope bag is cumbersome and probably dangerous because more rope than you need will likely end up in the water putting the swimmer at risk of entanglement. In this case, a short coiled rope throw is effective, or if available, a short-distance throw bag with 10 to 20 feet of line can also be used. The idea here is to use only enough rope to do the job.

to swing the swimmer to shore. Swimmers in river current exert a surprising amount of force on the rope and if a rescuer isn't prepared she can scramble to maintain her footing as river drags on the swimmer. Rescuers should be wary of retrieving swimmers from high rocks next to the river or any places that if they were to be pulled into the river they would put themselves in danger. Care should also be taken not to put the swimmer in increased danger through the rescuer's actions. Consider the path the swimmer will take to shore and make sure there are no strainers, bad holes or undercut rocks along the way.

There are several types of belays rescuers can use to secure their footing and better control the rope once the swimmer has grabbed it. Belaying

It's hard to see a river all at once, especially in the mountains. Down on the plains, rivers run in their course as straightforward as time, channeled toward the sea. But up in the headwaters, a river isn't a point where you stand. In the beginnings of the river, you teeter on the edge of a hundred tiny watersheds where one drop of water is always tipping the balance from one stream to another.

—Lynn Noel, Voyages: Canada's Heritage Rivers

comes from mountaineering and describes a variety of methods for controlling weighted ropes. The simplest belay, the one used in whitewater rescue, is the hip belay. It relies on proper technique and requires no extra equipment to perform. The rescuer uses her hips and holding the rope behind her back sits into it. The hand on the weighted side of the belay is the guide hand, and the hand with the loose rope is the control hand. Pointing her body (pointing the belay) toward the load, the rope bends around her hips just above the buttocks and she can lean her weight into it and against the load. To increase friction, she can move her control hand toward the inside of her legs. If she needs to give some rope, she can loosen her control hand grip and let some slide through. The belayer should be careful not to let the rope slide too high or too low on the body, and the guide hand can help with repositioning the rope on the body during the belay. She should also try to stay on the upstream side of the weighted rope to avoid entanglement, and if belaying from the middle of the rope, she should use a bight or loop of the rope around her back, rather than loop the whole rope around her.

Once proficient with controlling the rope in a hip belay, the rescuer needs to consider the way she will brace herself for the pull of the swimmer on the rope. The simplest way to do this is to stand with good footing and lean into the rope for a standing belay. It helps to have a rock, root or a depression in the ground where her feet can gain more purchase, and the rescuer should bend her knees to help ease the shock on the rope for her and the swimmer. If a second rescuer is available, he can grab the back of the belayer's PFD and give her some extra support by squatting and bracing his feet. The rescuer can also strengthen the standing belay by directing the rope around a tree or rock, using it to add friction to the system. There's little give in the friction belay, however, and the shock to the swimmer may be a lot for him to handle in swift current.

A more stable option is the sitting belay. The rescuer finds a good place to sit where she can brace her feet against a rock or a tree and belays from that position. A second rescuer can stabilize this belay by holding the back of the belayer's PFD and sitting with his legs outside of the belayer's legs. This is a powerful belay and good for pulling a swimmer to shore in heavy current. It's one that also has some give to it so the stresses on the swimmer usually won't be excessive.

Belays described above are commonly static belays, meaning the belayer can just hold the rope and swing the swimmer to shore, letting the swimmer take most of the shock from the current.

> *Gradient:* **The measure of how much a river drops over its course. Gradient is just one of the measures that will give a paddler a sense of what to expect. Many Class 3 runs are in the 20 to 40 foot per mile range, but that kind of drop can also be a lot of flat water hiding a steep Class 5 or 6 waterfall. Steep gradient is usually more that 100 feet per mile and steep creek paddlers are pushing the envelope at 400 and more feet per mile.**

Another option is the dynamic belay, in which the belayer finds a way to give rope to the swimmer to ease the shock on the system and gently slow the swimmer down on his swing into shore. The simplest way to do this is to move with the swimmer downstream while controlling the rope and slowly increasing tension on the system. This requires a riverbank with consistent footing, which is not always an option in many rescues.

Another option is to give some rope to the swimmer from the standing, seated or friction belay as the river drags him downstream. Without padding in the standing or seated belays, however, the belayer risks rope burns from this technique, but it's a good option to reduce the stress on the swimmer from the friction belay. Again it's a good idea to practice these more specific belays to get a sense of the forces involved. A poorly planned standing belay can become an unplanned dynamic belay once the rescuer loses her footing, knowing how to get the belay back under control is invaluable in real life rescues.

On most rope rescues, when the current is carrying the swimmer downstream, the river will do most of the retrieval work. With a good belay set, the swimmer will swing to shore to a point directly downstream of the rescuer. A second rescuer can follow the line downstream and pull the rope perpendicular to the load, coaxing the swimmer to shore across tricky eddy lines. Sometimes, however, a rescuer must take up rope to pull the swimmer out of trouble spots like holes or across dangerous channels that would be risky to let the swimmer cross with the float-and-swing method. The simplest

type of retrieval is pulling in line hand over hand. The natural tendency for most people is to grab the rope with their thumb pointed away from them and pull, but a more effective hand-over-hand pull is to aim the thumbs toward the chest and grab the rope. Pulling the rope this way, though at first awkward feeling, reduces slippage. A more dynamic retrieval can be made with multiple people walking the rope away from the shoreline, and with extra rescuers on the rope, the swimmer can be pulled quickly to shore. A word of caution: Overzealous rescuers using this technique can pull the rope out of the swimmer's hands, so be careful.

Belays allow rescuers to adapt the rescue system to the circumstances: the more static the system, the greater the jarring forces to a swimmer will be. Belayers should never tie off a rope. Entangled swimmers will plane underneath the water and risk drowning. Always be able to give rope and have a backup plan if things don't go as expected.

For the swimmer, this whole experience can be exhausting. Even the strongest swimmers, well versed in the swimmer's position, aggressive swimming, catching eddies and ferrying will still benefit from a rope in heavy water. Before they run the rapid, paddlers should know how rescuers plan to help and where they are in a rapid so if they're swimming, they know to look for help when it's available. Swimmers need to help rescuers by remaining calm and making eye contact so they can immediately spot the thrown rope and move to it. The swimmer shouldn't grab the bag—it may still hold rope and the swimmer will be carried much farther down river than necessary. Once the swimmer has the rope, he should hold tight and roll to his back so that the rope runs over his shoulder and his hands are at his chest on the surface of the water. In this position he will plane to the surface of the water and be able to breathe during the rescue. In heavy water with a firm belay an air pocket may form in front of the swimmer's face when he holds this position. The river will exert a lot of force on the swimmer, and he should hold tight. A swimmer should never wrap or tie the rope around any part of his body, and he should be ready to let go if the rescue carries him into trouble.

Rating Rivers

Paddlers rate rapids and rivers by a standard scale of difficulty. The idea is to help those unfamiliar with paddling or with the specific river make informed decisions about whether running a rapid or river fits their ability level. It also makes river stories a bit more consistent.

The International Scale of River Difficulty is the standard used the rivers of North America. Broken into six classes, from easy to extreme, it is meant to impose some order on river description and comparison. It is no substitute for experience, however, and should be used as a rough guide combined with water level, temperature and river character for a final judgement of whether the run or rapid is within your abilities. The American Whitewater Affiliation has adopted the following scale:

Class 1: Easy. Moving water with riffles and small waves. Few obstructions, all obvious and easily missed with little training. Risk to swimmers is slight; self-rescue is easy.

Class 2: Novice. Straightforward rapids with wide, clear channels that are evident without scouting. Occasional maneuvering may be required, but rocks and medium-sized waves are easily missed by trained paddlers. Swimmers are seldom injured and group assistance, while helpful, is seldom needed.

Flat water gives you the chance to absorb your surroundings— and work your paddling muscles.

Class 3: Intermediate. Rapids with moderate, irregular waves that may be difficult to avoid and can swamp an open canoe. Complex maneuvers in fast current and good boat control in tight passages or around ledges are often required; large waves or strainers may be present but are easily avoided. Strong eddies and powerful current effects can be found, particularly on large-volume rivers. Scouting is advisable for inexperienced parties. Injuries while swimming are rare; self-rescue is usually easy but group assistance may be required to avoid long swims.

Class 4: Advanced. Intense, powerful but predictable rapids requiring precise boat handling in turbulent water. Depending on the character of the river, it may feature large unavoidable waves and holes or constricted passages demanding fast maneuvers under pressure. A fast, reliable eddy turn may be needed to initiate maneuvers, scout rapids or rest. Rapids may require "must" moves above dangerous hazards. Scouting is necessary the first time down. Risk of injury to swimmers is moderate to high, and water conditions may make self-rescue difficult. Group assistance for rescue is often essential but requires practiced skills. A strong roll is highly recommended.

Class 5: Expert. Extremely long, obstructed or very violent rapids that expose a paddler to above average endangerment. Drops may contain large, unavoidable waves and holes or steep, congested chutes with complex, demanding routes. Rapids may continue for long distances between pools, demanding a high level of fitness. What eddies exist may be small, turbulent or difficult to reach. At the high end of the scale, several of these factors may be combined. Scouting is mandatory but often difficult. Swims are dangerous, and rescue is difficult

Fun rapids don't have to be scary; they just have to get your face wet. This ride on the Payette River in Idaho certainly does the trick.

Tougher runs often have waterfalls, like this drop on the Tygart River in West Virginia.

even for experts. A very reliable roll, proper equipment, extensive experience and practiced rescue skills are essential for survival.

Class 6: Extreme. These runs often exemplify the extremes of difficulty, unpredictability and danger. The consequences of errors are very severe and rescue may be impossible. For teams of experts only, at favorable water levels, after close personal inspection and taking all precautions. This class does *not* represent drops thought to be unrunnable but may include rapids that are only occasionally run.

The difficulty scale is great as a rough guide to what to expect on the river, but it struggles sometimes because in the end, it's a subjective rating.

Ratings change over time and between the perception of paddlers. They change with water level, season and remoteness. What was Class 5 a generation ago may be Class 3 now. This is especially true of the upper level of the rating system. Thirty years ago it was enough to say something was big, nasty and scary and call it Class 5. Now, however, equipment has improved and more people are paddling harder stuff and finding nuance among big, nasty and scary, and it's not enough for some to say a rapid is Class 5 if one Class 5 is harder than another. Rating it Class 6 won't solve the problem because Class 6 is a special category implying a distinct element of mortal danger while holding out the option that someone, somewhere might get down it and live. A Class 6 isn't unnrunnable, per se, but it's not commonly run or even considered. The Class 6 rating is also reserved for exploratory runs, and some of the more difficult Class 5's were Class 6's until recently.

Paddlers are trying to address this ambiguity problem, and there's movement to adopt breakdowns among the classes, similar to the decimal system of climbing routes. The problem is that the river is unlike the rock in that its difficulty changes with water level and season and a fixed number may not always be accurate. How do you account for flood? Or cold water and the risk of hypothermia? The system is in a flux and guide books often hedge their bets by offering a range. They'll call a river a Class 3 and say it's got one Class 4 in it that you might have the option of portaging. Or they'll say that the run is Class 4 during normal flows but goes to Class 5 at high water. If it says a rapid is 5.2, expect it to be significantly bigger, scarier and nastier than a garden-variety 5.

Another method assigns rapid ratings a plus or minus to give a better sense of the difficulty, which translates in speech to hard and easy. So a Class 3+, a "hard" Class 3, is almost Class 4—it might be technical with a blind move but not pushy or it could be straightforward but with a must-avoid dangerous river feature. Class 4- is harder than 3+ and will likely turn into a full-blown 4 (or more) with more water. This is perhaps a better system for rating an overall river as well because it implies a range of values. Still, it can be ambiguous. A Class 3+ river may be a collection of easy Class 3's with one Class 4 in it that you may have the option of walking or it may be hard Class 3's all the way down that you can't walk easily.

In the end it's a judgement call. Paddlers have been trying for years to impose a rating system on the rivers that has value, but if you listen closely to how they actually describe and learn about rivers you'll hear a different language. Ratings take a back seat to personal experience, and the comparisons roll in. "That river is like Five Falls stacked up for 10 miles," a paddler will say, comparing one run to another. "It's like Hell Hole only bigger."

Often it's raw description. "There are no pools, but there aren't any big drops either. It's just one big rapid. It falls 250 feet in a mile."

Or sometimes it's a recipe. "Take Jawbone, Corkscrew, and the Dog and put them together at

high water and you've got the run. It's like that all the way down."

At a loss, paddlers will revert to the numbers. "It's a Class 3 move that takes Class 5 nerve."

Paddling is a dangerous sport, especially so if the paddler's judgement falls short of his ability. Any yahoo can put on a Class 5 river, and he may come out okay. Or he may not. Survival is not an indication of skill. Running a hard rapid clean does not necessarily mean you have the ability to run it clean every time. Climbers are lucky because their rating system implies a barrier to entry—a 5.8 climber won't even be able to get on a 5.12 route and get in trouble. Not so with river running—someone who is proficient in Class 3 water can put on a Class 5 and quickly be in the thick of trouble and past the point of no return.

When looking for people to run the river with, cultivate paddling friends who share your river values. Paddling with people who are more skilled than you is a great way to learn, as long as they understand your limits. Paddling with people at your skill level who have a different perception of the river's perils can be dangerous. Trouble for someone in a group headed down the river is trouble for all. Don't be goaded into running something you don't feel good about.

In the end, you know your abilities and experience best. As you paddle more, you'll get a better sense of your limits. Start easy and push yourself only when you're ready. You are responsible for scouting your lines and making good judgement calls. You are responsible for yourself.

THE RIVER TRIP

The River Trip

To run a river you need a river to run. Word of mouth, guidebooks and advertisements can point you to the trip you want to do. If you've never paddled before, go with an outfitter or a very experienced friend. If you've been down a few rivers, but don't have much experience beyond outfitter trips, consider taking a class that will prepare you to use your own equipment. If you're experienced in one region but want to try out a new place, get a guidebook and talk to the locals. Nearby paddling shops can be a great resource, and if you get lucky, you might be able to tag along with a local.

Learn all you can about any unfamiliar rivers you want to run. Study maps and imprint the "hazards" section of the guidebook description on your brain. Identify what the landmarks are that signal a dangerous rapid and where the best place is to portage a sketchy drop. Try to compare descriptions of the unfamiliar river with features you know more about. Is the character of this river like those around where I live? Is the water colder? Is the river high volume? Many of the best-known runs have clear descriptions of rapids and hazards, but once you get off the beaten track, those descriptions become more vague. If you're unfamiliar with the river, scout often and expect the unexpected.

Don't boat alone. Even easy water holds hazards that you discount. A few small errors compound quickly into a problem, and without any help, that problem can become serious. Cultivate a river running friend of similar ability and go with him or her. You will learn each other's tendencies and habits, and on unfamiliar water, you'll know what to expect. Good paddling buddies help to make each other better paddlers and look out for each other in the tricky stuff.

RIVER TIME

When trying to figure out how long a river trip will take, be a pessimist. For a day trip, add at least two hours to the first time you think of. If your wife, hus-

I have never seen a river that I could not love. Moving water...has a fascinating vitality. It has power and grace and associations. It has a thousand colors and a thousand shapes, yet it follows laws so definite that the tiniest streamlet is an exact replica of a great river.
—Roderick Haig-Brown

band, mother, boss, asks what time you'll be back, don't say 5 p.m. if it's the first thing that comes to mind. Stop, breathe and add two hours. "I'll be home around seven," you say. Do this to account for everything that can and will go wrong and right with the day. Cars get flat tires and people forget helmets. Waves have never been better. You just had to run Hoo-Ha Falls one more time, and then you broke your paddle and had to walk out and Joey forgot the key to the take-out car... (all of which took exactly two hours) Your boss, husband, wife, mother nods appreciatively.

For longer trips, build in time for hikes or fishing or to sleep in. Set a doable agenda for the trip and then forget about time. You're there for escape, so put your watch in your drybag. That said, you may want to plan to have several options for campsites on the river because the one you really wanted may be taken (a lot of other people probably really want it, too). Try to time your run so that you don't find this out as the sun is setting, and you need to make three more river miles to the next site.

SHUTTLE

If you're going to run the river, you'll need to find some way to get to the put-in with your boats and

Large group trips can be an organizational challenge for even the most experienced paddlers. When traveling downriver with a large group, choose a couple of skippers to lead, keep your gear organized, and respect other paddlers on the river.

get home when you take out. If you hire an outfitter, they will take care of this for you. But if you have your own equipment and plan to run the river on your own wits and skill, you will have to shuttle cars. Statistically speaking, this will probably be the most dangerous part of your river trip, so take care and keep your eyes on that winding road. Actually stop the car to scout roadside rapids. You can learn a lot more about them this way than you can at 50 mph.

The shuttle seems like a simple matter, and it usually is. You'll need at least two cars to accomplish the shuttle, but depending on the size of your group and the type of boats you're using, you may need more cars to go to the put-in and unload. However, roads near rivers and access points can be remote, undeveloped places, and paddlers' cars are sometimes, well, *unreliable*.

If the road is particularly treacherous to one of the access points, you might need four-wheel drive, but try not to drive right down to the river's edge unless there's a developed access point. Cars and trucks can do a lot of damage to the river banks, promoting erosion and pollution. Try to pick shuttle cars that will get you to the river and home again and carry everyone and all the boats safely. Sure you *can* strap ten kayaks on a Subaru, but they may not stay there at highway speeds.

Think ahead—put dry warm clothes in the take-out car rather than leaving them in the put-in car. Towels are also a good idea to have in the take-out car if you're going to fill it with wet bodies to take back to the put-in. Your passengers on the ride home will thank you for not leaving a squishy seat. Having food and drinks at the take-out is nice too. Remember to bring the keys to the take-out vehicle or hide them on it somewhere—an eight- or ten-mile walk as night falls after a day on the river because you forgot your keys is no fun.

Personal cars and trucks are the most common shuttle vehicles, but you may want to consider other modes of shuttling to and from the put-in and take-out. On popular commercially run rivers you may be able to catch a ride up with one of the outfitters. They may charge you, but taking a bus up top eliminates much hassle.

You may also be able to pay someone at the river to shuttle your car. While it may seem a bit sketchy to hand your keys and $15 over to somebody at a rural gas station, on many rivers this is standard practice and local people make a tidy second income shuttling boaters' cars for them. On the Nolichucky River in North Carolina, through-hikers on the Appalachian Trail often shuttle vehicles for a few extra dollars and a chance to get off the trail for a while. On the Rogue River in Oregon, shuttling is bigger business for the multi-day trips on that river's most popular section. The shuttle is long and shuttle services there may charge $100 or more to run your car to the take-out.

On most rivers where this is feasible, rates range from $15 for a day trip to $100 or more depending on the length of shuttle and the season. Summer rates are sometimes cheaper because more people are running the river then, and shuttle services can arrange a van to return the hired drivers after they drop off your car.

In Alaska, bush plane shuttles are common to get boats and boaters to the put-in. This is significantly more expensive—hundreds of dollars per hour—but is the only practical way to get in to a lot of rivers, even rivers that are commonly run. Depending on how much gear, and money, you have, the pilot may have to make several trips. You'll be held to a maximum weight, and shuttling may take the better part of a day.

There may be other solutions to shuttling to cut down on the number of cars and amount of gas you use. Consider using a bicycle to shuttle if the distance and weather allow it. Running or walking the shuttle are options as well and can be a nice aerobic complement to a day on the river. Twisting, bending rivers are especially conducive to this because often the road distance is shorter than the river trip. The Loop on the Lower Youghiogheny in Pennsylvania offers a nice wooded walk between put-in and take-out that's much shorter than the section of river run.

On some remote creeks, you might have to hike your boat to the put-in. This is a practical, though strenuous, solution that can get you to beautiful and remote sections of creeks and rivers. Often the trail runs right next to the creek, offering a chance to scout carefully on the way up.

Whether it be for a day, a week or a lifetime, it's easy to lose yourself on the river.

Pulling into camp after a long day on the river is fun too. Dinner will be ready soon and your sleeping bag will be warm.

DAY TRIP

For a day trip, you won't need much beyond the appropriate warm and dry clothing for the river and season and your raft, kayak or canoe. Depending on the length of the trip, you may want to bring food. It's always a good idea to bring water, too. You can get thirsty out there and it's not a good idea to drink from the river, even pristine creeks in remote watersheds. Very little surface water in developed areas of North America is free from giardia and other nasty bugs that can wreak havoc with your gut.

You might also want to bring some extra warm clothing if you think you might get cold. All of this can fit into a small dry bag that will fit into most any boat. You may also want to have a first aid kit and rescue equipment that fits the difficulty and nature of the river you're running.

On remote rivers, or just to be on the safe side, you'll want to bring a spare paddle or oar. Kayak paddles are made in breakdown versions that you can stuff up under the back deck of your boat. Canoe paddles can be secured under the cord that holds the float bags in, and breakdown oars can be strapped to D-rings along a tube of the raft. The more gear you bring, the heavier your boat will be, and if it's a trip that may require a few portages, you'll want to minimize gear to the bare necessities.

OVERNIGHT

For overnight trips you'll need everything you bring on a day trip, plus the gear and food you need to stay out overnight or for as many days as you'll be going. On overnighters, the carrying capacity of bigger boats really shines. Canoes are good for overnighters, but for shear ability to haul the goods, rafts are king.

Rafts will haul coolers, big tents, lawn chairs and fresh food—not that you need all that where you're going, but for some it ain't wilderness adventure unless the two-burner Coleman stove is hissing beneath a sputtering pan full of bacon. Canoes can carry a lot of stuff, too, but they sacrifice a good bit of performance when loaded down. Multi-day kayak trips, in most boats, are tests of minimalism in which you'll need to make hard decisions about clothes, shelter and food. A few manufacturers are starting to cater to the expedition kayak crowd, making big boats that perform well loaded with 40 pounds of gear. The best situation for a kayaker who can't leave her boat at home but wants to do a multi-day section of river is to convince a rafter to carry her stuff. In exchange, she can run safety for the rafts.

Whatever boat you choose, you'll need to keep your gear dry. Bigger drybags designed to carry sleeping bags and extra warm clothes are essential. Some come with backpack straps to make portaging easier. Small dry boxes are good for valuables, first-aid kits, raft patch kits and other critical items. Big dry boxes can be handy for carrying food and odd-shaped hard kitchen gear if you're rafting. A big cooler is a nice addition to an overnight raft trip, as well. Canoes can carry smaller coolers on mellow rivers, but they're not advisable if there's any risk of going over in heavy water.

Overnight trips require food and you'll need to plan your spread in accordance with the boat and river you'll be paddling and the time out on the trip. On short trips, you might get by without cooking, but with small, light backpacking stoves—small enough to fit into a kayak—you can prepare a satisfying hot meal after a long day on the river. Rafts

> *Rafts can get you into some spectacular fishing between rapids. A patient hand at the oars and a steady ride can help even a beginning angler catch fish.*

Immerse yourself in the river experience. The rapids are great fun, but so is the scenery and the chance to be out and away from civilization.

Many a time have I merely closed my eyes at the end of yet another troublesome day and soaked my bruised psyche in wild water, rivers remembered and rivers imagined. Rivers course through my dreams, rivers cold and fast, rivers well-known and rivers nameless, rivers that seem like ribbons of blue water twisting through wide valleys, narrow rivers folded in layers of darkening shadows, rivers that have eroded down deep into the mountain's belly, sculpted the land, peeled back the planet's history exposing the texture of time itself.

—Harry Middleton

can haul coolers and supply fresh food many days into a river trip. The key to storing fresh food for multiple days on the river is to not open the cooler unless absolutely necessary. Those experienced with planning such trips break the food up into days and have packing lists for each cooler. Coolers meant for later in the trip are often sealed in duct tape so that no one will open them and the ice will last as long as possible.

It's important to plan carefully what you will bring on the river. Try to avoid as much packaging as possible to limit trash. Many rivers will require you to bring portable toilets and pack out waste. Fires may need to be made in fire pans or may be banned altogether. Make sure you have enough experienced paddlers on the trip to safely negotiate the river you want to run and consider bringing extra safety and rescue equipment if the river conditions warrant.

Many of the most beautiful multi-day runs are in limited to permit holders. A set number of permits are usually allotted to outfitters with the remaining left for private boaters. Depending on the river and the season, permitting may be a walk-up-and-sign-in deal such as on the Chattooga River in Georgia and South Carolina and off-season permits for the Rogue River in Oregon. Or permitting may be in such high demand that there's a lottery or a long waiting list. Private boaters wanting to run the Grand Canyon in prime months can expect to wait years before their names come up, and if you want to get on a river like that promptly, you'll need to buy a seat on an outfitter's trip. There's an up side to that, however, in that the outfitter will deal with most of the planning for the trip—shuttles, food, equipment—and you just need to show up.

INSTRUCTION

Consider taking a class or multiple classes on the fundamentals of whitewater. Only by doing it will you truly learn, and instructors are paid to help ease you into the whitewater experience. Classes range from nights at the pool learning to roll to week-long (or more) trips to exciting new paddle destinations where you'll be encouraged to push yourself. Whatever the format, instruction will help eliminate bad habits, and it provides a supervised environment for you to learn and challenge yourself. Find competent instruction, combine it with practical, safe and realistic experience and you'll be thrilled by your progress. See you on the river.

Just you, your friends and the river. What more is there?

Inn River, Switzerland/Austria

HEADWATERS: *Swiss Alps*

LENGTH: *30 miles*

DIFFICULTY: *Class 3+, 4, 5*

CHARACTER: *The Inn River is home to Europe's whitewater paddling scene. Fed by alpine glaciers, the river runs silty through several canyons offering a variety of whitewater challenges, from experts-only sections with portages to more intermediate-friendly water. Starting high in the Alps, by the time the river flattens out, in Austria, the Inn is big water and wide.*

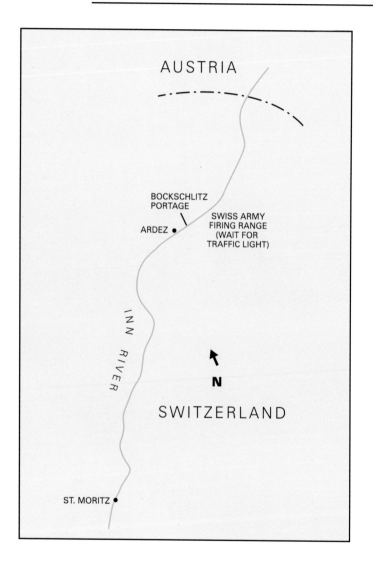

The Inn River is the mother of European whitewater boating. People have been navigating it for thrills for a century, and its rapids have had a strong influence on the development of whitewater paddling as a sport. The Oetz, Class 4-5, joins the Inn toward the bottom of the whitewater runs in Austria, increasing the river's volume substantially with the Oetz's own glacier-fed runoff.

The Class 5 Giarsun and Ardez gorges in Switzerland start the most commonly run sections of the Inn. Following that is the Scuol run, a hard Class 3 that's commercially run (though some trips are done on the higher sections). Boaters typically gather in the Austrian town of Landeck.

In the must-make eddy category of river hazards, paddlers on the Ardez section must run through a Swiss Army training ground and target range. There's a traffic signal for boaters here when the military is shooting over the river, and paddling down river before you're directed to is verboten. Paddlers should be aware of the many more normal river hazards on the runs of the Inn. From dams to log-choked drops, many have learned the hard way before you. Take all precautions on these runs and scout. The water is cold and can be high volume and pushy: swims, even on warm days, are dicey.

Switzerland's Inn River runs out of the heart of the Alps, one of many challenging rivers in the region. From creeks to big-water rivers, paddlers from around the world flock to Alpine rivers for the challenge and the beauty of river running in one of the world's great mountain ranges.

Salza River, Austria

HEADWATERS: *Austrian Alps*

LENGTH: *16 miles*

DIFFICULTY: *Class 3, 4*

CHARACTER: *Clear, cold water and challenging rapids make this run one of Europe's classics. The runs are challenging and the water is usually good through June.*

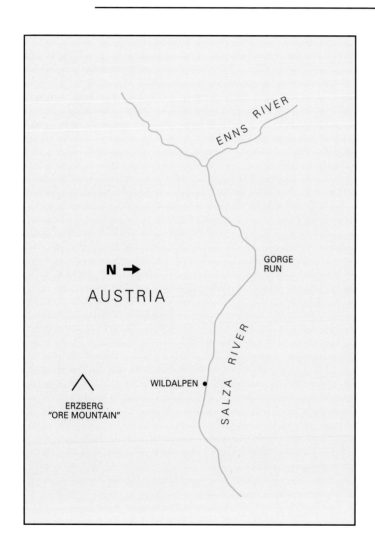

N ➡

AUSTRIA

ENNS RIVER

GORGE RUN

SALZA RIVER

WILDALPEN •

ERZBERG "ORE MOUNTAIN"

The Salza is the center of whitewater paddling and other river recreation near Vienna. A longtime classic run of the eastern Alps, the Salza flows through scenic forests and passes occasional signs of settlement. The water is clear and cold, mostly snowmelt runoff with a slight green tint, and most paddling on the river occurs in the wet months of April through June.

The runs start at Wildalpen and get progressively tougher the farther downriver you go. The first section of nine miles is a solid Class 3. That run is followed by the hard Class 3 section that starts at Erzhalden and goes four miles to Palfau. The final three miles run from Palfau to the Enns River and push into the Class 4 range. The river course may have undercuts and logs, especially in the upper reaches. The upper runs may also not have enough water late in the season, but some continue to scrape down it even in drier late-season months. Numerous runs can be combined from the three main sections and good surfing waves abound below Wildalpen especially at higher flows.

The Austrian Alps surrounding the Salza reach up to 7,000 feet around the river, and the river itself flows through protected alpine forestland. Wildalpen is the center of activity for the area and is a good place to find camping near the river.

The Salza River is a big-water Austrian run that tumbles through forbidding mountains and floods mightily.

RESOURCE GUIDE

Guides and Outfitters US

Alabama

Bear Creek Canoe Run
36676 US Highway 43, Phil
Campbell, AL 35581
(205) 993–4459

Canoe Livery
RR 3, Newton, AL 36352
(334) 299–3888

Canoe Livery
237 Henry Parker Road, Ozark,
AL 36360
(334) 445–2500

Styx River Canoe Rental
I 10 Wilcox Road, Robertsdale,
AL 36567
(334) 960-1161

Alaska

Alaska Cataraft Kayak & Raft CO
Anchorage, AK 99501
(907) 344–9453

Alaska Raft & Kayak
401 West Tudor Road,
Anchorage, AK 99503
(907) 561–7238

Alaska Raft Rentals
Anchorage, AK 99501
(907) 337–7238

Alaska Vision Quest Adventures
Anchorage, AK 99501
(907) 258–7238

Alaska Wildwater
Anchorage, AK 99501
(907) 345–4308

Anchorage Whitewater
Anchorage, AK 99501
(907) 333–3001

Class V White Water
Girdwood, AK 99587
(907) 783–2004

Denali Outdoor Center
Mi 238.9 Parks Highway Box 170,
Healy, AK 99743
(907) 683–1925
(888) 303–1925 (toll-free)
docadventure@hotmail.com
http://www.denali.com

Denali Raft Adventures
Mi 238 Parks Highway, Denali
National Park, AK 99755
(907) 683–2234

Gary Kings Sporting Goods
202 East Northern Lights
Boulevard, Anchorage, AK 99503
(907) 272–5401

Keak Rafting
Anchorage, AK 99501
(907) 243–0151

Marita Sea & Ski
1340 Rudakof Circle, Anchorage,
AK 99508
(907) 337–2744

McKinley Raft Tours
Mi 238.5 Parks Hwy Box 170,
Denali Park, AK 99755
(907) 683–2392
(888) 303–1925 (toll-free)
docadventure@hotmail.com
http://www.denaliparkrafting.com

Nova Riverrunners Inc
Mi 76.5 Glenn Highway, Sutton,
AK 99674
(907) 745–5753

Wild Alaska Rivers CO
2375 East 63rd Avenue,
Anchorage, AK 99507
(907) 344–9453

Arizona

Arizona River Runners
15211 North Cave Creek Road,
Phoenix, AZ 85032
(602) 867–4866

Bravo Guides & Outfitters
Peach Springs, AZ 86434
(520) 769–2612

Canyon Supply & Inflatables
505 North Beaver Street,
Flagstaff, AZ 86001
(520) 779–0624

Far Flung Adventures
Globe, AZ 85501
(520) 425–7272

Hualapai River Running
Peach Springs, AZ 86434
(520) 769–2219

Rivers & Oceans
12620 North Copeland Lane,
Flagstaff, AZ 86004
(520) 526–4575

Saguaro Lake Ranch River
Rentals
Mesa, AZ 85201
(480) 380-1239

Wilderness Outfitters Store
50 South Lake Powell Boulevard,
Page, AZ 86040
(520) 645–3279

Wilderness River Adventures
50 South Lake Powell Boulevard,
Page, AZ 86040
(520) 645–3279

Arkansas

Crooked Creek Canoe Service
Old Main Street # 62–B, Yellville,
AR 72687
(870) 449–6203

Gunga LA Lodge & River
Outfitters
River Road, Lakeview, AR 72642
(870) 431–5606

Many Islands Camp & Canoe
Rental
Many Islands, Hardy, AR 72542
(870) 856–3451

Martin Creek Adventures Inc
Highway 58 East, Williford, AR
72482
(870) 966–4703

Saddler Falls Canoe Rental
Hardy, AR 72542
(870) 856–2824

Southfork Resort
Highway 289, Mammoth Spring,
AR 72554
(870) 895–2803

Three River Outfitters
Hardy, AR 72542
(870) 856–4945

White Buffalo Resort
Mountain Home, AR 72653
(870) 424–6892

California

A Adventure for All River Journey
Inc
14842 Orange Blossom Road,
Oakdale, CA 95361
(209) 8474671
(800) 2922938 (tollfree)

A Current Adventure Kayak
School & Trips
Placerville, CA 95667
(530) 6429755

A Thrillsource
San Francisco, CA 94102
(415) 4744784

American River Raft Rentals
11257 South Bridge Street,
Rancho Cordova, CA 95670
(916) 6354479

American River Raft Rentals
11257 South Bridge Street,
Rancho Cordova, CA 95670
(916) 6356400

Baldt Anchor & Chain Corporation
Pier 54, San Francisco, CA 94102
(415) 8264433

Beyond Limits Adventures
5729 Terminal Avenue,
Riverbank, CA 95367
(209) 8696060
(800) 234raft (tollfree)

Boat People
1249 South 1st Street, San Jose,
CA 95110
(408) 2952628

Burkes Canoe Trips
Geyserville, CA 95441
(707) 8871222

Burkes Russian River Canoe Trips
Box # 602, Forestville, CA 95436
(707) 8871222

C B O C Whitewater Rafting
PO Box 554, Coloma, CA 95613
(530) 6211236
(800) 3562262 (tollfree)

Chili Bar Put In
1669 Chili Bar Court, Placerville,
CA 95667
(530) 6421669

Current Adventure Kayak School
& Trips
Placerville, CA 95667
(530) 6429755

Knights Ferry Rafting CO
1066 Sierra Road, Oakdale, CA
95361
(209) 8484800
(800) 8297238 (tollfree)

Rapid Descent Adventures
6015 Rafters Lane, Placerville,
CA 95667
(530) 6422370
(877) 4672386

River Journey Inc
14842 Orange Blossom Road,
Oakdale, CA 95361
(209) 8474671
(800) 2922938 (tollfree)

River Rat Raft And Mountain Bike
9840 Fair Oaks Boulevard, Fair
Oaks, CA 95628
(800) 5007238
(916) 9666777
rrraftbike@aol.com

River Runners Inc
4015 Magna Carta Road,
Calabasas, CA 91302
(818) 2224260

Russian River Canoe Trips Burkes
8600 River Road, Forestville, CA
95436
(707) 8871222

Sierra Outdoor Center
440 Lincoln Way, Auburn, CA
95603
(530) 8851844

Spirit Whitewater
P 559, Squaw Valley, CA 93675
(559) 3322227

Sunshine Raft Adventures
1066 Sierra Road, Oakdale, CA
95361
(209) 8484800

Tributary Whitewater Tours
20480 Woodbury Drive, Grass
Valley, CA 95949
(530) 3466812
(800) 6723846 (tollfree)

Whitewater Voyages
5225 San Pablo Dam Road, El
Sobrante, CA 94803
(800) 4887238
(510) 7587238 (fax)
fun@whitewatervoyages.com

Colorado

A1 Wildwater
317 Stover Street, Fort Collins,
CO 80524
(970) 2243379
(800) 3694165 (tollfree)

AAA Inflatable Repair
3264 Larimer Street, Denver, CO
80205
(303) 2988078

Acquired Tastes Rafting
27410 County Road 319, Buena
Vista, CO 81211
(719) 3952992

Adventure Company
101 Ski Hill Road, Breckenridge,
CO 80424
(970) 4530747

Adventure Quest Whitewater
Rafting
Canon City, CO 81212
(719) 2699807

Adventure Specialist
Frisco, CO 80443
(970) 6688321
(888) H20RAFT (tollfree)

Adventure Sports
2863 North Avenue, Grand
Junction, CO 81501
(970) 2452441

Alpine Kayak & Canoe
40690 US Highway 6 And 24,
Avon, CO 81620
(970) 9493350

Alpine Outside
635 6, Crested Butte, CO 81224
(970) 3495011

American Adventure Expeditions
228 North F Street, Salida, CO
81201
(719) 5392874

American Wilderness Experience
Inc
2820 Wilderness Place, Boulder,
CO 80301
(303) 4442622

Arkansas River Tours
19487 US Highway 50, Cotopaxi,
CO 81223
(719) 9424362

Arkansas Valley Adventures
40671 US Highway 24, Buena
Vista, CO 81211
(719) 3952338
(800) 3700581 (tollfree)

Aspen Outdoor Adventures Inc
Aspen, CO 81611
(970) 9251153

Avalanche Tours
842 North Summit Boulevard,
Frisco, CO 80443
(970) 6681689

Blue Sky Adventures
319 6th Street, Glenwood
Springs, CO 81601
(970) 9456605

Breckenridge Whitewater Rafting
Inc
842 North Summit Boulevard,
Frisco, CO 80443
(970) 6681665

Browns Rafting
45045 West US Highway 50,
Canon City, CO 81212
(719) 2755161

Buffalo Joe River Trips
113 North Railroad, Buena Vista,
CO 81211
(719) 3958757
(800) 3567984 (tollfree)

Buggywhips Fish & Float Service
Inc
720 Lincoln Avenue, Steamboat
Springs, CO 80487
(970) 8798033

Cannibal Outdoors
367 South Gunnison Avenue,
Lake City, CO 81235
(970) 9442559

Canyon Canoeing Adventures
41 Missouri Avenue, Steamboat
Springs, CO 80487
(970) 8708127

Canyon Marine Whitewater
Expeditions
135 West US Highway 50, Salida,
CO 81201
(719) 5397476

Canyon Passages Inc
675 South Downing Street,
Denver, CO 80209
(303) 7223061

Clear Creek Rafting CO
P 3178, Idaho Springs, CO 80452
(303) 5671000

Clear Creek Rafting CO
Canon City, CO 81212
(719) 2754500

Colorado Headwaters
2605 West 7th Avenue, Denver,
CO 80204
(303) 5927150

Colorado Rafting Expeditions
210 East Main, Oak Creek, CO
80467
(970) 7360054

Colorado RIFF Raft Whitewater
Rafting
54 Snwms Village Mill,
Snowmass Village, CO 81615
(970) 9232220

Colorado River Guides
123 West Williams, Oak Creek,
CO 80467
(970) 7362406

Colorado Whitewater Expeditions
1704 Rainbow Drive, Canon City,
CO 81212
(719) 2750534

Colorado Wilderness Sports
358 West Elkhorn Avenue, Estes
Park, CO 80517
(970) 5866548

Down River Equipment Company
12100 West 52nd Avenue,
Wheat Ridge, CO 80033
(303) 4679489
(888) 4672144 (tollfree)

Dvoraks Kayak & Rafting
Expeditions
17921 US Highway 285, Nathrop,
CO 81236
(719) 5396851

Echo Canyon River Expeditions
Inc
45000 West US Highway 50,
Canon City, CO 81212
(719) 2753154

Estes Park Adventures
Estes Park, CO 80517
(970) 5862303

Estes Park Mountain Shop
358 West Elkhorn Avenue, Estes
Park, CO 80517
(970) 5866548

Flexible Flyers Rafting
Durango, CO 81301
(970) 2472350

Four Corners Expeditions
22565 US Highway 285 South,
Buena Vista, CO 81211
(719) 3954137

Geo Tours
2515 South Fillmore Street,
Denver, CO 80210
(303) 7566070
(800) 6607238 (tollfree)

Gunnison River Expeditions
19500 South Highway 550,
Montrose, CO 81401
(970) 2494441

High Adventures
402 Lincoln Avenue, Steamboat
Springs, CO 80487
(970) 8798747

Highside Adventure Tours Inc
Frisco, CO 80443
(970) 6681228

Independent White Water Rafting
23850 US Highway 285 South,
Buena Vista, CO 81211
(719) 3952642

Lazy J Resort & Rafting CO Inc
16373 US Highway 50, Coaldale,
CO 81222
(719) 9424274

Mad Adventures Inc
523 Zerex, Fraser, CO 80442
(970) 7265290

Mile Hi Rafting
10626 Snowy Trail, Conifer, CO
80433
(303) 9670354
(303) 6730965
mile hi rafting@aol.com

Monarch Guides
78437 US Highway 40, Winter
Park, CO 80482
(970) 7264801

Mountain Sports Haus
Junction Highway 50, Poncha
Springs, CO 81242
(719) 5397618

Mountain Water Rafting Inc
Durango, CO 81301
(970) 2594191

Noahs Ark Whitewater Rafting CO
23910 US Highway 285 South,
Buena Vista, CO 81211
(719) 3952158

Nova Guides Inc
82 South Beaver Creek Road,
Golden, CO 80403
(970) 9494232

Pagosa Rafting Outfitters
Wilderness Journeys
P 222, Pagosa Springs, CO
81147
(970) 7314081

Raftmeister
641 West Lionshead Circle, Vail,
CO 81657
(970) 4767238

Rapid Transit Rafting
Estes Park, CO 80517
(970) 5868852
(800) 3678523 (tollfree)

Raven Adventure Trips
43659 West US Highway 50,
Canon City, CO 81212
(719) 2752890

Red Tail Rafting Inc
601 Zerex, Fraser, CO 80442
(970) 7261197

Rimrock Adventures
927 17 Road, Fruita, CO 81521
(970) 8589555

River Reach Youth Initiative
2303 East Dartmouth Avenue,
Englewood, CO 80110
(303) 3009598

Rock & Row Enterprises
Salida, CO 81201
(719) 5309165

Rock & Row Enterprises
Canon City, CO 81212
(719) 2769165

Rock N Roll Rubber Rentals &
Putt Putt Golf
Steamboat Springs, CO 80487
(970) 8467777

Rocky Mountain Adventures Inc
1360 Big Thompson Avenue,
Estes Park, CO 80517
(970) 5866191

Rocky Mountain Adventures Inc
1117 North US Highway 287,
Fort Collins, CO 80524
(970) 4934005

Rocky Mountain Adventures Inc
310 Charles Street, Buena Vista,
CO 81211
(719) 3958594
(800) 8586808 (tollfree)

Scenic River Tours
703 West Tomichi Avenue,
Gunnison, CO 81230
(970) 6413131

Sierra Outfitters & Guides
44650 West US Highway 50,
Canon City, CO 81212
(719) 2750128

Snowmass River Expeditions
Whitewater Rafting
54 Snwms Village Mill,
Snowmass Village, CO 81615
(970) 9232220

Southwest Whitewater
1430 Main Avenue, Durango, CO
81301
(970) 2598313

Splash Rafting of Buena Vista
27700 County Road 303, Buena
Vista, CO 81211
(719) 3952059

Steamboat Rafting Company
Steamboat Springs, CO 80487
(970) 8709632
(970) 8796699

Teluride Fly Fishing & Rafting
Expeditions
19500 South Highway 550,
Montrose, CO 81401
(970) 2494441

Tenderfoot Rafting & Outdoor
Adventures
133 East Tomichi Avenue,
Gunnison, CO 81230
(970) 6412200

Timberline Tours
23698 Highway 24, Minturn, CO
81645
(970) 4761414

Timberwolf Whitewater
Expeditions
4305 East US Highway 50,
Salida, CO 81201
(719) 5397508

Twin Lakes Expeditions
6559 Highway 82, Twin Lakes,
CO 81251
(719) 4863928

Wanderlust Adventures
3500 Bingham Hill Road, Fort
Collins, CO 80521
(970) 4841219

Whitewater Adventure Outfitters
50905 West US Highway 50,
Canon City, CO 81212
(719) 2755344
(888) 711raft (tollfree)

Whitewater Encounters
14825 US Highway 285, Salida,
CO 81201
(719) 5300937

Whitewater Voyageurs
Junction Highway 50, Poncha
Springs, CO 81242
(719) 5397618

Whitewater West
418 South 7th Street, Grand
Junction, CO 81501
(970) 2410441

Wilderness Aware Rafting
12600 Highway 24285, Buena
Vista, CO 81211
(719) 3952112
(719) 3956716 (fax)
(800) 4627238 (tollfree)
rapids@inaraft.com

Connecticut

AAA Whitewater
(207) 9233492
http://www.ncrivers.com

Magic Falls Rafting Co.
(207) 6632220
(207) 6634455
(207) 6634485 (fax)
(800) 2077238 (tollfree)
adventures@magicfalls.com
http://www.magicfalls.com

Cruisetime Inc
10 Fraser Drive, Woodbridge, CT
06525
(203) 3877694

Delaware

Wilderness Canoe Trips Inc
2111 Concord Pike, Wilmington,
DE 19803
(302) 6542227

Florida

Complete Inflatables & Life Rafts
9517 East US Highway 92,
Tampa, FL 33610
(813) 6204704

Dragonfly Watersports
20336 East Pennsylvania Avenue,
Dunnellon, FL 34432
(352) 4893046

Inflatable Boats by Avalon
9517 East US Highway 92,
Tampa, FL 33610
(813) 6204704

Georgia

Go With the Flow Sports
4 Elizabeth Way, Roswell, GA
30075
(770) 992–3200

Chattahoochee Canoe & Raft
Rental
199 Azalea Drive, Roswell, GA
30075
(770) 998–7778

Southeastern Expeditions Inc
50 Executive Park Drive
Northeast, Atlanta, GA 30329
(404) 329–0433

Whitewater Express
1240 Clairmont Road, Decatur,
GA 30030
(404) 325–5295
(800) 676–7238 (toll-free)

Idaho

Adventure Outfitters
570 Blue Lakes Boulevard North,
Twin Falls, ID 83301
(208) 736–8714

Bear Valley River CO
Banks, ID 83602
(208) 793–2272

Boise River Tours
111 Broadway Avenue 133,
Boise, ID 83702
(208) 333–0003

Brundage Mountainr Resort
Mccall, ID 83638
(208) 634–4151

Cabarton River Company
Cascade, ID 83611
(208) 382–5609

Canyon Cats Inc
Riggins, ID 83549
(208) 628–3772

Cascade Outfitters
604 East 45th Street, Garden
City, ID 83714
(208) 322–4411

Cascade Raft & Kayak
7050 Highway 55, Horseshoe
Bend, ID 83629
(208) 793–2221

Catacraft Inc
Mc Call, ID 83638
(208) 634–5934

Destination Wilderness
General Delivery, Salmon, ID
83467
(800) 423–8868
(541) 549–1297 (fax)
destwild@bendnet.com

Epleys Whitewater Adventures
1107 Davis Avenue, Mccall, ID
83638
(208) 634–5173

Erekson Outfitters
501 North 3rd Street, Mccall, ID
83638
(208) 634–4092

Exodus Wilderness Adventures
606 North Main Street, Pocatello,
ID 83204
(208) 628–3484

Headwaters River CO
PO Box 1, Banks, ID 83602
(208) 793–2348

Idaho Afloat
RR 1 Box 144, Grangeville, ID
83530
(208) 983–2414

Idaho River Sports
1521 North 13th Street, Boise, ID
83702
(208) 336–4844

Idaho Whitewater Unlimited Inc
Meridian, ID 83642
(208) 888–3008

Northwest Voyageurs
Lucile, ID 83542
(208) 628–3021

Northwest Voyages
Lucile, ID 83542
(208) 628–3780

R & R Adventures
504 Main Street, Lewiston, ID
83501
(208) 798–7693

River Odysseys West
Coeur D Alene, ID 83814
(208) 765–0841

River Rat White Water TOYZ
238 Blue Lakes Boulevard, Twin
Falls, ID 83301
(208) 735–8697

Rocky Mountain River Tours
Middle Fork
Boise, ID 83702
(208) 345–2400

Row River Odysseys West
Coeur D Alene, ID 83814
(208) 765–0841
(800) 451–6034 (toll-free)

S & S Whitewater Adventures
1711 Hemlock Avenue, Lewiston,
ID 83501
(208) 743–5245

Sobriety Adventures
RR 1 Box 144, Grangeville, ID
83530
(208) 983–2414

Three Rivers Motel & Rafting
Kooskia, ID 83539
(208) 926–4430

Whitewater Unlimited
Meridian, ID 83642
(208) 888–3008

Destination Wilderness
General Delivery, Salmon, ID
83467
(800) 423–8868
(541) 549–1297 (fax)
destwild@bendnet.com

Idaho Adventure River Trips
913 Highway 93 North, Salmon,
ID 83467
(208) 756–2986

Kookaburra Guided
Whitewater Trips
Salmon, ID 83467
(208) 756–4386

River Adventures for the Soul
Moscow, ID 83843
(208) 882–6517

Illinois

Ayers Landing Canoes
Wedron, IL 60557
(815) 434–2233

Bob's Riverside Inc
 (608) 588–2826
(608) 588–3476 (fax)
(888) 844–2206 (toll-free)
bobs@mhtc.net
http://www.bobsriverside.com

Cache Core Canoes
237 Dean Lane, Ullin, IL 62992
(618) 845–3817

Canoe Shack
Saint Charles, Elgin, IL 60120
(847) 289–8966

Chicagoland Canoe Base Inc
4019 North Narragansett Avenue,
Chicago, IL 60634
(773) 777–1489

Kickapoo Canoes
20842 Newtown Road,
Oakwood, IL 61858
(217) 354–2060

Schmidts Canoeing Service
Elgin, IL 60120
(847) 697–1678

Vertical Drop
116 West Main Street, Saint
Charles, IL 60174
(630) 584–1250

Will U Canoe Rental
110 North Charleton Street,
Willow Springs, IL 60480
(708) 839–2311

Indiana

Whitewater Canoe Rental
Box 2 Highway 52, Brookville, IN
47012
(765) 647–5434
(800) 634–4277 (toll-free)
http://www.whitewatercanoe.com

Hodges Canoe Trips
2761 North 1275 West, Delphi,
IN 46923
(765) 564–6806

Iowa

Iowa River Tube Rides
32488 215th Street, Eldora, IA
50627
(641) 858–5516

Rock N Row Adventures
32488 215th Street, Eldora, IA
50627
(641) 858–5516

Kansas

Kansas River Ouffitters
Ttl Creek St Park, Manhattan, KS
66502
(785) 537–8300

Kentucky

Sheltowee Trace Outfitters
Stearns, KY 42647
(606) 376–5567

Sheltowee Trace Outfitters
Whitley City, KY 42653
(606) 376–9992

Green River Canoeing
1145 South Main Street,
Brownsville, KY 42210
(270) 597–2031

J & J Bait & Tackle
1145 South Main Street,
Brownsville, KY 42210
(270) 597–2031

Ucanoe
Hc 35, Gray, KY 40734
(606) 545–6328

Barren River Canoe Rentals Inc
Bowling Green, KY 42103
(270) 796–1979

Cumberland River Canoe & Kayak
845 South Main Street,
Burkesville, KY 42717
(270) 864–1669

Galls Phillip & Son
1555 East New Circle Road,
Lexington, KY 40509
(859) 266–0469

Hoopers Outdoor Center
3791 Hinkleville Road, Paducah,
KY 42001
(270) 443–0019

Kentucky Kayak Kountry
2040 J H Obryan Avenue, Grand
Rivers, KY 42045
(270) 362–0081

Licking River Canoe Rentals US
Route 27, Butler, KY 41006
(859) 472–2000

Mammoth Cave Canoe & Kayak
1221 Old Mammoth Cave Road,
Cave City, KY 42127
(270) 773–3210

Quest Outdoors
128 Breckenridge Lane,
Louisville, KY 40207
(502) 893–5746

Rockcastle Adventures
London, KY 40741
(606) 864–940

Louisiana

Adventure Sports
333 North I 10 Service Road
East, Metairie, LA 70005
(504) 835–1932

Alligator Bayou Bait Shop &
Canoe Rentals
9980 Manchac Road, Baton
Rouge, LA 70801
(225) 642–9448

Bayou Barn Cajun Canoeing &
Dancing
313 Highway 45 H, Marrero, LA
70072
(504) 689–2663

Big Creek Outfitters &
Expeditions Inc
880 Mary Barron Road, Pollock,
LA 71467
(318) 765–3060

Campbells Canoe Rentals
772 King Road, Dry Creek, LA
70637
(337) 328–7121

Canoe Crystal
1607 Sunburst Lane, Pineville, LA
71360
(318) 445–3455

Delta Wilderness Outfitters
333 North I 10 Service Road
East, Metairie, LA 70005
(504) 835–1932

Norris Canoe Outfitters
6240 Highway 80, Princeton, LA
71067
(318) 949–9522

Ship To Shore CO
4313 Lake Street, Lake Charles,
LA 70605
(337) 474–0730

Tack A Paw Expedition
Toro Road, Anacoco, LA 71403
(337) 286–9337

Waynes World Canoeing &
Tubing
51439 Camp Circle Road,
Franklinton, LA 70438
(504) 795–2004

Whiskey Chitto Canoe Rental
624 Dave Smith Road, Mittie, LA
70654
(337) 639–4959

Maine

Magic Falls Rafting Co.
P O Box 9, West Forks, ME
04985
(207) 663–2220
(207) 663–4455
(207) 663–4485 (fax)
(800) 207–7238 (toll-free)
adventures@magicfalls.com
http://www.magicfalls.com

AAA Whitewater
Route 201, West Forks, ME
04985
(207) 663–4476
(207) 923–3492
(800) 649–7238 (fax)
(800) 348–8871 (toll-free)
raftmaine@ncrivers.com
http://www.ncrivers.com

Adventure Bound Inc
1094 US Route 201, Caratunk,
ME 04925
(207) 672–4300

Adventure Rafting Expedition
Route 201, West Forks, ME
04985
(207) 663–2249

Downeast Whitewater
RR 201, West Forks, ME 04985
(207) 663–2281

Great Adventures
Route 201, West Forks, ME
04985
(207) 663–2251

Maine Whitewater Inc
Gadabout Gaddis Airport,
Bingham, ME 04920
(207) 672–4814

Mountain Magic Expeditions
Route 201, Bingham, ME 04920
(207) 672–3994

Moxie Outdoor Adventures
Route 201, West Forks, ME
04985
(207) 663–2231

North Country Rivers
East, East Vassalboro, ME 04935
(207) 923–3492

River Rentals
PO Box 11, Yarmouth, ME 04096
(888) 723–8788
rivers8@usa.net

North Country Rivers
West Forks, ME 04985
(207) 663–4476

Northeast Rafting Expeditions Inc
Moosehead Lake, Rockwood,
ME 04478
(207) 534–2242

Northern Outdoors OFC
Route 201, West Forks, ME
04985
(207) 663–4466

River Rentals
PO Box 11, Yarmouth, ME 04096
(888) 723–8788
rivers8@usa.net

Three Rivers Whitewater Inc
Route 201, West Forks, ME
04985
(207) 663–2104

Unicorn Rafting Expeditions
Route 201, Jackman, ME 04945
(207) 668–7629

Wilderness Expeditions
Moosehead Lake, Rockwood,
ME 04478
(207) 534–2242

Wilderness Expeditions Inc
North Main, Greenville, ME
04441
(207) 695–0738

Maryland

Precision Rafting Expeditions
Morris Avenue, Friendsville, MD
21531
(301) 746–5290

Massachusetts

Magic Falls Rafting Co.
(207) 663–2220
(207) 663–4455
(207) 663–4485 (fax)
(800) 207–7238 (toll-free)
adventures@magicfalls.com
http://www.magicfalls.com

Buzzards Bay Kayak Instruction
PO Box 144, Fairhaven, MA
02719
(508) 996–8885
(617) 627–3861
(617) 627–3862 (fax)
http://www.bbk.baweb.com

North Shore Kayak & Outdoor
Center
9 Tuna Wharf, Rockport, MA
01966
(978) 546–5050

Zoar Outdoor
7 Main Street, Charlemont, MA
01339
(413) 339–4010
(413) 337–8436 (fax)
(800) 532–7483 (toll-free)
info@zoaroutdoor.com
http://www.zoaroutdoor.com

Michigan

A A A Rogue River Canoe Rental
12 East Bridge Street, Rockford,
MI 49341
(616) 866–9264

Areawide Canoe Raft & Tube
Rental by Wisner
25 Water Street, Newaygo, MI
49337
(231) 652–6743

Canoe Raft & Tube Rental by
Wisner
101p, Newaygo, MI 49337
(231) 652–6743

Duggans Canoe Livery &
Campground Inc
501 North 1st Street, Harrison,
MI 48625
(517) 539–7149

Grand Rogue Campgrounds &
Canoes
6400 West River Road Northeast,
Belmont, MI 49306
(616) 361–1053

Heavner Canoe Rental
13461 State Parkway, Brighton,
MI 48116
(248) 437–9406
(810) 685–2379

Heavner Canoe Rental
2775 Garden Road, Milford, MI
48381
(248) 685–2379

Indian Valley Campground &
Canoe
8200 108th Street Southeast,
Middleville, MI 49333
(616) 891–8579

Mountainside Canoe Livery
4700 West Remus Road, Mount
Pleasant, MI 48858
(517) 772–5437

Old Allegan Canoe Rental
2722 Old Allegan Road, Fennville,
MI 49408
(616) 561–5481

Raupp Campfitters
421 South Washington Avenue,
Royal Oak, MI 48067
(248) 547–6969

River Raisin Canoe Livery
Dundee, MI 48131
(734) 529–9029

Rollway Canoe Rental
Hale, MI 48739
(517) 728–3322

Salmon Run Campground
Canoes & Tubes
8845 Felch Avenue, Grant, MI
49327
(231) 834–5494

Sawmill Tube & Canoe
230 Baldwin Street, Big Rapids,
MI 49307
(231) 796–6408

Sharon Hollow Acres Canoe
Livery
17055 Bethel Church Road,
Manchester, MI 48158
(734) 428–0100

Skips Huron River Canoe Livery
3780 Delhi Court, Ann Arbor, MI
48103
(734) 769–8686

U Rent Em Canoe Livery
805 West Apple Street, Hastings,
MI 49058
(616) 945–3191

VICS Canoes
8845 Felch Avenue, Grant, MI
49327
(231) 834–5494

Wisner Rent Canoes
25 Water Street, Newaygo, MI
49337
(231) 652–6743

Wolynski Canoe Rental
2300 Wixom Trail, Milford, MI
48381
(248) 685–1851

Minnesota

Actionsport Canoe & Kayak
Saint Paul, MN 55101
(651) 994–9029

Bear Track Outfitting CO
2011 East Highway 61, Grand
Marais, MN 55604
(218) 387–1162
(800) 795–8068 (toll-free)

Colonial Outdoors
1990 North Lake Shore Drive,
Glenwood, MN 56334
(320) 634–5977

Country Camping
750 273rd Avenue Northwest,
Isanti, MN 55040
(763) 444–9626

Duluth Pack Store
365 Canal Park Drive, Duluth, MN
55802
(218) 722–1707

Gloeges Northern Sun Canoe
Outfitters
RR 2, Sebeka, MN 56477
(218) 472–3250

Gods Country Outfitters
29745 State Highway 38, Grand
Rapids, MN 55744
(218) 326–9866

Huntersville Outfitters
23516 280th Street, Menahga,
MN 56464
(218) 564–4279

IRV Funk Canoe Outfitters
RR 2, Sebeka, MN 56477
(218) 472–3272

Kedros Canoes
2107 West Superior Street,
Duluth, MN 55806
(218) 720-3886

Lacroix Outfitters
5713 Crane Lake Road, Crane
Lake, MN 55725
(218) 993–2642

Lanesboro Canoe Rental
301 Fillmore Avenue North,
Lanesboro, MN 55949
(507) 467–2948

Little River General Store
104 Parkway Avenue North,
Lanesboro, MN 55949
(507) 467–2943

Midwest Mountaineering
Outdoor Equipment Canoes & CL
309 Cedar Avenue South,
Minneapolis, MN 55454
(612) 339–3433

North Star Bikes & Boards
6002 East Superior Street,
Duluth, MN 55804
(218) 525–7357

Northwest Canoe Company
308 Prince Street, Saint Paul, MN
55101
(651) 229–0192

Northwoods Outfitters Inc
1400 5th Place Northwest,
Rochester, MN 55901
(507) 288–2552

Odyssey Design Works
207 East 1/2 Superior Street,
Duluth, MN 55802
(218) 720-6061

Out N About Gear
47 4th Street Northeast, Waite
Park, MN 56387
(320) 251–9036

Raven Moon Adventures
1632 London Road, Duluth, MN
55812
(218) 724–8914

Recreational Equipment Inc
1955 West County Road 52,
Saint Paul, MN 55112
(651) 635–0211
(612) 884–4315

Red Rock Wilderness Store
Fernberg Road, P.O. Box 690, Ely,
MN 55731
(218) 365–5489
(218) 365–4512 8AM-8PM Daily
(218) 365–4114 (fax)
(800) 280-1078 (toll-free) 8AM- 8
PM Daily
norec@northernnet.com

Rei-Recreational Equipment Inc
1955 County Road B2 West,
Saint Paul, MN 55113
(651) 635–0211
(612) 884–4315

River Ridge Custom Canoes
5865 River Ridge Court
Northeast, Rochester, MN 55906
(507) 288–2750

Root River Bait & Tackle
307 Industrial Drive, Rushford,
MN 55971
(507) 864–7004

Ski Hut
1032 East 4th Street, Duluth, MN
55805
(218) 724–8525

Sport Zone
32339 Harris Town Road, Grand
Rapids, MN 55744
(218) 326–8956

Welch Mill Canoeing & Tubing
26389 County 7 Boulevard,
Welch, MN 55089
(651) 388–9857

Western Lake Superior Kayaks
23 East 7th Street, Duluth, MN
55805
(218) 720-3577

Wild Mountain Canoe & Boat
Rental
37350 Wild Mountain Road,
Taylors Falls, MN 55084
(651) 465–6365

Wilderness Canoe Base
2301 Oliver Avenue North,
Minneapolis, MN 55411
(612) 522–6501

Mississippi

Adventure Outfitters
4919 Poplar Springs Drive,
Meridian, MS 39305
(601) 693–1478

Biloxi River Canoes
Gulfport, MS 39501
(228) 832–0412

Black Creek Canoe Rental
Brooklyn, MS 39425
(601) 582–8817

Buffalo Peak Outfitters
Highland Village, Jackson, MS
39211
(601) 366–2557

Canoe & Trail Outpost
Dillon Bridge Road, Tylertown,
MS 39667
(601) 876–6964

Canoe Rentals Okatoma
Seminary, MS 39479
(601) 722–4297

Indian Cycle Fitness & Outdoor
I 55 At County Lane Road North,
Jackson, MS 39201
(601) 956–8383
(800) 898–0019 (toll-free)

Leaf River Canoe Rental
5627 Highway 42, Hattiesburg,
MS 39401
(601) 584–9070

Okatoma Canoe Rental
Seminary, MS 39479
(601) 722–4297

Pearl River Canoe Co
112 Fishermans Lane, Florence,
MS 39073
(601) 845–1965

Red Creek Canoe Rental
1566 Highway 49, Wiggins, MS
39577
(601) 928–7007

Wolf River Canoe & Kayak
21640 Tucker Road, Long Beach,
MS 39560
(228) 452–7666

Missouri

Akers Ferry Canoe Rental
Eminence, MO 65466
(800) 333–5628
(573) 858–3224
(573) 858–3341 (fax)
akers@currentrivercanoe.com
http://www.currentrivercanoe.com
http://www.currentrivercanoe.com

Bass Canoe Rental
PO Box, Steelville, MO 65565
(573) 786–8517

Big Elk Camp & Canoe Rentals
Highway 71, Pineville, MO 64856
(417) 223–4635

Birds Nest Lodge & River Resort
P 1158, Steelville, MO 65565
(573) 775–2606

Blue Springs Resort
33261 Melrose Drive, Eldridge,
MO 65463
(417) 426–5512

Brown Canoe Rental
586 Highway East, Steelville, MO
65565
(573) 775–5542

Cowskin Canoe Rental &
Campground
RR 2 Box 2, Tiff City, MO 64868
(417) 775–2448

Dubes Three River Campground
Inc
P 697, Pineville, MO 64856
(417) 223–4746

Eagles Nest Campground
RR 2, Noel, MO 64854
(417) 475–3326

Elk River Floats & Campground
Noel, MO 64854
(417) 475–3561

Fagans Meramec River Canoe &
Raft Rental
247 Thurman Lake Road,
Steelville, MO 65565
(573) 775–5744
(800) 324–2674 (toll-free)

Garrisons Canoe Rental & RV
Campground
P 1069, Steelville, MO 65565
(573) 775–2410

Mountain Creek Campground
11564 Kinfolk Road, Eldridge,
MO 65463
(417) 426–5641

Ozark County Canoe & Kayak
107 E 3rd St, Gainesville, MO
65655
(417) 679–4296
offhours@aol.com
http://www.rockthat.com

Rafting CO Camping RV Resort
95 McCormick Road, Steelville,
MO 65565
(573) 775–2628

Robs Canoe Rental
2 1/2 Mills South On Highway K,
Windyville, MO 65783
(417) 345–2912

Sugar Island Camp & Canoe
Rental
Pineville, MO 64856
(417) 223–4410

Tree House RV Park & Canoe
Rental
15 Highway M, Steelville, MO
65565
(573) 775–2475

Montana

Absaroka River Adventures
Absarokee, MT 59001
(406) 328–4608

Adventure Whitewater
310 West 15, Red Lodge, MT
59068
(406) 446–3061

Adventures Big Sky Raft
Company
Big Sky, MT 59716
(406) 995–2324

All Seasons Sport Shop
1092 Helena Avenue, Helena, MT
59601
(406) 443–2978

Beartooth Whitewater
217 West 10, Red Lodge, MT
59068
(406) 446–3142

Big Sky River Sports
5575 Estate Lane, Belgrade, MT
59714
(406) 388–6410

Bitterroot Fly Company
Darby, MT 59829
(406) 821–1624

Flathead Raft Company Inc
Highway 93, Polson, MT 59860
(406) 883–5838

Geyser White Water
Gallatin Gateway, MT 59730
(406) 995–4989

Kootenai Country Bed &
Breakfast
264 Mack Road, Libby, MT 59923
(406) 293–7878

Lewis & Clark Trail Adventures
912 East Broadway Street,
Missoula, MT 59802
(406) 728–7609

Montana River Guides Inc
210 Red Fox Road, Lolo, MT
59847
(406) 273–4718
(800) 381–raft (toll-free)

Montana River Outfitters
923 10th Avenue North, Great
Falls, MT 59401
(406) 761–1677

Montana Whitewater
Gallatin Gateway, MT 59730
(406) 763–4465

North West Force
2019 Meridian Road, Victor, MT
59875
(406) 642–3251

Panda Sports Rentals
621 Bridger Drive, Bozeman, MT
59715
(406) 587–6280

Pangaea Expeditions
1617 Stoddard Street, Missoula,
MT 59802
(406) 721–7719

Rapid Discoveries Inc
81805 Gallatin Road, Bozeman,
MT 59718
(406) 582–8110

River Services Inc
Livingston, MT 59047
(406) 222–3746

Rocky Mountain Whitewater
1905 Ola Drive, Missoula, MT
59802
(406) 728–2984

Rubber Ducky River Rentals &
Shuttles
Livingston, MT 59047
(406) 222–3746

Sunshine Sports
304 Moore Lane, Billings, MT
59101
(406) 252–3724

Water Master Products
5000 US Highway 93 South,
Missoula, MT 59804
(406) 251–3337

Western Waters
Missoula, MT 59801
(406) 543–3203

Western Waters
5604 Bridger Court, Missoula,
MT 59803
(406) 251–5212

Wild West Rafting
US Highway 89 South, Gardiner,
MT 59030
(406) 848–2252

WW Outfitters
2811 Old Darby Road, Darby, MT
59829
(406) 821–3622

Yellowstone Raft CO
406 Scott Street West, Gardiner,
MT 59030
(406) 848–7777

Yellowstone Raft Company
Big Sky, MT 59716
(406) 995–4613

Nebraska

Canfields Sporting Goods
8457 West Center Road, Omaha,
NE 68124
(402) 393–3363
(800) 333–2263 (toll-free)

Graham Canoe Outfitters
603 East C Street, Valentine, NE
69201
(402) 376–3708

L JS Outpost
Arlington, NE 68002
(402) 478–4764

Little Outlaw Canoe & Tube
Rentals
1005 East Highway 20, Valentine,
NE 69201
(402) 376–1822

McRabbit Canoe Sales
405 South Front Street, Waterloo,
NE 68069
(402) 779–3136

Outdoor Services Limited
8035 Irvington Road, Omaha, NE
68122
(402) 571–1915

Rocky Ford Camp & Canoe Base
PO Box 3, Springview, NE 68778
(402) 497–3479
(712) 642–4422

Sunny Brook Camp & Canoe
Outfitters
RR, Sparks, NE 69220
(402) 376–1887

Supertubes
310 West Highway 20, Valentine,
NE 69201
(402) 376–2956

Nevada

Rebel Adventure Tours
713 East Ogden Avenue, Las
Vegas, NV 89101
(702) 380-6969

Kayaks Etc
Reno, NV 89501
(775) 849–2714

Reno Mountain Sports
155 East Moana Lane, Reno, NV
89502
(775) 825–2855

New Hampshire

Contoocook River Canoe CO
Canoe and Kayak Rentals
9 Horse Hill Road, Concord, NH
03303
(603) 753–9804

Country Canoeist Inc
1005 School Street, Dunbarton,
NH 03046
(603) 774–7888

Hannahs Paddles Canoe Livery
15 Hannah Dustin Drive,
Concord, NH 03301
(603) 753–6695

AAA Whitewater
 (207) 923–3492
http://www.ncrivers.com

Magic Falls Rafting Co.
(207) 663–2220
(207) 663–4455
(207) 663–4485 (fax)
(800) 207–7238 (toll-free)
adventures@magicfalls.com
http://www.magicfalls.com

New Jersey

Delaware River Country
(570) 588–5650
(877) 570-6700 (toll-free)
paul-langenbach@hotmail.com
http://www.erivercountry.com

New Mexico

Big River Raft Trips
15 Camino De Las Vacas, Taos,
NM 87571
(505) 751–7248

Far Flung Adventures
Highway 522, Taos, NM 87571
(505) 758–2628

Known World Guide Service
Velarde, NM 87582
(505) 852–3579
http://www.knownworldguides.c
om

Los Rios River Runners
Ski Valley Road, Taos, NM 87571
(505) 776–8854

Native Sons Adventures
1033 Paseo Del Pueblo Sur, Taos,
NM 87571
(505) 758–9342

New Wave Rafting Company
RR 5 Box 302, Santa Fe, NM
87501
(505) 984–1444
(800) 984–1444 (toll-free)

Rio Grande River Tours
3994 State Road 68, Ranchos De
Taos, NM 87557
(505) 758–0762
(800) 525–4966 (toll-free)

Santa Fe Detours
54 East 1/2 San Fransisco, Santa
Fe, NM 87501
(505) 983–6565

Santa Fe Rafting CO & Outfitters
1000 Cerrillos Road, Santa Fe,
NM 87501
(505) 988–4914
(800) 467–RAFT (toll-free)

Southwest Wilderness
Adventures
Santa Fe, NM 87500
(505) 983–7262

White Water Adventures
Albuquerque, NM 87101
(505) 298–0698

Wolf Whitewater
4626 Palo Alto Avenue
Southeast, Albuquerque, NM
87108
(505) 262–1099

New York

Pride of The Hudson
Monroe, NY 10950
(914) 782–0685
hudrivad@frontiernet.net

Als Sport Store
Downsville, NY 13755
(607) 363–7740

Bay Creek Paddling Center
1099 Empire Boulevard,
Rochester, NY 14609
(716) 288–2830

Bayside Boat&Tackle
1200 Empire Boulevard,
Rochester, NY 14609
(716) 224–8289

Canoe Center
6477 North Avon Road, Honeoye
Falls, NY 14472
(716) 624–4240

Landers River Trips
Route 97, Narrowsburg, NY
12764
(845) 252–3560

Moose River Company
RR 28, Old Forge, NY 13420
(315) 369–3682

Mountain Man Outdoor Supply
CO
2855 Route 28, Thendara, NY
13472
(315) 369–6672

Mountainman Outdoor Supply
CO
RR 28, Inlet, NY 13360
(315) 357–6672

North River General Store
4527 State Route 28, North
Creek, NY 12853
(518) 251–5678

Oak Orchard Canoe & Kayak
Experts
40 State Street, Pittsford, NY
14534
(716) 586–5990
(800) 452–9257 (toll-free)

Tickners Moose River Canoe
Trips
Riverside Drive, Old Forge, NY
13420
(315) 369–6286

North Carolina

Adventurous Fast River Rafting
Nantahala
Nantahala Riv, Bryson City, NC
28713
(828) 488–2386

Blue Ridge Outing
5472 West US Highway 74,
Whittier, NC 28789
(828) 586–3510

Blue Ridge Rafting & Lodging
Bridge Street, Hot Springs, NC
28743
(828) 622–3544

Brookside Campground
Topton, NC 28781
(828) 321–5209

Endless River Adventures
14157 Highway 19 West, Bryson
City, NC 28713
(828) 488–6199

Fast River Rafting Nantahala
River
Nantahala Riv, Bryson City, NC
28713
(828) 488–2386
(800) get-raft (toll-free)

Foothills Adventure Inc
5050 NE Us 25/70 Hwy, Marshall,
NC 28753
(828) 656–2978
http://www.foothillsadventures.c
om

Great Smokies Rafting CO
9405 Highway 19 West, Bryson
City, NC 28713
(828) 488–6302

Huck Finn Adventures
260 Bridge Street, Hot Springs,
NC 28743
(828) 622–9645
http://www.pisgahweb.net/huck-
finn

Nantahala Expeditions
11044 Highway 19 West, Bryson
City, NC 28713
(828) 488–3316

Nantahala Rafts Inc
Bryson City, NC 28713
(828) 488–2325
(828) 488–3627

Native River Expeditions
20 Bridge Street, Hot Springs,
NC 28743
(828) 622–9731

Rafting Nantahala Whitewater
14690 Nantahala Gorge, Bryson
City, NC 28713
(828) 488–2386

River Runners Retreat Inc
1349 US Highway 19, Topton, NC
28781
(828) 321–2211

Rolling Thunder River Company
10160 Highway 19 West, Bryson
City, NC 28713
(828) 488–2030
(800) 344–5838
(800) 408–7238 (toll-free)
rafting@rollingthunderriverco.com

Smokey Mountain Tubing &
Rafting CO
Big Cove Road, Cherokee, NC
28719
(828) 497–9773

USA Raft
11044 Highway 19 West, Bryson
City, NC 28713
(828) 488–3316

Whitesell Canoes
14690 Nantahala Gorge, Bryson
City, NC 28713
(828) 488–2386

North Dakota

Dakota Cyclery
1606 East Main Avenue,
Bismarck, ND 58501
(701) 222–1218

Oklahoma

Riverside Canoe Rental
Highway 70 East, Eagletown, OK
74734
(580) 835–7130

Oregon

A Float On the River
Eugene, OR 97401
(541) 338–9338

Adventure Center
Ashland, OR 97520
(541) 488–2819

Bend Whitewater Supply
413 Northwest Hill Street, Bend,
OR 97701
(541) 389–7191

C & J Lodge Whitewater Rafting
304 Bakeoven County Road,
Maupin, OR 97037
(541) 395–2404

Cascade River Adventures
Bend, OR 97701
(541) 382–6277

Cascade River Runners
PO Box 86, Klamath Falls, OR
97601
(541) 883–6340

Cool Runnings Rafting
1273 Northwest Wall Street,
Bend, OR 97701
(541) 389–5327

Custom Adventure Trips
8320 Southwest Canyon Drive,
Portland, OR 97225
(503) 297–5005

Deschutes River Adventures
602 Deschutes Avenue, Maupin,
OR 97037
(541) 395–2238

Deschutes Share-A-Raft
2328 Southeast Hale Drive,
Gresham, OR 97030
(503) 669–4942
(541) 395–2488
(503) 661–2985 (fax)
sharearaft@aol.com

Deschutes U Boat Inc
501 Hy 197 South, Maupin, OR
97037
(541) 395–2503

Deschutes White Water Service
Bakeoven Road, Maupin, OR
97037
(541) 395–2232

Ewings Whitewater
P 265, Maupin, OR 97037
(541) 395–2697

Ferrons Fun Trips
585 Rogue Rim Drive, Merlin, OR
97532
(541) 474–2201

Freewind Sports
56771 Lunar Drive, Bend, OR
97707
(541) 593–1912

Galice Resort & Raft Rentals
11744 Galice Road, Merlin, OR
97532
(541) 476–3818

Wayne Gardner Outfitter & Guide
Service
89807 Greenwood Drive,
Walterville, OR 97489
(541) 896–3615

Half Moon Bar Lodge
Gold Beach, OR 97444
(541) 247–6968
(541) 247–3486 (fax)
(888) 291–8268 (toll-free)
una@harborside.com
http://www.halfmoonbarlodge.com

Helfrich River Outfitters
37855 Shenandoah Loop,
Springfield, OR 97478
(541) 741–1905

In the Wild Wilderness
Adventures
5513 Southeast Yamhill Street,
Portland, OR 97215
(503) 232–8795

J CS Raft Repair
607 Southeast Riverside Avenue,
Grants Pass, OR 97526
(541) 479–8933

Jims Oregon Whitewater Inc
56324 McKenzie Highway, Blue
River, OR 97413
(541) 822–6003

Justus Outfitters
Eugene, OR 97401
(541) 342–1755

Lindas River Shuttle
Hy 197 And L Rod Street,
Maupin, OR 97037
(541) 395–2488

Magnum Adventures
Springfield, OR 97477
(541) 746–1454

McKenzie River Adventures
Blue River, OR 97413
(541) 822–3806

McKenzie River Rafting CO
7715 Thurston Road, Springfield,
OR 97478
(541) 726–6078

McKenzie River Adventures
Sisters, OR 97759
(541) 549–1325

Morrisons Rogue River Lodge
8500 Galice Road, Merlin, OR
97532
(541) 476–3825

Ncat Whitewater
Walterville, OR 97489
(541) 896–3468

Noahs Rafting & Fishing Trips
PO Box 11, Ashland, OR 97520
(541) 482–2811

Noahs Rafting & Fishing Trips
P 11, Ashland, OR 97520
(541) 488–2811

North Umpqua Outfitters
P, Roseburg, OR 97470
(541) 673–4599

Northwest Drifters
7000 Steelhead Place, Gold Hill,
OR 97525
(541) 855–2336
nwd@cdsnet.net

Oregon Ridge & River Excursions
Glide, OR 97443
(541) 496–3333

Oregon River Experiences
Beavercreek, OR 97004
(503) 632–6836
(800) 827–1358 (toll-free)

Oregon River Sports
1640 West 7th Avenue, Eugene,
OR 97402
(541) 334–0696

Oregon Whitewater Adventures
39620 Deerhorn Road,
Springfield, OR 97478
(541) 746–5422

Osprey Adventures
114 Northwest Congress Street,
Bend, OR 97701
(541) 330-6776

Otter Industries Inc
7605 4th Street, White City, OR
97503
(541) 830-4710

Ouzel Outfitters River Trips
Bend, OR 97701
(541) 385–5947

Portland River Company
315 Southwest Montgomery
Street, Portland, OR 97201
(503) 229–0551

Quests of the West
Bend, OR 97701
(541) 389–0323

Raft Rite Rentals
31 Maple Drive, Shady Cove, OR
97539
(541) 878–4005

Rainman Excursions
143 Belindy Circle, Grants Pass,
OR 97527
(541) 474–7131

Rapid Pleasure Raft Rental
7474 Crowfoot Road, Trail, OR
97541
(541) 878–2500

Ridgeline Mountain Sports
2210 Northwest Stewart Parkway
1, Roseburg, OR 97470
(541) 677–1777

River Dance Raft Rentals & Sales
105 Merlin Road, Merlin, OR
97532
(541) 472–9506

River Riders NW
Hood River, OR 97031
(541) 386–7238
(800) 448–raft (toll-free)

River Runner Supply
78 Centennial Loop, Eugene, OR
97401
(541) 343–6883

River Trails Deschutes
Bakeoven Road, Maupin, OR
97037
(541) 395–2545

River Trails Raft & Canoe
336 East Historic Columbia Ri,
Troutdale, OR 97060
(503) 667–1964
(888) 324–8838 (toll-free)

Rogue Rafting Company
7725 Rogue River Drive, Shady
Cove, OR 97539
(541) 878–2585

Rogue River Trips at Galice
11744 Galice Road, Merlin, OR
97532
(541) 476–3818

Rogue Wilderness Inc
325 Galice Road, Merlin, OR
97532
(541) 479–9554

Rogueklamath River Adventure
Medford, OR 97501
(541) 779–3708

Santiam Outdoor Supply
Salem, OR 97301
(503) 362–6315

Share A Raft
Hy 197 And L Rod Street,
Maupin, OR 97037
(541) 395–2488

Sotar
1700 Nebraska Avenue, Grants
Pass, OR 97527
(541) 476–1344

Sun Country Tours
Bend, OR 97701
(541) 382–6277

Sunset On the Rogue
26876 Highway 62, Trail, OR
97541
(541) 878–3330

TMS Outdoor Specialties
11833 Southeast Harold Street,
Portland, OR 97266
(503) 760-6575

Wet N Wild Raft Rental
22175 Highway 62, Shady Cove,
OR 97539
(541) 878–2889

White Water Cowboys
209 Merlin Road, Merlin, OR
97532
(541) 479–0132

White Water Manufacturing
1700 Nebraska Avenue, Grants
Pass, OR 97527
(541) 476–1344

White Water Warehouse
625 Northwest Starker Avenue,
Corvallis, OR 97330
(541) 758–3150

Whitewater Unlimited
501 Hy 197 South, Maupin, OR
97037
(541) 395–2503

Wilderness River Outfitters
1567 Main Street, Springfield,
OR 97477
(541) 726–9471

Pennsylvania

Adventure Sports
Route 209, Marshalls Creek, PA
18335
(570) 223–0505

Anglers Roost & Hunters Rest
Lackawaxen, PA 18435
(570) 685–2010

Chamberlain Canoes
Minsnk Acres, Minisink Hills, PA
18341
(570) 421–0180

Great Rivers of the East
Star Route 903, Jim Thorpe, PA
18229
(570) 325–4100

Hot Pursuit Inc
Route 940, White Haven, PA
18661
(570) 443–9532

Laurel Highlands River Tours Inc
Farmington, PA 15437
(724) 329–4501

Laurel Highlands River Tours Inc
Sherman, Ohiopyle, PA 15470
(724) 329–8531
(800) 472–3846 (toll-free)

Mountain Streams & Trails
Outfitters
Main, Ohiopyle, PA 15470
(724) 329–8810

Ohiopyle Recreational Rentals
Main, Ohiopyle, PA 15470
(724) 329–8810

Ohiopyle Trading Post Inc
Whitewater, Ohiopyle, PA 15470
(724) 329–1450

Outdoor Adventures Inc
Route 940, White Haven, PA
18661
(570) 443–9532

Pocono Whitewater Photos
Star Route 903, Jim Thorpe, PA
18229
(570) 325–3654

Two River Junction
Lackawaxen, PA 18435
(570) 685–2010

White Water Adventurers Inc
RR 381, Ohiopyle, PA 15470
(724) 329–8850

Whitewater Challengers Inc
Route 940, White Haven, PA
18661
(570) 443–9532

Whitewater Raft Adventures
101 West Adventure Trail,
Nesquehoning, PA 18240
(570) 669–9127

Whitewater Rafting
243 Main Street, White Haven,
PA 18661
(570) 443–0604

Whitewater World
Star Route 903, Jim Thorpe, PA
18229
(570) 325–3654

Wilderness Voyageurs
200 Main, Dawson, PA 15428
(724) 529–0202

Wilderness Voyageurs Inc.
PO Box 97, Ohiopyle, PA 15470
(724) 329–1000
(724) 329–5517
(724) 329–0809 (fax)
(800) 272–4141 (toll-free)
rafting@wilderness-
voyageurs.com

Rhode Island

AAA Whitewater
(207) 923–3492
http://www.ncrivers.com

Compass Canoe CO
73 Gooding Avenue, Bristol, RI
02809
(401) 247–1200

Fin & Feather Hunting & Fishing
Lodge
95 Frenchtown Road, East
Greenwich, RI 02818
(401) 885–8680

Kayak Centre
562 Charlestown Beach Road,
Charlestown, RI 02813
(401) 364–8000

Kayak Centre
518 Thames Street, Newport, RI
02840
(401) 848–2920

Kayak Centre
9 Phillips Street, North
Kingstown, RI 02852
(401) 295–4400

Kayak RI
99 Poppasquash Road, Bristol, RI
02809

Magic Falls Rafting Co..
(207) 663–2220
(207) 663–4455
(207) 663–4485 (fax)
(800) 207–7238 (toll-free)
adventures@magicfalls.com
http://www.magicfalls.com

Ocean State Adventures
99 Poppasquash Road, Bristol, RI
02809
(401) 254–4000
(877) KAY-AKRI

Paddle Providence Inc
Prvdnc Rvr Wlk, Providence, RI
02906
(401) 453–1633

URE Outfitters
Main, Hope Valley, RI 02832
(401) 539–4050

South Carolina

Chattooga River Adventures
14544 Long Creek Highway,
Mountain Rest, SC 29664
(864) 647–0365

Chattooga Whitewater Shop
14239 Long Creek Highway, Long
Creek, SC 29658
(864) 647–9083

Rafts
1251 Academy Road, Mountain
Rest, SC 29664
(864) 647–9587

Star Inflatables
Travelers Rest, SC 29690
(864) 836–2800

Wildwater Limited Outdoor
Adventures
1251 Academy Road A, Long
Creek, SC 29658
(864) 647–9587

Wildwater Limited
1251 Academy Road, Mountain
Rest, SC 29664
(864) 647–9587

South Dakota

Pedal & Paddle
411 South Pierre Street, Pierre,
SD 57501
(605) 224–8955

Tennessee

Cherokee Rafting Service Inc
869 Highway 64, Ocoee, TN
37361
(423) 338–5124

Eagle Adventure CO
375 Eagle Ranch Road,
Copperhill, TN 37317
(423) 496–1843

Five River Adventures
3385 Hartford Road, Hartford, TN
37753
(423) 487–3701

Funyaks
Highway 64, Ocoee, TN 37361
(423) 338–0100

High Country Adventures
430 Highway 64, Ocoee, TN
37361
(423) 338–8634
(800) 233–8594 (toll-free)

Hiwassee Outfitters Reservations
Office
Highway 30, Reliance, TN 37369
(423) 338–8115

Kayak Instruction
Highway 64, Ocoee, TN 37361
(423) 338–0100

Lake Ocoee Inn & Marina MNC
US Highway 64 East, Benton, TN
37307
(423) 338–2064

Ocoee Adventure Whitewater
Rafting
Highway 64, Ocoee, TN 37361
(423) 338–2438

Ocoee Inn Rafting Inc
US Highway 64 East, Benton, TN
37307
(423) 338–2064

Ocoee Outdoors Inc
Highway 64, Ocoee, TN 37361
(423) 338–2438

Ocoee Rafting Inc
Hghwy 64 And Stt, Copperhill,
TN 37317
(423) 496–3388

Ocoee River Eagle Ranch
375 Eagle Ranch Road,
Copperhill, TN 37317
(423) 496–1843
(800) 288–3245 (toll-free)

Ocoee River Rats
899 Parksville Road, Benton, TN
37307
(423) 338–4264

Ocoee River Whitewater Rafting
Welcome Valley Road, Benton,
TN 37307
(423) 338–8388

Outland Expeditions White Water
Rafting
6501 Waterlevel Highway,
Cleveland, TN 37323
(423) 478–1442

Pigeon River Outdoors
2470 East, Gatlinburg, TN 37738
(865) 436–5008

Quest Expeditions
Highway 64, Ocoee, TN 37361
(423) 338–2979

Rafting in the Smokies
2470 East, Gatlinburg, TN 37738
(865) 436–5008

Rapid Descent River Company
3195 Hartford Road, Hartford, TN
37753
(423) 487–2105

Rip Roaring Adventures White
Water Rafting CO
3375 Hartford Road, Hartford, TN
37753
(423) 487–4277

River Runners Retreat Inc
420 Trentham Lane, Gatlinburg,
TN 37738
(865) 436–3478

Smoky Mountain River Run
3249 North River Road, Pigeon
Forge, TN 37863
(865) 428–4403

Southeastern Expeditions
1242 Highway 64, Benton, TN
37307
(423) 338–8073

Webb BROS Float Service Inc
3708 Highway 30, Reliance, TN
37369
(423) 338–2373

White Water Express
196 Eagle Ranch Road,
Copperhill, TN 37317
(423) 496–9126

Whitewater Company
Gatlinburg, TN 37738
(865) 436–4303

Whitewater Company
3485 Hartford Road, Hartford, TN
37753
(423) 487–2030

Wildwater Limited
9472 Highway 64, Savannah, TN
38372
(423) 496–4904

U S A Raft
3630 Hartford Road, Hartford, TN
37753
(423) 487–4303

USA Raft
1278 Welcome Valley Road,
Benton, TN 37307
(423) 338–2381

Texas

Big Bend River Tours Boardwalk
P 317, Terlingua, TX 79852
(915) 424–3219

Dudleys
206 East Mansfield, Sanderson,
TX 79848
(915) 345–2503

Rio Grande Adventures
Terlingua, TX 79852
(915) 371–2567

Scott Canoe & Raft Expeditions
Sanderson, TX 79848
(915) 345–2268

Utah

Adrift Adventures
9500 East 6000 South, Jensen,
UT 84035
(435) 789–3600

Adrift Adventures
378 North Main Street, Moab, UT
84532
(435) 259–8594

Anglers Inn
2292 Highland Drive, Salt Lake
City, UT 84106
(801) 466–3921

Canyon Voyages Adventure CO
211 North Main Street, Moab, UT
84532
(435) 259–6007

Coyote Shuttle
Moab, UT 84532
(435) 259–8656

Destination Sports
738 Main, Park City, UT 84060
(435) 645–5336

Flaming Gorge Lodge
Eendale Highway 191, Dutch
John, UT 84023
(435) 889–3773

Hatch Don & Meg River
Expeditions
55 East Main Street, Vernal, UT
84078
(435) 789–4316

High Country Rafting
Highway 189 Provo Canyon,
Provo, UT 84601
(435) 649–7678

Holiday Expeditions
544 East 3900 South, Salt Lake
City, UT 84107
(801) 266–2087

Moab Bed & Breakfast
PO Box 801, Moab, UT 84532
(435) 259–7238

Moab Rafting
44001 Stocks, Moab, UT 84532
(435) 259–7238

Navtec Expeditions
321 North Main Street, Moab, UT
84532
(435) 259–7983

North American River
Canyonland Tours
543 North Main Street, Moab, UT
84532
(435) 259–5865

Park City Rafting
Park City, UT 84060
(435) 655–3800

Rent A Raft
Moab, UT 84532
(435) 259–7019

River Rafts Inc
3031 South 500 East, Salt Lake
City, UT 84106
(801) 466–1912

Roadrunner Shuttle of Moab
Moab, UT 84532
(435) 259–9402

Sidsports Inc
3025 East 3300 South, Salt Lake
City, UT 84109
(801) 486–9424

Splore
610 Cermak Street, Moab, UT
84532
(435) 259–4338

Tag-A-Long Expeditions
452 North Main Street, Moab, UT
84532
(435) 259–8946

Texs Riverways
691 North 500 West, Moab, UT
84532
(435) 259–5101

Wasatch Paddle Sports
697 West Riverdale Road,
Ogden, UT 84405
(801) 392–0862

Western River Expeditions
Moab, UT 84532
(435) 259–7019

Wild Rivers Expeditions
Bluff, UT 84512
(435) 672–2244

World Wide River Expeditions
625 Riversands Road, Moab, UT
84532
(435) 259–7515

Vermont

Adventure Outfitters
97 Main Street, Brattleboro, VT
05301
(802) 254–4133

Alpine Shop
1184 Williston Road, South
Burlington, VT 05403
(802) 862–2714

Battenkill Canoe Limited
Route Box # A, Arlington, VT
05250
(802) 362–2800

Canoe Imports
370 Dorset Street, South
Burlington, VT 05403
(802) 651–8760

Clearwater Sports Inc
Route 100, Waitsfield, VT 05673
(802) 496–2708

Craftsbury Outdoor Center
535 Lost Nation Road, Craftsbury
Common, VT 05827
(802) 586–7767
(800) 729–7751 (toll-free) reserva-
tion info

Downhill Edge Ski Rack
65 Main Street, Burlington, VT
05401
(802) 862–2282

Green River Canoe
Jeffersonville, VT 05464
(802) 644–8336

Kayak King Rentals
Killington, VT 05751
(802) 422–2070

Mad River Canoe Inc
Mad River Green, Waitsfield, VT
05673
(802) 496–3127

Moose Caboose
79 Birch Landing Road,
Plymouth, VT 05056
(802) 228–4957

Mountain Travelers Hike & Ski
Shop
147 US Route 4 East, Rutland, VT
05701
(802) 775–0814

Northern Excursions
79 Birch Landing Road,
Plymouth, VT 05056
(802) 228–4957

Northern Forest Canoe Trail
Waitsfield, VT 05673
(802) 496–2285

Small Boat Exchange
16 Kilburn Street, Burlington, VT
05401
(802) 864–5437

Three Rivers Canoe CO
74 Broad Street, Windsor, VT
05089
(802) 626–8648

Umiak Outdoor Outfitters
849 South Main Street, Stowe,
VT 05672
(802) 865–6777

Vermont Canoe & Kayak
Pudding Hill Road, Lyndonville,
VT 05851
(802) 626–7230

Vermont Canoe Touring Center
451 Putney Road, Brattleboro, VT
05301
(802) 257–5008

Vermont Pack & Paddle Outfitters
Route 100, Waitsfield, VT 05673
(802) 496–7225

Village Sport Shop
RR 5, Lyndonville, VT 05851
(802) 626–8448

Voyageur
Mad River Green, Waitsfield, VT
05673
(802) 496–3127

Wildwater Outfitters
97 Main Street, Brattleboro, VT
05301
(802) 254–4133

Virginia

Adventure Challenge
Richmond, VA 23219
(804) 276–7600

Richmond Raft CO
Richmond, VA 23219
(804) 222–7238

Massanutten Canoe & Kayak
Voyages
Mc Gaheysville, VA 22840
(540) 289–9453

Massanutten Tour Company
Mc Gaheysville, VA 22840
(540) 289–9453

Outdoor Adventure Experiences
Inc
Dayton, VA 22821
(540) 879–9030

Downriver Canoe CO
884 Indian Hollow Road,
Bentonville, VA 22610
(540) 635–5526

James River Basin Canoe Livery
Limited
1870 East Midland Trail,
Lexington, VA 24450
(540) 261–7334

James River Canoe & Tube Trips
10082 Hatton Ferry Road,
Scottsville, VA 24590
(804) 286–2338

James River Reeling & Rafting
Main And Ferry Street,
Scottsville, VA 24590
(804) 286–4386

Shenandoah Outfitters
6502 South Page Valley Road,
Luray, VA 22835
(540) 743–4159

Shenandoah River Trips
2047 Rocky Hollow Road,
Bentonville, VA 22610
(540) 635–5050

Wilderness Canoe CO
Natural Bridge Stati, VA 24579
(540) 291–2295

Washington

AAA Rafting
860 Highway 141, Husum, WA
98623
(509) 493–2511

Alpine Adventures
Leavenworth, WA 98826
(800) 723–8386
info@alpineadventures.com
http://www.alpineadventures.com

Alpine Adventures
Leavenworth, WA 98826
(509) 782–7042
(800) 926–7238 (toll-free)

Carrots
1107 Fruitvale Boulevard, Yakima,
WA 98902
(509) 248–3529

Downstream River Runners
13414 Chain Lake Road, Monroe,
WA 98272
(360) 805–9899

Enchanted Water Tours
PO Box 611, Leavenworth, WA
98826
(509) 548–5031
(888) 723–8987 (toll-free)
ewtours@enchantedwatertours.c
om
http://www.enchantedwater-
tours.com

Intrepid Excursions
Kennewick, WA 99336
(509) 582–1864

Northwest River Adventures
Nine Mile Falls, WA 99026
(866) 528–7800
(509) 325–1396 (fax)
(866) 528–7800 (toll-free)
charco98@hotmail.com

Oar House
11734 State Highway 2,
Leavenworth, WA 98826
(509) 548–2304

Orion Expeditions
5111 Latona Avenue Northeast,
Seattle, WA 98105
(206) 547–6715

Phil Zollers White Water
Adventures
38 Northwestern Lake Road,
White Salmon, WA 98672
(509) 493–2641

Renegade River Rafters
Stevenson, WA 98648
(509) 427–7238

River Recreation Inc
6850 Olalla Canyon Rd,
Cashmere, WA 98815
(509) 782–7238
(509) 782–RAFT
(800) 464–5899 (toll-free)
office@riverrecreation.com
http://www.riverrecreation.com

River Riders
Monroe, WA 98272
(360) 794–8782

Swiftwater
4235 Fremont Avenue North,
Seattle, WA 98103
(206) 547–3377

White Water Market
860 Highway 141, Husum, WA
98623
(509) 493–2511

Wild & Scenic River Tours
Seattle, WA 98101
(206) 323–1220

Wildwater River Tours
(800) 522–9453
(253) 939–2151
(800) 522–9453 (toll-free)
http://www.wildwater-river.com

West Virginia

Mountain River Tours Inc.
Sunday Road, Hico, WV 25854
(304) 658–5266
(304) 658–5817 (fax)
(800) 822–1386 (toll-free)
mail@raftmrt.com
http://www.raftmrt.com

Blue Ridge Outfitters
RR 340, Charles Town, WV 25414
(304) 725–3444

River Riders Inc
Alstadts Hill, Harpers Ferry, WV
25425
(304) 535–2663

Adventour L L C
211 North Court Street,
Fayetteville, WV 25840
(304) 574–0201

Adventure Pursuit Inc
Parkersburg, WV 26101
(304) 485–0911

Appalachian Guide Service
White Sulphur Spring, WV 24986
(304) 536–2536

Greenbrier River Campground
Fort Spring, WV 24936
(304) 645–2760

Mountain State Outfitters
4112 Maccorkle Avenue
Southeast, Charleston, WV
25304
(304) 925–5959

Pedals & Paddles
1100 Murdoch Avenue,
Parkersburg, WV 26101
(304) 422–2453

Starrk Moon Kayaks
139 South Court Street,
Fayetteville, WV 25840
(304) 574–2550
(304) 574–2533 (fax)
(304) 574–2550 (toll-free) 2
starrkmoonwv@aol.com

Wisconsin

Blackhawk River Run
Highway Y, Mazomanie, WI
53560
(608) 643–6724

Big Smokey Falls Rafting
Hc 1, Keshena, WI 54135
(715) 799–3359

Wildman Whitewater Ranch
N12080 Allison Lane, Athelstane,
WI 54104
(715) 757–2888

Wyoming

Acme Boat Rentals
P 125, Jackson, WY 83001
(307) 739–8899

Barker Ewing Float Trips Scenic
P 100, Moose, WY 83012
(307) 733–1800

Barker Ewing River Trips
Whitewater
P 450, Jackson, WY 83001
(307) 733–1800

Lewis & Clark River Expeditions
P 720, Jackson, WY 83001
(307) 733–4022

Rent A Raft
P 1864, Jackson, WY 83001
(307) 733–2728

Wind River Canyon White Water
210 US Highway 20 South,
Thermopolis, WY 82443
(307) 864–9343

Wyoming Choice River Runners
513 North Lennox Street, Casper,
WY 82601
(307) 234–3870

Jackson Hole Kayak School
1035 Broadway, Jackson, WY
83001
(307) 733–2471

Platte River Outfitters
1725 Sycamore Street, Casper,
WY 82604
(307) 265–2843
Rendezvous River Sports
PO Box 9201, Jackson, WY
83002
(307) 733–2471

Snake River Kayak & Canoe
School Inc
P 4311, Jackson, WY 83001
(307) 733–9999

Wyoming River Raiders
300 Salt Creek Highway, Mills,
WY 82644
(307) 235–8624

Wyoming River Raiders
Post Office Box 50490, Casper,
WY 82604
(307) 266–7723
dan@net-impress.com

Guides and Outfitters Canada

Alberta

Adventure Hotline
Canmore
AB T1W 1A0
Phone: (403)678–7238

Altitude Outdoor Sports Rentals
& Service
1302 Bow Valley Trail
Canmore
AB T1W 1N6
Phone: (403)678–1636

Banff Adventures Unlimited
Banff
AB T0L 0C0
Phone: (403)760-3196

Blast Adventure
115 Elk Run Blvd
Canmore
AB T1W 1G8
Phone: (403)609–2009

Bow Valley School of Kayaking,
1302 Bow Valley Trail
Canmore
AB T1W 1N6
Phone: (403)678–1636

Canadian Rockies Rafting
Company
Canmore
AB T1W 1A0
Phone: (403)678–6535

Canadian Whitewater Adventures
79 Douglas Park Blvd SE
Calgary
AB T2Z 2K9
Phone: (403)720-8745

Chinook River Sports
341 10 Av SW
Calgary
AB T2R 0A5
Phone: (403)263–7238

Dans Rafting & Tours
Grande Cache
AB T0E 0Y0
Phone: (780)827–4454

Hunter Valley Adventure Tours
PO BOX 310
Water Valley
AB T0M 2E0
Phone: (403)637–2777

Hydra-River Guides
211 BEAR ST
Banff
AB T0L 0C0
Phone: (403)762–4554

Inside Out Experience
Bragg Creek
AB T0L 0K0
Phone: (403)949–3405

Jasper Raft Tours
Jasper
AB T0E 1E0
Phone: (780)852–2665

Kananaskis River Adventure
KANANASKIS
AB T0L 2H0
Phone: (403)591–7301

Kimball River Sports
PO BOX 2622
Cardston
AB T0K 0K0
Phone: (403)382–0997

Maligne Rafting Adventure
627 Patricia St
Jasper
AB T0E 1E0
Phone: (780)852–5208

Maligne Tours
626 Connaught Dr.
Jasper
AB T0E 1E0
Phone: (780)852–3370

Mirage Adventure Tours
999 Bow Valley Trail
Canmore
AB T1W 1N4
Phone: (403)678–4919

Otter Rafting Adventure
Red Deer
AB T4P 3A0
Phone: (403)342–4699

Rainbow Riders Adventure Tours
Canmore
AB T1W 1A0
Phone: (403)678–7238

Raven Adventure
Jasper
AB T0E 1E0
Phone: (780)852–4292

Rocky Mountain Raft Tours
PO BOX 1771
Banff
AB T0L 0C0
Phone: (403)762–3632

Sekani Rafting
224 Colin Cr.
Jasper
AB T0E 1E0
Phone: (780)852–5211

Sunwest River Guides Co
4424 16 Av NW
Calgary
AB T3B 0M4
Phone: (403)276–5388

Western River Runners
PO BOX 1771
Banff
AB T0L 0C0
Phone: (403)762–3632

Wild Water Adventure
Lobby, Chateau Lake Louise
Lake Louise
AB T0L 1E0
Phone: (403)522–2211

British Columbia

Adventure Ranch
1642 Sea to Sky Hwy 99
Pemberton
BC V0N 2L0
Phone: (604)894–5200

Alpine Rafting CO
1020 Trans-Canada
Fairmont Hot Springs
BC V0B 1L0
Phone: (250)344–6778

Apex Raft Co
216 2ND ST E
Revelstoke
BC V0E 2S0
Phone: (250)837–6376

Big White Canadian Outback
Adventure CO
657 Marine DR
West Vancouver
BC V7T 1A4
Phone: (604)921–7250

Canadian Rockies River
Expeditions
232 Spokane St
Kimberley
BC V1A 2E4
Phone: (250)427–3266

Canyon Raft Company
Fernie
BC V0B 1M0
Phone: (250)423–7226

Chilko River Expeditions
285 Donald Rd
Williams Lake
BC V2G 4K4
Phone: (250)398–6711

Chilliwack River Rafting
Adventures
49704 Chilliwack Lake Road
Chilliwack
BC V4Z 1A7
Phone: (604)824–0334

Chilliwack River Rafting
Adventures
Vancouver
BC V5K 2B0
Phone: (604)874–5542

Desert Pedal Mountain Bike &
Rafting Adventures
118A 1ST ST
Ashcroft
BC V0K 1A0
Phone: (250)453–9602

Destiny River Adventure
3948 Dillman Road
Cambell River
BC V9H 1H5
Phone: (250)923–7238

Drifters Rod & River Adventures
Rock Creek
BC V0H 1Y0
Phone: (250)446–2442

Fraser River Raft Expeditions
PO BOX 10
Yale
BC V0K 2S0
Phone: (604)863–2336

Glacier Raft Company
Golden
BC V0A 1H0
Phone: (250)344–6591

Hyak Wilderness Adventures
2009 4TH AVE W
Vancouver
BC V6J 1N3
Phone: (604)734–8622

Interior Whitewater Expeditions
73 Old N Thompson Hwy W
Clearwater
BC V0E 1N0
Phone: (250)674–3727

Kootenay River Runners
Riverview Dr
Edgewater
BC V0A 1E0
Phone: (250)347–9210

Kumsheen Raft Adventures
Lytton
BC V0K 1Z0
Phone: (250)455–2297

Osprey Adventures
1520 16TH Ave S
Cranbrook
BC V1C 6R5
Phone: (250)426–6805

Panorama Mountain Village
1921 Panorama Drive
Invermere
BC V0A 1K0
Phone: (250)342–6941

Pro-Fish Guiding & Rafting Tours
5 MT Minton Street RR 3
Fernie
BC V0B 1M0
Phone: (250)423–3526

Reo Rafting Adventures
Vancouver
BC V5K 2B0
Phone: (604)684–9536

River Quest
1320 Zenith
Brackendale
BC V0N 1H0
Phone: (604)898–4633

Rivers & Oceans Unlimited
Expeditions
802 BAKER ST
NELSON
BC V1L 4J7
Phone: (250)354–2056

Rocky Mountain Rafting
1105 Trans Canada
Fairmont Hot Springs
BC V0B 1L0
Phone: (250)344–6979

Rogues Rafting
Frontage Road North
Spences Bridge
BC V0K 2L0
Phone: (250)458–2252

Spicy Sports
4557 Blackcomb Way
Whistler
BC V0N 1B4
Phone: (604)938–1821

Sunwolf Outdoor Centre
70002 Squamish Valley
Brackendale
BC V0N 1H0
Phone: (604)898–1537

Suskwa Adventure Outfitters
Tatlow Road
Smithers
BC V0J 2N0
Phone: (250)847–2885

Wedge Rafting
Whistler
BC V0N 1B0
Phone: (604)932–7171

Wet N' Wild Adventure
Golden
BC V0A 1H0
Phone: (250)344–6546

Whistler Connection
Whistler
BC V0N 1B0
Phone: (604)938–9712

Whistler River Adventures
Whistler
BC V0N 1B0
Phone: (604)932–3532

Whitewater Voyageurs
Golden
BC V0A 1H0
Phone: (250)344–7335

WOS Water & Outdoor Sports
International
6048 Paradise Valley
Winlaw
BC V0G 2J0
Phone: (250)226–7900

Manitoba

Adventure Junkie Tours
Winnipeg
MB R2C 0A1
Phone: (204)487–0004

Caddy Lake Resort
Falcon Beach
MB R0E 0N0
Phone: (204)349–2596

North River Outfitters
80 Deerwood Drive
Thompson
MB R8N 1E1
Phone: (204)778–6979

Red River Canoe & Paddle
19 River RD
Lorette
MB R0A 0Y0
Phone: (204)878–2524

New Brunswick

Cedarwood Canoes
2285 Route 105
Mouth Of Keswick
NB E0H 1N0
Phone: (506)363–3410

Nepisiguit River Company
96 Main
Bathurst
NB E2A 1A3
Phone: (506)548–5575

O'Donnell's Cottages &
Expeditions
439 Storeytown Rd
Doaktown
NB E0C 1G0
Phone: (506)365–7636

South East Paddlesport
NB
Phone: (877)627–4837

Adventure High
North Head
NB E0G 2M0
Phone: (506)662–3563

Ammon Water Sports
48 Ammon Rd
Moncton
NB E1G 2K4
Phone: (506)852–3822

Arbor Vitae Canoes
4B Court
Sussex
NB E0E 1P0
Phone: (506)433–2013

Betts Kelly Canoe & Kayak
Rentals
615 Storeytown Rd
Doaktown
NB E0C 1G0
Phone: (506)365–8008

Canotier Le
8 Parc P'tiso
Edmundston
NB E3V 3X7
Phone: (506)735–7173

Cattail Canoes & Fibreglassing
Darlings Island
Hampton
NB E0G 1Z0
Phone: (506)832–2200

Chamcook Boat & Canoe
39 Glebe Rd
St. Andrews
NB E0G 2X0
Phone: (506)529–4776

Eastern Outdoors
165 Water
St Andrews
NB E0G 2X0
Phone: (506)529–4662

Eastern Outdoors
Brunswick Sq
Saint John
NB E2L 4V1
Phone: (506)634–1530

Eastern Water Sports
Mactaquac Lake, NB
Phone: (506)363–2993

Eddy Out Depot
60 Rosebank Dr
Nelson-Miramichi
NB E0C 1H0
Phone: (506)622–5050

FreshAir Adventures
Alma
NS B2N 5A9
Phone: (506)887–2249

Inch Arran Expeditions
Phone: (800)576–4455

Lennon Canoes
Andover
Perth-Andover
NB E0J 1V0
Phone: (506)273–3759

M A G Aventures Plein Air
207 Bd J D Gauthier
Shippagan
NB E8S 2K8
Phone: (506)336–8836

Moore's Canoes
8710 Route 3
St. Stephen
NB E3L 2Y2
Phone: (506)466–3561

Nashwaak Outfitters
Brookside Mall
NB E6C 1M4
Phone: (506)450-2628

Nepisiguit River Company
96 Main
NB E2A 1A3
Phone: (877)548–5575

Old Town Canoes
48 Ammon Rd
NB E1G 2K4
Phone: (506)852–3822

Outdoor Adventure Company
St. George
NB
Phone: (506)755–6415

Paulin Ventures
9864 Route 17
St-Jean-Baptiste
NB E0K 1H0
Phone: (506)284–1113

Piskahegan River Company
St George
NB
Phone: (506)755–6269

Port City Outfitters
89 Acamac Backland Rd
Saint John
NB
Phone: (506)672–1413

Restigouche River Clothing
Company
41 Water
Campbellton
NB
Phone: (506)753–5737

River Marsh Tours
611A Darlings Island Rd
NB E5N 8B4
Phone: (506)832–1990

River Valley Adventures
Quispamsis
Rothesay
NB E2E 4J5
Phone: (506)849–8361

Scout Shop The
201 Union
Saint John
NB E2L 1A9
Phone: (506)646–9123

Small Craft Aquatic Center Of
Fredericton
Woodstock Rd
NB
Phone: (506)460-2260

Tobique River Tours
NB
Phone: (506)356–2111

Nova Scotia
Shubenacadie River Adventure
Tours
South Maitland
Halifax
NS B3M 2S4
Phone: (902)261–2222

Shubenacadie River Adventure
Tours
NS
Phone: (888)878–8687

Shubenacadie River Runners
8681 Highway 215
NS
Phone: (902)261–2770
Phone: (800)856–5061

Tidal Bore Rafting Park
Maitland Rd
Shubenacadie
NS B0N 2H0
Phone: (902)758–4032
Phone: (800)565–7238

Ontario

Aventures En Eau Vive Quebec
Ltée
120 Ch De La Riviere Rouge
Calumet
QC J0V 1B0
Phone: (819)242–6084
Phone: (800)567–6881

Aventures Outaouais-Ottawa
Adventures
18 Ch Wilson
Bryson
QC J0X 1H0
Phone: (819)648–5200
Phone: (800)690-7238

Base De Plein Air Nouvelle
Aventure
Calumet
QC
Phone: (819)242–1708

Equinox Adventures
5334 Yonge
North York
ON M2N 6V1
Phone: (416)222–2223
Phone: (800)785–8855

Esprit Rafting Adventures
3 Ch Esprit
Davidson
QC J0X 1V0
Phone: (819)683–3241
Phone: (800)596–7238

Extrême Plein Air De L'Outaouais
153 Commerciale
Maniwaki
QC J9E 1P1
Phone: (819)441–2726

Madawaska Kanu Centre
39 First Av
Ottawa
ON K1S 2G1
Phone: (613)594–5268

Madawaska Kanu Centre
Barrys Bay
ON K0J 1B0
Phone: (613)756–3620

New World River Expeditions
Harrington Harbour
QC J0V 1B0
Phone: (819)242–2168

Owl Rafting
39 First Av
Ottawa
ON K1S 2G1
Phone: (613)238–7238
Phone: (800)461–7238

Owl Rafting
Foresters Falls
Cobden
ON K0J 1K0
Phone: (613)646–2263
Phone: (800)461–7238

Rafting Action Rivière Rouge
Montréal
QC
Phone: (514)942–8791

River Rat Rentals
RR 2 Harston Dr
Kakabeka Falls
ON P0T 1W0
Phone: (807)473–9117

River Run
Beachburg
Cobden
ON K0J 1K0
Phone: (613)646–2501

River's Edge Tours
2800 John
Markham
ON L3R 0E2
Phone: (905)946–8438

Wilderness Tours
Foresters Falls
ON
Phone: (613)646–2291
Phone: (800)267–9166

Yukon

Kanoe People
P O Box 5152
Whitehorse
YT Y1A 4S3
Phone: (867)668–4899

Access Yukon
Whitehorse
YT Y1A 1A6
Phone: (867)668–1233

Prospect Yukon Wilderness
Adventures
3123–3rd Ave
Whitehorse
YT Y1A 1E6
Phone: (867)667–4837

Up North Boat & Canoe Rentals
86 Wickstrom Rd
Whitehorse
YT Y1A 3H6
Phone: (867)667–7905

Outfitters for International Trips

As whitewater adventures have become more popular, more outfitters have begun to offer trips on rivers around the world. Some specialize in a single region or river, others take expeditions to all corners of the globe. Look around, talk to people who have gone on large-scale international expeditions, and do a lot of reading before you go. Here are a few outfitters to get you started.

O.A.R.S. (Outdoor Adventure River Specialists):
trips to Chile, Fiji, Africa
PO Box 67
2687 S. Hwy. 49
Angels Camp, CA 95222
Phone: 800-346-6277 or
209-736-4677
Fax: 209-736-2902
Email: reservations@oars.com

Hidden Trails: trips to Chile, Zimbabwe, Ethiopia, Uganda, Turkey, Nepal, Ecuador & others
202-380 West 1st Ave
Vancouver, BC V5Y 3T7
1-888-9-TRAILS
Fax: 604-323-1148

Bio Bio Expeditions World Wide: trips to Nepal, Chile, Zimbabwe, Siberia, Turkey and others
5225 San Pablo Dam Rd.
El Sobrante, California
94803-3309
1-800-2-GO-RAFT

Splash Whitewater Rafting: trips to the Italian Alps, Nepal, UK
Dunkeld Road,
Aberfeldy, PH15 2AQ
01887 829706 (phone and fax)

Mountain Travel Sobek U.S.: trips all over Europe, Asia, Africa and the United States
6420 Fairmount Avenue
El Cerrito, CA 94530-3606
1-888-MTSOBEK (687-6235)
Fax: 1-510-527-7710
Email: info@mtsobek.com

Mountain Travel Sobek U.K.
67 Verney Avenue
High Wycombe Bucks
HP12 3ND
44-(0)1494-448901
Fax: 44-1494-465526
Email: sales@mtsobekeu.com

Earth River Expeditions: trips to Patagonia, Peru, Chile, Yukon, Ecuador, Tibet
180 Towpath Road
Accord, NY 12404
1-800-643-2784

Safaraid: trips on the Dordogne, Cele and Allier rivers in France
Tel: 05 65 30 74 47
fax: 05 65 30 74 48
email: Safaraid@aol.com
web: www.canoe-dordogne.com

Expediciones Chile:
trips on the Futaleufu
tel: 888-488-9082
email: office@kayakchile.com
web:
www.raftingchile.com/home.html

ProAdventure
Tel: 01978 861912
23 Castle Street, Llangollen,
Great Britain. LL20 8NY
email:
sales@adventureholiday.com
web: www.adventureholiday.com

Naturally New Zealand
Holidays Ltd.
P O BOX 94
Darfield, Canterbury
Tel: +64 3 318 7540
Fax: +64 3 318 7590
web: http://nzholidays.co.nz
email: info@nzholidays.co.nz

Clubs, Associations and River Centers

United States and Canada

American River Outdoor Center
11257 South Bridge Street,
Rancho Cordova, CA 95670
(916) 6380808

Denali Outdoor Center
Mi 238.9 Parks Highway Box 170,
Healy, AK 99743
(907) 683–1925
(888) 303–1925 (toll-free)
docadventure@hotmail.com
http://www.denali.com

River Skills Center
1104 Firenze, Mccloud, CA
96057
(530) 9642544

Kayak School of Boulder
2510 47th Street, Boulder, CO
80301
(303) 4448420
(800) 3649376 (tollfree)

Boulder Outdoor Center Inc
2510 47th Street, Boulder, CO
80301
(303) 4448420
(800) 3649376 (tollfree)

Mountain Sports Kayak School
1450 South Lincoln Avenue,
Steamboat Springs, CO 80487
(970) 8798794

River Heritage Society
Denver, CO 80202
(303) 4770379

Chattahoochee Outdoor Center
Inc
1990 Island Ford Parkway,
Atlanta, GA 30350
(770) 395–6851

New England Outdoor Center
Medway Road, Millinocket, ME
04462
(207) 723–5438

New England Outdoor Center Inc
Route 201, Caratunk, ME 04925
(207) 672–5506

Penobscot Outdoor Center
Millinocket Road, Millinocket, ME
04462
(207) 723–5861 U S Kayak &
Canoe Center
31 Highway 210, Carlton, MN
55718
(218) 384–3404
Carolina Mountains Outdoor
Center
18 Macktown Road, Sylva, NC
28779
(828) 586–5285

Cascade Adventure Center
22297 Highway 62, Shady Cove,
OR 97539
(541) 878–3339

Nantahala Outdoor Center
851 Chattooga Ridge Road,
Mountain Rest, SC 29664
(864) 647–9014

Nantahala Outdoor Center Ocoee
Outpost
Highway 64, Ocoee, TN 37361
(423) 338–5901

Ocoee Adventure Center
Highway 64, Ducktown, TN
37326
(423) 496–4430

American Canoe Association
7432 Alban Station Blvd, Suite B-
232
Springfield, VA 22150
Phone: (703) 451–0141
Fax: (703) 451–2245
General Email: aca@acanet.org
http://www.acanet.org/acanet.ht
m

Manitoba Recreational Canoing
Association
Winnipeg
MB R2C 0A1

Manitoba Paddling Association
Winnipeg
MB R2C 0A1
Phone: (204)284–4646
Phone: (204)338–6722

WORLDWIDE

Uk British Canoeing Association
Adbolton Lane
West Bridgford
Nottingham
NG2 5AS
01159 821100

International Rafting Federation
Tel: 27–21–761–9298
Fax: 797–9633
PO Box 18634
Wynberg, 7824
South Africa

Australian Canoeing
Suite 210, Sports House,
Wentworth Park Sporting
Complex
Wattle Street, Ultimo 2007
PO Box 666
Glebe NSW 2037, Australia
Tel: (02) 9552 4500 (International:
+61 2 9552 4500)
Fax (02) 9552 4457 (International:
+61 2 9552 4457)
Email to:
auscanoe@canoe.org.au

World Kayak Federation: news,
links, articles and information for
kayakers around the world.
http://www.worldkayak.com/

Alpine Kayak Club: an international group based in Germany
that has been sponsoring races,
trips, and other whitewater
events for almost 30 years.
http://www.alpine-kayak-club.org

International Whitewater
Federation: association for
freestyle kayakers—sponsors pro
and amateur races and events.
Tel/Fax: 418 - 667 0915
CP 63 St Augustin
Quebec, G3A 1V9
Canada
http://city.hokkai.or.jp/~njwwf/ei
wf.html

Spanish Canoe Federation:
Spain's best whitewater organiza-
tion—check with them for news,
competitions and events for
whitewater canoeing, wildwater,
raft races, slalom and marathon
races plus a number of great
links for European paddling.
http://www.sportec.com/fep/

British Canoe Union ®: Britain's
governing body for canoeing and
kayaking.
Adbolton Lane
West Bridgford, Nottingham.
NG2 5AS
Tel: 0115 9821100
Fax: 0115 9821797
http://www.bcu.org.uk/member-
ship/whatis.htm

The Scottish Canoe Association:
Caledonia House
South Gyle, Edinburgh
EH12 9DQ
Tel: 0131–317–7314
Fax: 0131–317–7319
www.scot-canoe.org

Canoe Association for Northern
Ireland (CANI)
The House of Sport
Upper Malone Road
Belfast BT9 5LA
Tel: 01247 469907

Welsh Canoeing: resources for
whitewater paddling in Wales—
as well as information about the
Canolfan Tryweryn, the whitewater center on the banks of the
Tryweryn river.
http://www.welsh-
canoeing.org.uk/

Glossary

360: To spin a boat in a complete circle. Also called a spin or flat spin. Two spins in a row are sometimes called 720s, but after that the arithmetic is usually beyond most spin dizzy paddlers.

Backstroke: Any stroke done against the direction of travel. They can stop or slow a boat if done on both sides or turn the boat if done on one side only. Also called back paddling.

Big Water: High volume flows tend to spawn large and chaotic river features such as exploding waves, boiling eddies, dramatic eddy lines, whirlpools. Some rivers are big water runs all the time—the Zambezi or the Grand Canyon of the Colorado being two notable examples—but most rivers have the potential for big water features when flooding.

Boil line: When water reverses on itself in a hole or hydraulic creating a cyclical current, the boil line is the point at which the water rises up to the surface and either falls back into the hole or flows on downstream. It literally looks like boiling water and is the highest point of the surrounding water. To escape the hole, you may have to find a way over or under the boil.

Boil: Boiling water looks like boiling water in a pot and is an indicator of a turbulent and unpredictable flow. The water is subjected to tremendous pressure and abandons the water-always-flows-downhill dynamic that powers rivers. Instead it surges and pushes to the surface, forming unpredictable currents and seams that surge and pull at a boat.

Boiling eddy: An eddy filled with boiling water. Usually a big water feature or one where water is subjected to unusual pressure. A boiling eddy is usually not a friendly place to hang out and rest.

Bombproof: A one hundred percent, absolute, combat-tested river skill or piece of equipment. A bombproof roll means you roll up when you need to and (almost) never have to swim. Bombproof gear doesn't break (right). A variant, "bomber," is another synonym for river reliability. *My van is bomber dude—did you see me boof that rock on the takeout road?*

Boof: To skip a boat off a rock to get lift (or *air*). Boofs are named for the sound a boat's hull makes when it lands in the water below—boof! like a bass drum. It's a useful move for avoiding nasty holes or other unfriendly features in the main channel of a drop. Done correctly, a boof will land a paddler clear of the hole below the drop and usually in the eddy. Care should be taken on especially tall drops not to land flat, however, because you can hurt your back.

Boulder garden: A type of rapid clogged with boulders. Passage is usually not straightforward and may take eddy hopping to run cleanly. Expect pourover holes and many quick moves, especially in steep boulder gardens.

Bow: The part of the boat in front of you. Most of the time you want it pointed downstream.

Brace: A type of paddle stroke used to add stability or keep from tipping over. What looks like a slap of the paddle on the surface of the water is really accomplished with a flick of the head and snap of the hips.

Brain Wave: A monstrous wave that boils on top and looks a bit like a brain. It's a variant of the exploding wave.

Busy water: Busy water requires a lot of tight, quick technical moves. A waterfall with a technical lead in and followed by a steep boulder garden with no real eddies would be pretty busy water.

C-1: A decked canoe. The C-1 paddler, a canoeist (never canoer), kneels in his or her boat and uses a one-bladed paddle. The boat looks like a kayak and often is a kayak with the seat removed and a foam pedestal glued in its place.

CFS: Cubic feet per second is the standard measure of flow of U.S. rivers. See also River Levels.

Chine: On a kayak or canoe, the chine is the transition between the side of the boat and its bottom. Hard chined boats have sharp corners or edges that define this transition and are made to carve in the water. They are also more edgy and feel more likely to "catch" in a hole and flip the paddler. Soft chines are more subtle and rounded and allow more margin for error but may sacrifice some performance.

Chundered: What a hole does to you when it "keeps" you in its recirculating current and you lose control. Characterized by a spontaneous cartwheeling, barrel rolling ride. To be chundered is to get a real thrashing. It has many regional variations—getting worked, munched, eaten and clobbered among them.

Combat roll: To complete a roll in real river conditions. A combat roll is a necessary step for kayakers and canoeists looking to safely run Class 3 and harder water.

Continuous: Continuous flows have few pools between rapids. River gradient is distributed fairly evenly throughout the course. High volume continuous rivers can make for difficult rescues and long swims.

Creek: Any tight and narrow flow of water. Usually creeks are steeper than their neighboring rivers and often hold waterfalls, slides and technical passages that demand sharp skills. Creeks are also often remote and beautiful and their access can be arduous.

Curler: A wave that curls like an ocean wave. It may be a small feature used to gain bearings while running a river or it might be something you can surf.

Deck: The top of a kayak or C-1.

Drain Plug: The plug at one end of a kayak that can be removed to drain water.

Draw: A draw stroke pulls the boat to the paddle.

D-ring: A metal ring attached to inflatable boats that's used to fix gear and flip lines.

Drop: Another name for a rapid or for the gradient of a river or a rapid. A paddler will fall 30 feet over the course of a 30-foot drop.

Dry Bag: A bag usually made of coated nylon with a roll top used to store gear, food and clothes that must remain dry on the river. A must for long day and multi-day trips.

Dry Box: A box that is used to keep gear, food and clothes dry on the river. As it's usually more durable, dry boxes are often used for more valuable items or gear that might punch a hole in a dry bag.

Ducky: An inflatable kayak. See IK.

Duffeck: A type of kayak stroke in which the paddler plants the paddle in a different flow than the one she's in and uses the power of the river to turn the boat and pull it into that new flow.

Eddy Fence: A dramatic eddy line that will take extra power to cross.

Eddy Line: The separation of slack and downstream flows at the edge of an eddy. Requires a specific technique for crossing effectively.

Eddy: A seemingly slack flow of water bounded by downstream current. Usually formed behind obstructions such as rocks, bridge pilings and bends in the river, eddies and moving from eddy to eddy, called eddy hopping, is an essential river running strategy.

Eskimo Roll: The technique kayakers and canoeists use to right flipped boats while staying in them.

Ferry angle: The angle at which a boat needs to be to the current to move laterally across it without being swept downstream.

Ferry: Moving laterally across a river without going downstream. Ferrying works on the principle of river ferries connected to cables. By altering the angle of the boat, the paddler can use the river's power to move the boat across it.

Float bags: Inflated bags in kayaks and canoes intended to displace water in the event the boat fills with water, usually after a flip or swim. Float bags make recovering boats much more simple.

Funny Water: Funny water is boiling unpredictable water that surges and sucks at a boat. Often a big water feature, funny water can make for an unstable feeling ride and is a notorious kayak and canoe flipper. To an extent, poorly formed eddy lines are examples of funny water.

Grab Loop: The loop of nylon webbing or rope at the bow and stern of kayaks and whitewater canoes.

Grabby: Any river feature that wants to hold a boat. Usually used in reference to holes.

Gradient: The measure of how much a river drops over its course. Gradient is just one of the measures that will give a paddler a sense of what to expect. Many Class 3 runs are in the 20 to 40 foot per mile range, but that kind of drop can also be a lot of flat water hiding a steep Class 5 or 6 waterfall. Steep gradient is usually more that 100 feet per mile and steep creek paddlers are pushing the envelope at 400 and more feet per mile.

Green Water: Un-aerated water. Usually used to describe the water coming into a hole or the face of a wave.

Guard rocks: Hidden rocks in eddies that may keep a boat out. It's good to know where guard rocks are in a must-make eddy.

Gunnel: The rail that goes along the top edge of a canoe's hull. Usually gunnels are made of wood or plastic.

Haystack: A big wave with whitewater on top.

Head dink: A flick of the head used to change a paddlers center of gravity when she's off balance.

High side: Rafters move to the high side of the boat when it gets up against a rock or in a hole. Highsiding keeps the downstream current from catching a tube and flipping the raft.

Hole: When water flows over an obstruction in the river, it often causes the surface water to reverse flow and move upstream, creating a hole. The upstream flow causes a circular action that can hold floating objects. There are friendly holes that will let go of a paddler with little effort and are fun to surf and dangerous "terminal" holes that can recirculate boats and bodies for hours. Learn to spot the difference.

Horizon line: The farthest point downriver that you can see. If it's very close and you can only see treetops beyond, expect a steep slide or waterfall.

Hull: The shell of a canoe or kayak.

Hydraulic: Another term for hole.

IK: Inflatable kayak is a mouthful, so the term has been shortened to IK (or ducky) for inflatable boats paddled as a kayak. They may hold on or two people and usually have two tubes and an inflatable or foam floor.

Indexing: Most whitewater paddles are slightly oval-shaped at the point where the hand grips the shaft. This indexing allows the paddler to feel the orientation of his blades without looking at them.

J-lean: When you lean a kayak or canoe and keep your center of gravity over the top of it, your body makes a shape like a j. The j-lean is useful in surfing holes and for learning the effects of leans in holes.

Keeper: A type of hole that won't let go. Keepers are sticky, but not necessarily big, holes that you may or may not be able to swim out of. It's generally good practice to avoid these.

Kick: A hole often has a current within it that tends to push a floating object laterally across its face. This kick can be useful for escaping a hole because it often leads where the current breaks the hole. Holes may also kick into their stickiest part, so beware and scout.

Lean: Tipping the boat on edge in the water. Learning how to lean effectively in whitewater is a fundamental skill.

Meltdown: When a paddler runs through a hole and completely disappears, she has melted down. She's actually caught the downstream current *under* the hole and taken it for a ride.

Munchy: A colorful adjective that describes a hole that's likely to stick and keep a paddler, at least for a short time.

Mystery move: Skilled paddlers in low volume boats can use the river's currents, usually on strong eddy lines, to make their boats corkscrew down into the water. A really good mystery move makes the paddler completely disappear.

Oar lock: The attachment point for oars to the rowing frame on a raft.

Oar: A one-bladed device used to row a boat. Used in pairs, one hand holds each oar and the rower uses leverage against the oar lock to pull or push against the water.

OC-1: An open whitewater canoe for one person.

Off-side: The side of the boat opposite your dominant hand.

On-side: The side of the boat where your dominant hand feels most comfortable.

Paddle: A one- or two-bladed device used to paddle a canoe or kayak. A paddle is gripped with two hands and is pulled through the water using body twist.

Peel-out: To exit an eddy using an eddy turn.

Pencil: To enter the water vertically off a steep drop. If you pencil into shallow water, you will hit bottom. Ouch.

Pile: The foamy part of a hole. The water here is actually flowing upstream.

Pillow: Water stacked up in front of a rock. It forms a pressure wave that is useful for riding away from the rock.

Playboat: Any boat designed mainly for surfing and playing on river features.

Pool-drop: A type of riverbed that drops in short steep sections into pools. On rivers that aren't too steep, pool-drop rapids offer paddlers a chance to collect themselves after each drop. As the river gets more steep, the pools will likely get shorter and the drops more vertical. Waterfalls are almost guaranteed on steep gradient pool-drop rivers.

Pourover: A rock with water flowing over the top of it forms a pourover and usually a sticky hole.

Power face: The face of a paddle blade that pushes against the water in most strokes.

Pressure wave: A pressure wave is formed when water pushes against an immobile object and stacks up against it.

Push stroke: Pushing against oars rather than pulling them.

Pushy: Powerful water that tends to push boats around and demands decisive moves.

Rapid: Where the riverbed gets more steep, it tends to form rapids, which are any collection of waves, holes, rocks and other features that paddlers must negotiate.

Ride: The amount of time spent surfing or playing on a feature.

Rise: The amount that a raft is upswept in the bow and stern. Rise can help a boat turn more quickly and ride over holes.

River Left: The left side of the river as you face downstream.

River Levels: The amount of water in the river as measured by a gauge or personal experience. River levels in the U.S. are usually measured in cubic feet per second, by feet and inches on an established gauge, by a calculation derived from a downstream or nearby river's gauge, by a power company formula, and by eyeballing the river from the road at 40 mph while trying to avoid a head-on collision with a hay truck. High and low are the rough criteria of river levels. More specifically, gauges report actual data on the flow. A typical river usually flows between 1,000 and 3,000 cfs. Creeks may hold flows as low as 200 cfs and be runnable. Big water is often 10,000 cfs or more, but that's entirely dependent on the character of a riverbed. Some rivers are low at 10,000 cfs while others may be washing out the put-in bridge. Read guidebooks and check online with real time streamflow gauges and look at a lot of rivers to get a sense of what different flows look like. In the jargon of dam controlled rivers, a standard flow in the whitewater section may be a set

number of "tubes" or turbines that the power company is running. It may also be expressed in megawatts or some other derivative of the river's energy. For safety, find out how many tubes, turbines or megawatts is fun, and how many is scary and how much the rain has had an effect on the flow. Calculations of the flow can be handy but are also highly variable and should be verified by personal inspection. Cumecs, cubic meters per second, are the metric counterpart of CFS.

River Right: The right side of the river as you face downstream.

Road Scout: To inspect rapids from the road. Expect them to be a lot bigger than they looked from your car.

Rocker: The amount that a canoe or kayak is upswept at the ends. Rocker lets a boat turn and resurface quickly but makes it harder to paddle in a straight line.

Roostertail: A plume of water shooting up from an irregular river feature. Roostertails are often used as reference points in rapids.

Rowing frame: The metal frame strapped to a raft that provides leverage and support for oars. It also tends to stiffen the boat, making it less likely to bend when it hits a river feature.

Rudder: Using a paddle blade to steer like the rudder of a ship.

Scull: A paddle stroke used to make a canoe or kayak move laterally. The motion describes an hourglass shape and the paddle doesn't leave the water.

Sideslip: Moving a boat move laterally on the water by a short distance.

Sieve: When rocks and logs obstruct passage of objects but not water through a channel.

Ski jump: Making a boat clear the water and the hole below on a vertical drop. See also Boof.

Skirt: A removable deck on a kayak or C-1 that seals out water. Whitewater skirts are made of thick neoprene rubber with heavy duty rubber bands around their edges that clip into the boat's cockpit.

Slick: A deep, unobstructed channel forms a glossy patch of water that comes to a point at the downstream end where the channel is fastest. Also called the V or the tongue.

Slicy: Whitewater playboats have thin bows and sterns that allows them to slice into the water, making moves like cartwheels easier.

Slide: Slides are waterfalls' not-quite-vertical cousins. They're formed when the river pours over a solid smooth rock formation that slopes at an angle into the pool below. The water is usually only a few inches deep, making maneuvering difficult, and boats on tall slides can get going very fast.

Spin: To spin a boat around 360 degrees. Also called a flat spin or 360.

Stern: The end of the boat behind you.

Sticky: A hole that tends to want to hold a floating object. Sticky is usually not as severe an adjective as keeper or terminal when used to describe a hole, but sticky holes can lead to some unintended surfs.

Stoppers: Similar to a sticky hole but often used to describe big breaking wave-hole combinations that may stop a boats going through them.

Strainer: A tree or log that's fallen into the river. So named for the branches that may hide under the water that let water pass but not much else. Strainers are NOT good features to play near or have to swim through. Give them a wide berth: they're like the icebergs of the river environment—what you see above the surface may only be a hint of the nasty stuff below.

S-turn: A type of rapid or move in a rapid that requires a boater to turn one way and then back the other quickly, describing an S.

Surf: To hang on a wave or stick in a hole and ride it. Surfing is a great way to hone skills for river running and learn the fundamentals of boat control. It's also a lot of fun. In fact, surfing and playboating is a whole subculture of whitewater paddling, with international competitions and an ever-growing list of moves to perfect.

Sweep: The sweep is used to turn a boat. It's done with the shaft of the paddle nearly parallel to the surface of the water.

Sweeper: Another word for strainer.

Terminal: Bad. End of game. Don't go there.

T-grip: The grip at the top of a whitewater canoe paddle. It's shaped like a t to allow your fingers to wrap on it and get a more positive grip.

Thwart: The crosspieces in a canoe that run between the sides of the hull from gunnel to gunnel. They're usually made of wood and they help to make the boat stiff. Rafts have inflatable thwarts that may be removable and provide extra stability for the boat, keeping it from twisting and folding during rough rides.

Tongue: An alternate name for the slick or the V that marks the deepest fastest part of a channel.

Tube: Tubes give rafts their characteristic shape. Tubes are usually made of coated fabric with multiple chambers, so that the raft can maintain its shape and buoyancy if one is punctured. Tubes are also integral to the design of catarafts and inflatable kayaks, serving the same purpose.

Typewriter: To be displaced laterally across a river channel like the carriage return on a typewriter.

V: River channels are marked by a surface feature that looks like a V pointing downstream. The point of the V is the fastest and deepest part of the channel. Also called a slick or a tongue.

Waterfall: Any vertical or mostly vertical drop more than six to eight feet tall. Many waterfalls are fun and relatively safe to run, but always scout. The record for the tallest waterfall intentionally run is 98 feet by Tao Berman.

Wave train: Waves tend to form in series in the deepest part of the channel.

Wave: River waves are formed by water in the channel slowing down. Waves can be great fun to surf and ride through, though they are notorious raft flippers if a big wave catches a raft out of position.

Whitewater: Literally it's the white frothy stuff that splashes and tumbles through a rapid. In more general terms, it's used to describe a type of river where you can expect to find rapids.

Suggested Reading

There's some great literature on rivers—but perhaps none so useful to the river runner than a good guide-book. Here are a few good ones to get you started.

Amaral, G. *Idaho: The Whitewater State*. Watershed Books, 1990.

Anderson, F. And A. Hopkinson. *Rivers of the Southwest: A Boater's Guide to the Rivers of Colorado, New Mexico, Utah and Arizona*. Pruett, 1987.

Armstead, L.D. *Whitewater Rafting in Eastern America: A Guide to Rivers and Outfitters for Beginning and Advanced Whitewater Rafters*. The Globe Pequot Press, 1974.

Armstead, L.D. *Whitewater Rafting in North America: More Than 100 River Adventures in the United States and Canada*. The Globe Pequot Press, 1997.

Armstead, L.D. *Whitewater Rafting in Western America: A Guide to Rivers and Professional Outfitters*. The Globe Pequot Press, 1990.

Banks, G. and D. Eckardt. *Colorado Rivers and Creeks*. Moenkopi Digital Formations, 1995.

Belknap, Buzz. *Grand Canyon River Guide*. Westwater, 1974.

Benner, B. and D. Benner. *Carolina Whitewater: A Paddler's Guide to the Western Carolinas*. Menasha Ridge Press, 1993.

Bennett, J. *A Guide to the Whitewater Rivers of Washington: A comprehensive Handbook to Over 150 Runs in the Cascades and Beyond*. Swiftwater Publishing Co., 1991.

Bennett, J. *Class Five Chronicles: Things Mother Never Told You 'Bout Whitewater*. Swiftwater Publishing Co., 1992.

Campbell, A. *John Day River: Drift and Historical Guide*. Frank Amato Publishers, 1980.

Cassady, J. and D. Dunlap. *World Whitewater: A Global Guide for River Runners*. Ragged Mountain Press, 1999.

Cassady, J. and F. Calhoun. *California Whitewater: A Guide to the Rivers*. North Fork Press, 1990.

Cassady, J., B. Cross, and F. Calhoun. *Western Whitewater: From the Rockies to the Pacific*. North Fork Press, 1994.

Charles, G. *New Zealand Whitewater*. Craig Potton Publishing, 1996.

Connelly, J. and J. Porterfield. *Appalachian Whitewater: The Northern Mountains*. Menasha Ridge Press, 1987.

Corbett, H.R. *Virginia Whitewater*. Seneca Press, 1977.

Crumbo, K. *History of the Grand Canyon: A River Runner's Guide*. Johnson, 1981.

Davidson, P. and W. Eister. *Wildwater West Virginia: The Northern Streams*. Menasha Ridge Press, 1985.

Davidson, P. and W. Eister. *Wildwater West Virginia: The Northern Streams*. Menasha Ridge Press, 1985.

Embick, A. *Fast and Cold: A Guide to Alaska Whitewater*. Valdez Alpine Books, 1994.

Fischer, H. *The Floater's Guide to Montana*. Falcon Press, 1986.

Foss, J. *The Whitewater Rivers of Chile*. Blue Sky Press, 1998.

Fox, A. *Run River Run*. Diadem Books, 1990.

Garren, J. *Idaho River Tours*. Touchstone Press, 1980.

Garren, J. *Oregon River Tours*. Garren Publishing.

Grove, E. et al. *Appalachian Whitewater: The Central Mountains*. Menasha Ridge Press, 1987.

Hamblin, W.K. and J.K. Rigby. *Guidebook to the Colorado River, Part I: Lee's Ferry to Phantom Ranch in Grand Canyon National Park*. Brigham Young University Press, 1969.

Hamblin, W.K. and J.K. Rigby. *Guidebook to the Colorado River, Part II: Phantom Ranch in Grand Canyon National Park to Lake Mead*. Brigham Young University Press, 1969.

Harrington, R. River Rafting in Canada. Alaska Northwest Publishing Co., 1987.

Hass, J. *Gems of the High Alps*. Rosgarten Verlag/Suderkurier, 1990.

Holbeck, L. and C. Stanley. *A Guide to the Best Whitewater in the State of California*. Friends of the River Books, 1984.

Holbek, Lars. *The Rivers of Chile*. American Whitewater, 1992.

Hulick, K. and L. Wright. *Paddler's Atlas of U.S. Rivers*. Stackpole Books, 1993.

Jettmar, K. *The Alaska River Guide: Canoeing, Kayaking, and Rafting in the Last Frontier*. Graphic Arts Center Publishing Center, 1993.

Kennon, T. *Ozark Whitewater: A Paddler's Guide to the Mountain Streams of Arkansas and Missouri*. Menasha Ridge Press.

Kirkley, G. *A Guide to Texas Rivers and Streams*. Lone Star Books, 1983.

Knowles, Peter. *White Water Europe*. Rivers Publishing, 1996.

Korb, G. *A Paddler's Guide to the Olympic Peninsula: A Comprehensive Guide to 69 River Runs on Washington's Beautiful Olympic Peninsula*. 1992.

Lewis, D. *Paddle and Portage: The Floater's Guide to Wyoming Rivers.* The Wyoming Naturalist, 1991.

Margulis, R. K. *The Complete Guide to Whitewater Rafting Tours: California Edition*. Aquatic Adventure Publications, 1986.

Maurer, S.G. *A Guide to New Mexico's Popular Rivers and Lakes*. Heritage Associates, 1983.

Moore, G. and D. McClaren. *Idaho Whitewater: The Complete Guide for Canoeists, Rafters and Kayakers*. Class VI Whitewater, 1989.

Nealy, W. *Whitewater Home Companion, Volume I*. Menasha Ridge Press, 1981.

Nealy, W. *Whitewater Home Companion, Volume II*. Menasha Ridge Press, 1984.

Nichols, G.C. *River Runner's Guide to Utah and Adjacent Areas*. University of Utah Press, 1986.

Nolen, B.M. and R.E. Narramore. *Texas Rivers and Rapids*. Ben Nolen Graphics, 1983.

North, D. *Washington Whitewater*. The Mountaineers, 1992.

Penny, R. *The Whitewater Sourcebook: A Directory of Information on American Whitewater Rivers*. Menasha Ridge Press, 1989.

Sehlinger, B. et al. *Appalachian Whitewater: The Southern Mountains*. Menasha Ridge Press, 1986.

Shears, N. *Paddle America: A Guide to Trips and Outfitters in All 50 States*. Starfish Press, 1992.

Smith, S. *Canadian Rockies Whitewater*. Headwaters Press, 1995.

Willamette Kayak and Canoe Club. *Soggy Sneakers: A Guide to Oregon Rivers*. Willamette Kayak and Canoe Club, 1994.

Wood, P. *Running the Rivers of North America: A Guide to Canoeing, Kayaking, and Rafting Down More Than 50 U.S. and Canadian Rivers*. Barre Publishing, 1978.

Photo Credits

Imagestate: p. 12: Eric Evans, p. 112: Scott Spiker, p. 113: Rick Ridgeway, p. 133: Emily Hart-Roberts

Steve Bly: p. 13, p. 24, p. 27, p. 37, p. 47, p. 55, p. 67, p. 91, p. 97, p. 100, p. 125, p. 131, p. 179, p. 185, p. 195

Flashfocus: p. 25, p. 105

National Geographic Society: p. 17: Johan Reinhard, p. 88: Raymond Gehman, p. 99: Barry Tessman, p. 157: George Mobley

Corbis: p. 19, p. 31, p. 51, p. 53, p. 65, p. 77, p. 107, p. 114, p. 123, p. 165, p. 168, p. 172, p. 177, p. 203

James Kay: p. 120, p. 184, p. 193

Proadventure: p. 33

Skip Brown: p. 40, p. 75, p. 83, p. 147

Gary Valle: p. 20, p. 23, p. 29, p. 39, p. 63, p. 78, p. 85, p. 109, p. 151, p. 154, p. 174, p. 175, p. 178

Lee Peterson: p. 21, p. 28, p. 48, p. 61, p. 70, p. 71, p. 79, p. 80, p. 84, p. 116, p. 135, p. 136, p. 140, p. 141, p. 149, p. 160, p. 163, p. 169

Adventure Photo & Film: p. 119: William Campbell, p. 186: Steven Wayne Rotsch

David Gluns: p. 22, p. 34, p. 110, p. 115, p. 126, p. 127, p. 152, p. 194, p. 199

Jessica MacMurray: p. 35, p. 36, p. 38, p. 48, p. 49, p. 56, p. 58, p. 190

Gnass Images: p. 43: Sandy Lonsdale, p. 82: Fred Pflughoft

Naturally New Zealand: p. 45

Mark Blaine: p. 54

Photodisc: p. 72, p. 102, p. 128, p. 144, p. 166, p. 170, p. 188, p. 196

AP/Wide World Photos: p. 87, p. 93: Jon Hancock, p. 191: Ted Anthony

Eric Evans: p. 94, p. 95, p. 139, p. 155, p. 158

Index